Certified So

Redefining Happiness

Roland J Coleman

Certified So Publications, LLC ™
Tonasket, WA USA

Copyright © 2013 by Roland J Coleman

Certified So: Redefining Happiness
By Roland J Coleman

Author photo and cover photo and effects by Charles Coleman
www.rapidfyre.com/certifiedso/

All rights reserved. This book is protected under the copyright laws of the United States of America. This book may not be copied or reprinted for commercial profit or financial gain. The use of short quotations or occasional page copying for personal use or group study is encouraged and permitted. Permission to do so will be granted upon request.

Unless otherwise noted all Bible verses are from the New King James Version (NKJV) Copyright © 1982 by Thomas Nelson, Inc. Used by Permission. All rights reserved. Bible verses paraphrased by the author are not enclosed with quotation marks.

Scripture references marked KJV are from the King James Version of the Bible (with permission, Cambridge University Press)

Published by Certified So Publications, LLC ™
www.certifiedsopublications.com.

Printed and distributed by Ingram, Spring Arbor
www.ingramcontent.com.

Library of Congress Cataloging-in-Publication Data

Coleman, Roland J. 1954-

ISBN 978-0-9897831-0-1 (Perfect Bound)

Library of Congress Control Number: 2013908106

Table of Contents

Note From Author vii

Acknowledgments ix

Introduction 1

Feed Me First 5

Much Fruit 29

The Curse 53

The Waiter 69

Rest 85

The Still Small Voice. 103

Seven Times 123

Summary 148

Certified Signatures 165

Note From Author

It all began with an accident.

Visiting in a cozy living room, I offered a comment about the source of total contentment that surprised even myself. *What if,* I asked, *our peace of mind can be derived from what we don't have?*

I hadn't intended to ask that question, nor did I envision the chain of events that soon occurred. This accidental question led right to the root of what we all want... happiness. My paradigm was shifting. I started to view happiness in a new light. I began to understand how it propagates, and where it goes when it hides. Instead of accidental, now my passing comment seemed more providential!

As I shared my discoveries, others agreed. They wanted me to write my thoughts down, but every attempt was like attacking a sealed can of chili with a spoon. Three years passed and I was on the verge of giving up, when another "accident" occurred. A question in my email inbox, which simply said: "*I will be joining the Church of Satan in two weeks. Do you think that is a good idea?*"

Nearly seventy emails ensued. Halfway through I knew I had to wait until the person I was writing to decided what to do. For this reason, my sentences became shorter and shorter as I sought to emphasize the most important parts. Eventually, a sentence only had two or three words, and a paragraph was equally pared down. And then it clicked: *This* was the gold plated can opener I was looking for!

You have probably already guessed by now, that I do not believe in accidents. Not when something this profound occurs. In hindsight, I can also see the reason why it took so long to write this book. Nearly nine years. This was by design, too. Because I had to fully *live it*, before I could fully *give it*. In a very real sense, every chapter had to be taste tested, field tested and lived in the laboratory of life before it passed inspection.

But all of this is just the back story. You see, this book isn't about me; it is about you and the amazing changes that occur when you seek to certify this paradigm. In the end it will help you redefine the source of true happiness!

Roland Coleman

Acknowledgments

It would take many pages to list the names of all the family and friends who helped this book become a reality. I am deeply in debt to all of you. Especially my wife, without whose support this never would have happened. Thank you!

But, to give credit where credit is truly due, my greatest praise really belongs to God. He alone is the inspiration for writing this book!

Introduction

Despite how trite
Or overused,

Clichés that shape
Religious views

Are seldom subject
To review

Because they seem
To state the obvious.

But how can *anything*
That sounds so logical

Accurately describe
An act of faith

That seems so illogical?

Like when Peter
Tried to walk on water? Matthew 14:25-31

Or when David
Taunted he

Who hid behind

His iron armor? 1 Samuel 17:4-8, 41-51

Or when
Holy men of old

Defied the king
When they were told

That they would die

If they did not deny the Lord
Or heed an evil order? Daniel 3:14-26

Or,

What about the widow
Who said she never
Knew the Lord,

And yet she had
An order from the Lord

To feed all the food
She had
To a total stranger? 1 Kings 17:8-16

As we ponder on
These themes and thoughts

And think about
These observations,

It underscores
The reason for this
Little dissertation

Where we take clichés
That seem to be above reproach
Or condemnation,

And subject them to
A thorough cross-examination

In the light
Of what we learn about
The Mustard Seed Concept.

The Mustard Seed Concept…

That most amazing,
Life changing concept

That permeates
Every page of the Bible!

Feed Me First

If we are fully committed
And filled with the Spirit,

Happiness
Will overflow
On everyone we meet.

But if we aren't,
It won't.

Because spiritually speaking,
We cannot give away
Something we do not have.

Or can we?

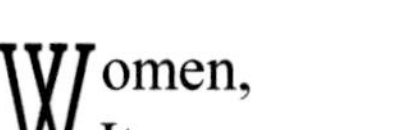

Women,
It seems,

Were deemed inferior
In Bible times.

But not by God.

For when those He had chosen
Rebelled
And went their own way,

He looked for,
And found,

More faith
In a heathen widow

Than in a nation
Of professedly
God fearing men.

Our story begins
When Elijah the Tishbite,
Prophet of God,

Delivered this message
To wicked king Ahab,
Ruler of reprobate Israel.

"As the LORD God
Of Israel lives,
Before whom I stand,

There shall not be
Dew nor rain
These years,

Except at my word." 1 Kings 17:1

Then he ran and hid
By a little brook,
As the Lord instructed him to.

Ravens
Brought him food,

And there was an abundance
Of water to drink.

But eventually,
The creek dried up. 1 Kings 17:7

Now what?

" 'Arise,

Go to Zarephath,
Which belongs to Sidon,
And dwell there,'

The LORD said.

'Behold,

I have commanded
A widow there
To provide for you.' " 1 Kings 17:9 KJV/NKJV

So he arose.
And went.

And indeed
A widow was gathering sticks
By the city gate.

But was she the one?

And if so,
How would he know?

All he could do was ask,
So he said,

"Please bring me
A little water in a cup,
That I may drink."

And,
As she was going to get it,
He called to her and said,

"Please bring me
A morsel of bread
In your hand." 1 Kings 17:10-11

Then the widow
Answered him and said,

"As the LORD
Your God lives,
I do not have bread,

Only a handful
Of flour in a bin,

And a little oil
In a jar;

And see,
I am gathering
A couple of sticks

That I may go in
And prepare it for myself
And my son,

That we may eat it,
And die." 1 Kings 17:12

On the surface,
Elijah's next request
Seems so selfish

We often wonder
Why he said it?

Was it just
To test her faith?

Or was there
A more important
Underlying reason?

"And Elijah said to her,

'Do not fear.

Go and do
As you have said,

But make me a small cake
From it first,
And bring it to me.

Afterward

Make some
For yourself
And your son.

For thus says
The LORD God of Israel;

'The bin of flour
Shall not be used up,

Nor shall the jar of oil
Run dry,

Until the day
The LORD sends rain
On the earth.' '

So she went away
And did according to

The word of Elijah;

And she
And he
And her household

Ate for many days.

The bin of flour
Was not used up,

Nor did the jar of oil
Run dry,

According to the word
Of the LORD

Which He spoke
By Elijah." 1 Kings 17:13-16

"Feed me first!"

Elijah
To the widow said.

Elijah,
To she whose child
Cried for bread.

She did,
But what about you?

Would you have fed
All the food you had

To a total stranger?

Not if you had been
Her friend or neighbor.

They hoarded their food,
And refused to share.

But could you blame them?

Because nobody knew
How long the drought
Would last.

But,
The fact that she lacked
Sufficient food

Tells us something else
Besides.

It tells us,
What every soul
In Zarephath said

Whenever the widow
Asked for food.

They said,

"I'm sorry neighbor,
But I cannot give you
Something I do not have."

Or they answered her
And said,

"We'd love to help you friend,
But our cupboards

Are not exactly
Overflowing either."

Note the kinds of things

Her neighbors told her.

Do they seem
To sound familiar?

They should,

Because we still hear
The same today.

That "*we cannot give,*
What we do not have,"

Or that "*our cup*
Of love from God
Must be so full,

It overflows
On others everyday."

But is this
Even remotely close
To what the Savior said

When the twelve disciples
Begged for spiritual bread?

"*And the apostles*
Said to the Lord,

'Increase our faith.'

So the Lord said,

'If you have faith
As a mustard seed,

You can say to this
Mulberry tree,

'Be pulled up by the roots

And be planted in the sea,'
And it would obey you.'" Luke 17:5-6

A mustard seed of faith?

Perhaps.
But surely only
At the start.

Because aren't we supposed
To water it?
And weed it?

And nurture it
And feed it?

Until our tiny
Seed of faith sprouts,

And grows to be
As mighty as a tree?

But no,
This isn't what
The Savior said at all.

Nor did He ever indicate,
That our seed of faith
Would need to grow so tall.

And the only time
It seems He did,

The tiny seed He spoke of
Did not refer to faith at all.

Instead,
It symbolized
The growth and spread

Of the kingdom of God
On earth.

Matthew 13:31-32
Mark 4:30-32
Luke 13:18-19

Okay,
Then perhaps what Jesus
Really meant was

That a mustard seed of faith
Can move a mountain,

Matthew 17:20

But only if it's genuine,
And certified as true.

And only if there's not
An ounce of doubt
In our heart

That disbelieves
What God can do.

But no,
Jesus never ever
Said it this way.

Nor did He ever indicate
That it's the quality,

And not the quantity
That matters.

And the reason why He didn't
Might surprise you.

Because how much
Flour and oil

Did the widow
Say she had?

About a mustard seed's worth,
Perhaps?

And yet,
Even though
Elijah knew this,

Did he apologize
Because he asked her?

Or hypothesize
On how she ought to find
More food a little faster?

Or did he simply sigh
And say the Lord
Must have meant someone else?

No,
He didn't.

In fact,
He seemed to think
A mustard seed-sized meal—

Was just enough for her
To do what with?

It was just enough for her
To have something in her hand
To give away!

But,

What became of
Her meager measure,
The very moment that she did?

We call her
The destitute widow
Of Zarephath.

But what can we surmise
About the size of her faith?

As in,
How much
Do you think she really had?

Because Elijah,
Was a total stranger.

So could she really put
Her total trust in him?

No.
The truth be known,
We know she couldn't.

For in her dire situation
What she really had

Was just *an ounce* of faith,
And *a ton* of desperation.

And yet,
Even though
Elijah knew this,

Did he chide her
To increase it?

Or advise her
On how she ought to
Strengthen it?

Or did he simply sigh,

And say the Lord
Must have meant someone else?

No,
He didn't.

In fact,
He seemed to think
A mustard seed of faith,

Was just enough for her
To do what with?

It was just enough for her,
To have something in her heart
To give away!

But,

What became of
Her feeble faith
The very moment that she did?

So what are we
To think then?

That she was just
An ordinary widow,

With no extraordinary reason
To explain the reason
She was singled out?

Surely not!

Perhaps it was because
She was so full of happiness,
It overflowed,

And everyone around her
Wanted what she had?

But no,
Not from what
She told Elijah.

Okay,

Then what about the strength
Of her relationship
With the Lord?

Was this the reason
Why the God of Heaven
Honored her,

Because she had it
All figured out?

No.
Not from what
She told Elijah.

For in the land of Sidon,
Ashtoreth reigned supreme, 1 Kings 11:5

Whom everyone
Believed to be the goddess

Of sensual love
And virility,

And everyone around her
Worshiped her.

Everyone,
Including Sidon's

Heathen king,

Who was the father
Of her royal wickedness,

Queen Jezebel,

Israel's evil queen,
And a major reason
For the drought. 1 Kings 16:31

So,
In light of all
We've come to know,

There is still one thing
We would really like to know.

Which is…

Why was she
Who knew not God,

And who had so little
Faith in God,

So richly blessed?

Simply put,

It was because
She understood the meaning of
The Mustard Seed Concept.

That it's not about
How much we have to have,

But rather
How little we have to have,

To have something

In our heart or hand
To give away!

This is why
The Savior said

That just
A mustard seed of faith
Will do. Matthew 17:20

And this is why the widow,
Who thought she had so little,

Actually had
A whole lot more
Than she knew. 1 Kings 17:12

Because how much,
Of anything at all
Must we have

To have something
In our heart or hand
To give away?

Just a mustard seeds' worth
Of anything at all
Will do.

Anything!

Because if faith
Is a Fruit of the Spirit, Galatians 5:22-23

And if just a mustard seed
Of faith will do, Luke 17:6

Then the very same

Principle applies

To all the other Fruits
And spiritual attributes too! James 1:17

And the Fruits
Of the Spirit are,

Love,
Joy,
Peace,

Patience,
Kindness,
Goodness,

Faithfulness,
Gentleness,
And self-control. Galatians 5:22-23

But how,
Pray tell,

Can just a mustard seed
Of patience be enough?

Or how can half an ounce
Of peace of mind suffice?

Or how

Can having hardly any
Happiness at all
Make anybody happy?

The only reason
Why it can,

Is because,

Even if we only have
An infinitesimal amount,

When we share it,

God has promised
To renew it

So we never
Run out!

This,

Is the secret He concealed
In the mustard seed-sized
Meal,

The widow fed Elijah.

And yet God has promised
To reveal it

To all who seek
To do the same.

To all

Who seek to feed the needs
Of others first,

Instead of being focused
On their own needs first,

Or on the things
They think they need
Or must attain.

For would the miracle
Have occurred

If the widow had insisted

That she eat first?

Or if she had demanded
That she had to have
Some proof first?

Or,
If she had asserted
That she had to have

An overflowing measure
In her own cup first?

No.
It never would have.

Instead,
God waited till her flour bin
Had been completely emptied,

For the needs
Of others first,

Before He spoke the word
That re-infused it.

No.
It never would have.

Instead,
God waited till her heart
Had been completely emptied,

For the needs
Of others first,

Before He spoke the word
That re-imbued it.

"Increase our faith"
Is what the twelve disciples said. Luke 17:5

But had they learned a lesson
From the widow,

Whose needs
Would they have been
More focused on instead?

Their own needs?
Or the needs of others?

Others!

"Increase my faith"
Is a prayer
We've often heard or said.

But when we learn a lesson
From the widow,

Whose needs
Will we tend to be
More focused on instead?

Our own needs?
Or on the needs of others?

Others!

Because it's never been about
How much we have to have,

Instead
It has always been about
How little we have to have

To have something

In our heart or hand
To give away!

So knowing this,
Now how should we pray?
And now what should we say?

We should pray and say,

"Thank You Lord,
For the promise
I will always have

At least a mustard seed's worth
Of everything I need to have.

Now please help me find someone
Who needs these very things,

And teach me how to try
To give them all away."

And how do we
"Give them all away"?

By simply seeking
To encourage or increase

The very things we think
We have the very least of

In the hearts and minds
Of others every day.

And how do we
"Give them all away"?

By saying something
Just as simple as,

"I'm sorry."

Or, "Please forgive me."
Or, "What can I do
To help today?"

Even when it *seems like*
It's the hardest thing
We've ever had to say!

But we say it anyway.

And the reason
Why we say it

Is because
Now we know

That there is really
Only one way

To truly walk with God
And grow in grace.

And that's by letting
Someone who's impatient
Cut in line.

Or by sharing just a moment
Of our time.

Or by a thousand other
Little things

The Lord empowers us
To do or say

To help and bless
The lives of others everyday!

But isn't it,
A little hypocritical

To encourage others
To be happy
When we're not?

Or to try
To nurture patience
In the hearts of others

When we ourselves
Are overwrought?

No,
Because *the very instant,*
That we do,

In faith
However small,

A miracle occurs.

And even though
It seemed like

We had hardly any
Happiness at all,

God gives us yet another,
And then another,

And then another
Mustard seed of happiness
To share with those around us,

Until the magnitude
Of what the Lord has wrought
Confounds us.

Because we just gave away
A heaping wheelbarrow full

Of the very thing
We thought we had
The very least of,

And yet now we know
Is boundless! Galatians 5:22-23

Only then,

Can we ever start
To comprehend
Or discover

That it's never been
About the greatness
Of our faith

Or the sum
Of all our grandiose
Endeavors. Titus 3:5-6

But rather,

It has always been about
The fact that,
With God,

Just a mustard seed

Of anything at all
Is all we ever need

To always have enough
To feed the needs
Of those around us! Luke 6:38

Much Fruit

The Fruit of the Spirit
Should be found
In every Christian's life. Galatians 5:22-23

For if these things
In us abound,

The Father's name
Is glorified. John 15:8

But,
Will God bequeath us
Peace of mind,

Or buoy our faith,
Or make us kind

If we only offer up
A rushed or shallow prayer
From time to time?

Or is there something
To be said
About sincerity?

And a spirit of humility?

And the *earnestness,*
With which we pray
And seek?

Sleepy streets yawned,
And darkened houses
Dreamed on,

As Jesus
And eleven pensive men
Passed by,

Softly walking
On the shadows
Of the night.

And yet even though
Gethsemane

They could faintly see
In feeble light,

For reasons only
Jesus knew,

Judas,
Was nowhere in sight. John 18:1-3

Which meant

That it was almost all
But over now.

His hour
Had nearly come. Matthew 26:45-47

But what could He say

That He hadn't said?

Or do
That He hadn't done?

As Jesus slowly walked,

And calmly talked
With His disciples
As they wend their way,

The moonlight,
Shone like a spotlight

On a fruitful vine
Beside the garden gate.

And this
Is what it prompted Him
To say.

"I am the vine,
You are the branches.

He who abides
In Me,

And I in him,

Bears much fruit;

For without Me
You can do nothing.

If anyone
Does not abide in Me,

He is cast out
As a branch

And is withered;

And they gather them

And throw them
Into the fire,

And they are burned." John 15:5-6

And then
For added emphasis
He added,

"By this
My Father is glorified,
That you bear much fruit;

So you will be
My disciples." John 15:8

"That you bear much fruit."
It still resounds today!

But how can we be
More productive vines

Or fruitful trees
From day to day?

For in the Sermon on the Mount
The Savior also spoke
Of bearing fruit this way,

Saying,

"Even so,
Every good tree
Bears good fruit,

But a bad tree
Bears bad fruit.

A good tree
Cannot bear bad fruit,

Nor can a bad tree
Bear good fruit.

Every tree
That does not bear
Good fruit

Is cut down
And thrown into the fire.

Therefore
By their fruits
You will know them." Matthew 7:17-20

The good fruit,
Is the Fruit of the Spirit
Of course. Galatians 5:22-23

But does the Word of God
Enumerate the bad?

"Now the works
Of the flesh
Are evident,

Which are:

Adultery,
Fornication,
Uncleanness,

Lewdness,
Idolatry,
Sorcery,

Hatred,
Contentions,
Jealousies,

Outbursts of wrath,
Selfish ambitions,
Dissensions,

Heresies,
Envy,
Murders,

Drunkenness,
Revelries,
And the like;

Of which
I tell you beforehand,

Just as I also told you
In time past,

That those who practice
Such things

Will not inherit
The kingdom of God." Galatians 5:19-21

Condensed,
Distilled and coalesced,
It sounds like this:

That even though we know
We're saved by grace through faith
In Jesus Christ alone,

The things we do
Or do not do,

Are *never* unimportant. Ephesians 2:8 Titus 3:1-8

For if the God of all
Has promised all
The power to obey, Philippians 4:13 Romans 1:16-17

Then what will happen
If we won't let Him change
Our wicked ways? Zechariah 7:8-13

Will barren branches,

Or those who choose
To bear bad fruit,

Survive? Luke 13:6-9

Or will those who say
They love the Lord,

And yet whose deeds
Deny His holy name,

Be saved? Matthew 7:22-23

The Bible abounds
With stories

Of those who thought
They could.

And it tells of the woes
Of those who walked
With those who walked with God,

But they themselves,
Never did. Genesis 4:3-12 2 Kings 5:15-27

And yet,
Even though we know

Their stories never end well, Matthew 27:1-5 Acts 5:1-10

Are we always confident
We know the way
Our story will?

Or has it ever *seemed* like

The more we try
To be like Him,

The less we seem
To do His will? Romans 7:18-19, 24

For even though we know
The Lord forgives us

When we have to ask Him
For forgiveness, 1 John 1:9

What about our neighbor?
Or our friend?
Or our spouse?

Do we ever start to wonder
If they doubt us

When we have to say
We're sorry
For the very same thing,

Over,
And over again?

What then?

Eventually,
If we do not gain
The victory,

Don't our words begin
To sound a little hollow?

And our apologies,
Start to seem a little shallow?

Even to the point where

We are loath
To say we're sorry
Yet again?

Or what if,

Even when we claim
The promises of God
To make us strong, 2 Peter 1:2-4

We do the very thing
We vowed we'd never do,

Over,
And over again?

What then?

Eventually,
If we do not gain
The victory,

Don't we start to question
Our sincerity?

And forfeit peace of mind
For insecurity?

And in the end,
Decide to our chagrin

That we simply seem

To love the sin

More than we say
We love the Savior? John 14:15 1 John 5:2-4

Hearts hurt
And heads ache

Thinking these defeated
Sinking thoughts.

Sometimes

We wonder if we'll ever
Find the victory
That we sought,

The "much fruit"
Jesus spoke of—

The Fruit of the Spirit
Abounding in our life
That we long for. John 15:8 Galatians 5:22-23

If you have ever had
Such fleeting thoughts

Or pondered on
Your fruitless situation,

Then perhaps the reason
For your consternation

Is just a simple
Misinterpretation

Of what it means,
To be a fruit tree.

The Fruit Tree Analogy:

Please stop reading
Right now,

And find two pieces
Of your favorite
Kinds of fruit.

An apple
Or an orange
Will do,

But if it's something
Like the latter,

Please peel one
As if prepared to eat,

And then do the following.

First,
Please name each one

For a Fruit of the Spirit
That you feel like you need
Or know you often lack. Galatians 5:22-23

One could be
The fruit of faith
That's hard to find,

While the other one
Could symbolize
The fruit of happiness,

Or patience,

Or a fleeting sense

Of peace of mind.

And now,
Holding one in either hand,

Please stand,

And when you slowly
Lift your limbs
On either side,

What have you just become?

A fruit tree,
Right?

A fruit-bearing
Fruit of the Spirit
Fruit tree,

Just like we're
Supposed to be!

Well,
Not exactly.

Because there really isn't
"Much fruit"
Hanging on your branches,

Is there?

And yet don't you really
Long for more?

And yet don't you often
Pray and plead for more?

And don't you *hunger*
To be filled

With the very
Fruit of the Spirit
That you hold?

If so,
Then freely eat!

Eat,
And keep on eating

Until your stomach is as full
As your heart longs to be.

Filled,
With the Fruits of the Spirit!

But wait a minute.
Isn't something wrong here?

Because aren't we
Supposed to be

A spiritual fruit tree?

Or at least resemble those
Who say they try to be?

And yet,
If so,

Have you ever seen
A fruit tree
Eat its own fruit?

No,
And that's because
They don't.

And yet whom do we

Seek to feed

When we say or pray
The following?

"*I need* more of this Fruit.
And *I need* more of that Fruit.

And please Lord,

Please *fill me* with
The Fruits of the Spirit,
Today!"

This prayer

Exemplifies
The reason why
The Lord used parables.

And it summarizes
Why He said
Our lives are comparable

To fruit trees.

Because a fruit tree,
Doesn't ever eat
Its own fruit.

And a lowly fruit tree,
Never seeks to feed
Its own root.

Nor does it ever try
To multiply
Or bear more fruit,

Just so it can satisfy
Its branches.

Instead,

A fruit tree
Always seeks to feed
The needs of others first.

And a faithful fruit tree,
Always tries to satisfy
The lives of those around it first,

Even if there's
Very little fruit
Growing on its branches.

So can we really
Claim to be a fruit tree?

Or can we truly
Say we aim
To be a fruit tree

If our happiness depends
Upon the quantity of fruit
Hanging on our branches?

In the Sermon
On the Mount,

The Savior said
Something else
That applies here.

For when He wanted
Those who heard Him

To know the way
They'd heard it all their life
Wasn't so,

He started out by saying
Something similar
To the words we read below.

"You have heard it said of old,"
He said,

And then,

He reiterated
What they always said. Matthew 5:21-22

"But I say unto you …"

And then He boldly told them
What they should have said.

Now let's say the same ourselves
To illustrate

What Jesus might have said
To set the record straight

Today.

"You have heard it said of old,
That you need to feed
Your own needs first,

Before you seek to feed
The needs of others.

But I say unto you

That a fruit tree
Never eats its own fruit.

Instead it always seeks to feed
The needs of those around it,
First,

Even if
There is very little fruit
Growing on its branches."

Based on :
Matthew 5:43-48 .
and Romans 13:8-10

Some say,

That feeding others first
Sounds *way too*
Impossible.

Or that it seems
Way too implausible
To ever really work.

But is it?

Yes.

But only in
The very same sense,

That every miracle
The Lord ever did,
Or ever will do,

Is utterly impossible
For us to fabricate,

Or imitate,
Or do.

Simply put,

The ways of God
Are way beyond
Our comprehension.

And yet even though
They far exceed

What mortal minds can mention,

There is still one thing

That the God of all
Wants all His followers
To know about redemption.

And that is

The irrefutable,
Unexplainable,

"Much fruit" miracle
That changes our condition

The very moment
We believe

And serving others first
Becomes our mission.

So go ahead,
By the grace of God,
Become a fruit tree!

And seek to feed
The needs of others first,

And try to help
And bless the lives
Of others first,

Even when it *seems like,*

It's the very opposite
Of everything you think
You ought to do!

But why,

Even try

To feed the needs
Of others first?

Or why should we
Even strive

To strengthen faith
And hope in others first

When our own faith
Feels feeble,

Or is faltering,

Or when there's hardly
Any fruit at all
Clinging to our branches? Galatians 5:22-23

It's just because
That's what
Fruit trees do!

They mimic Him
Who made them, John 1:1-3

And gave them
All He had, John 3:16 Philippians 2:5-8

So they could bless
The lives of others first,

And make the hearts
Of others glad! Matthew 15:32-38

So the final
Answer is,

No.

The miracle of "much fruit"
Doesn't ever happen

Just because our faith
Feels strong.

Or just because
We can't imagine
Anything we're doing wrong.

If we could,
We'd need to ask forgiveness
Of course. Ezekiel 18:30-32

And then abide in Him
And He in us,
Of course. John 15:4, 10

But then,
A nanosecond later,

And even when it *feels*
As if our faith
Is very small,

Or even if it *seems*
As if we've hardly any
Happiness at all,

Even then,

If we seek to feed
The needs of others first,

We will start to see
And comprehend

Why the miracle
Of "much fruit"

Is really very,
Very little us,
And very everything Him! 2 Corinthians 12:7-10 Psalm 71:14-19

Because

Now we know,
From what the Lord Himself
Has shown us,

That even if we only have
An apple's worth
Of happiness

Today,

With God,
It is utterly
Impossible

To ever give it all away!

"And Elijah
Said to her,

'Do not fear.

Go and do
As you have said,

But make me a small cake
From it first,
And bring it to me.

Afterward

Make some
For yourself
And your son.' " 1 Kings 17:13

"So she went away
And did according
To the word of Elijah;

And she
And he
And her household

Ate for many days.

The bin of flour
Was not used up,

Nor did the jar of oil
Run dry,

According to the word
Of the LORD
Which He spoke by Elijah." 1 Kings 17:15-16

God's Eternal Word
Is sure: Psalm 119:89

If we do the same
Today,

We will see the same today.

The same supernatural
Miracle of "much fruit"

That Jesus spoke of

On the night the moonlight
Shone like a spotlight

On the deed that Judas did
When he betrayed Him.

For even then

When He knew
The very ones He spoke to

Would soon run away
Or say they never knew Him, Mark 14:29-72

And even though
His own heart broke

With the very thought,
That His Father
Might disown Him, Mark 15:34

Even then,
Jesus,

Still sought
To soothe the hearts of those

Who really should have sought
To soothe Him. Matthew 26:36-41

And He steadfastly
Focused on the needs
Of those around Him first. John 13:2-5

And He first and lastly
Spoke of hope

And how we ought to feed
Our neighbor first. John 14:1-3 John 15:12-13

And then,

To summarize
The reason why
He simply said,

"These things
I have spoken to you,

That My joy
May remain in you,

And that your joy,
May be full." John 15:11

For His joy

Has always been
The joy of showing us

That even if we only have
An apples worth
Of happiness,

Today,

With God,
It is utterly
Impossible

To ever give it
All away! Matthew 14:15-21

The Curse

Some have said that faith
Is like the gas in our car.

  Without it
    We cannot go very far

    And that the way
      To keep our tank full

      Is to read the Word
        And be more prayerful

        And to keep our thoughts
          On God throughout the day.

But what happens,
  If the busy-ness of life
    Interrupts these things

  And deprives us
    Of the time

    We set aside
      To meditate
        And pray?

Will we tend to be

Impatient?

Or way too
Complacent?

Or unable to resist
Because our faith is weak?

Yesterday,
When Jesus rode
Into the city,

The cloaks of those
Who waved and cheered

Were cast upon the street
The donkey trod. Matthew 21:1-8

And yet even though
The Pharisees

Complained,

Jesus
Offered no apologies,

For what the people
Proclaimed.

"Hosanna
To the Son of David!

Blessed is He
Who comes in the name
Of the LORD!

Hosanna
In the highest!" Matthew 21:9

Then He went
Into the Temple

And chased
The moneychangers out

And overturned the seats
Of those who sold doves. Matthew 21:12-13

The lame,
And halt

Were welcomed in instead,

And He healed
Everyone who knew
They needed to be healed, Matthew 21:14

While the hearts of those
Whose minds were filled
With avarice

And greed Luke 11:39-41

Prowled around
The outside,

Waiting for
An opportunity

To pounce. Matthew 21:15-16
Matthew 26:1-5

But that
Was yesterday.

Today,
The Lord had something
Rather harsh to say

To a fig tree?

"Now in the morning,
As He returned
To the city,

He was hungry.
And seeing a fig tree
By the road,

He came to it
And found nothing on it
But leaves,

And said to it,

'Let no fruit
Grow on you
Ever again.'

Immediately
The fig tree
Withered away.

And when the disciples
Saw it,

They marveled,
Saying,

'How did the fig tree
Wither away
So soon?' " Matthew 21:18-20

Why,
Pray tell,

Did Jesus
Seem to say something

That sounded so

Un-Christlike?

Because if fruit
Was truly out of season, Mark 11:13

Then why curse
The fig tree?

To understand,

We need to know a few
Fig tree facts
First.

Fact:

Fig trees
Bear two crops.

The *breba crop,*
Matures in early Spring
Before the leaves appear.

It is very small,
And inferior.

While the main crop,
Which are the *true figs,*
Ripens in the Fall.

Fact:

A fig tree
With no *breba crop*
In the Spring

Will not bear
True figs in the Fall.

The tree

Is totally barren.

Okay,
So what are we
To think then?

That Jesus cursed
The fig tree

Because it made
Him angry,

Because He was
So hungry?

No,
Not at all.

Instead,

It was because
It symbolized
The lives of the Pharisees,

By identifying
Why they bore
No fruit.

No spiritual fruit. Galatians 5:22-23

In this respect,

It was precisely like
Another fig tree
That Jesus spoke of.

The Parable
Of the Barren Fig Tree.

"A certain man
Had a fig tree
Planted in his vineyard,

And he came
Seeking fruit on it
And found none.

Then he said
To the keeper
Of his vineyard,

'Look,

For three years
I have come seeking fruit
On this fig tree

And find none.

Cut it down;
Why does it
Use up the ground?'

But he answered
And said to him,

'Sir,
Let it alone
This year also,

Until I dig around it
And fertilize it.

And if it bears fruit,
Well.

But if not,
After that
You can cut it down.' " Luke 13:6-9

The question,
Jesus seems to pose
Here is:

"Where were
The little figs

That should have fed
The hungry farmer?"

It is very clear
For all to see,

That they were *in the tree,*
Instead of *on the tree,*

Tightly sealed in the sap
That flowed *inside*
The barren branches.

For the roots had "eaten"
Everything the tree needed,
To bear much fruit, Isaiah 5:1-7

But like the Pharisees,
This tree's priorities,
Were backwards,

And from day to day
Its barren branches
Seemed to say,

"*I need* a little more
Of the sun's bright rays,

And *I need* a gentle wind
To move me.

I need another drink
Of the dew or rain,

And *I need* a longer root
To feed me."

Essentially,
We could say this was
A fig tree

That ate its own fruit

Because it used
All the nutriments
That God had given it

To feed itself,
Instead of others.

But then again,

Don't we too
Do the same

If we only offer leaves
To those who look for love
And understanding? James 2:14-17

Or if we fail to feed
The needs of those

We deem to be impatient
Or demanding? Matthew 5:38-42

And then,
Notwithstanding,

We say the reason
Why we swore
Or have a temper

Is because
"I didn't get to
Pray enough today."

Or because
"I didn't get to
Meditate enough today."

Or because
"I didn't get to
Eat, or drink, or sleep enough,

Or to read
The Word of God enough
To make me strong enough,

To make it through the day!"

When Elijah
Met the widow,
She felt the same way too.

For she echoed everything
That everyone around her,
Said we ought to do. 1 Kings 17:8-12

But would the miracle
Have occurred

If she had mimicked
What her neighbors
Said we ought to do?

Or
If she had done

The very same things

That we still are taught
We ought to do?

For every reason
We can think of

To explain the reason
Why *we think* we need
To feed our own needs first,

There is a withered,
Barren fig tree

Standing by
The road of life

That warns us
Of the final end
Of those who do.

This
Is why the Savior
Cursed the fig tree.

No,
Not because there wasn't
A bumper crop of fruit.

But rather,
Because it sought to feed
Its own needs first

Instead of feeding others
Any fruit.

For even if the Maker
Of the fig tree

Had only found
One little tiny fig
Clinging to its branches,

Do you think
He would have cursed it?

No,

Because it's never been
About how many figs
Are *on the tree.* Mark 12:41-44

But rather,

It has always been about
The infinite amount
The Lord can make

If He is *in the tree,*

When the tree
Seeks to feed the needs
Of others first.

And *we* are
The fig trees,
The planting of the Lord, Isaiah 61:1-3

If our deeds feed
Our neighbors need
For love and understanding. 1 Peter 3:8-9

Or if we seek to sow
A seed of patience

In those we deem to be
Impatient or demanding. Galatians 5:13-16

Notwithstanding,

The overwhelming fact
That we *feel like*
We only have

One little tiny fig
Of happiness
Clinging to our branches.

But why,
Should we even try,

To do the things
That often seem
So impossible? Isaiah 58:6-12

Because
The very instant

That we seek to feed
The needs of others first,

In faith,
However small,

A miracle occurs.

And even though
It *seemed like*

We had hardly any
Figs of happiness
At all, Galatians 5:22-23

God will always give us
Just enough

To always have enough
To feed the needs
Of one and all!

So are you bothered
By your barren branches?

Or by the lack
Of the Fruit
Of the Spirit in your life?

If so,
Then *don't wait*

Until you feel like you have
A bumper crop
Of patience.

Or *don't wait*

Until you feel like you have
An apple bin full
Of happiness.

Or an overflowing
Bushel basket
Full of faith.

Or,

Until you think
You finally feel
Strong enough

To have the strength
To feed the needs
Of those around you.

Instead,
Be like she
Who fed Elijah Luke 4:24-27

And seek to feed

The needs of others first,

All the time. Matthew 25:31-46
1 Corinthians 9:19-22

For when we seek
To certify the way He keeps
His promises,

We will surely find

That He who made
The very first fig tree,
And then pronounced it good, Genesis 1:11-12

Will give us just exactly
What we need,

Just exactly
When we need it,

And just exactly like
He said He would! Romans 8:31-32

The Waiter

The fiber of our faith
Has been compared
To a muscle,

Where it's said
That exercise

Will increase the size
And make it stronger

And inactivity,
Will lead to weakness
And decay.

If so,
Then are bulging
Spiritual biceps

Our ultimate aim
And highest goal?

The twelve disciples
Seemed to think so.

Day after day
They watched
And listened,

Amazed
And awed,

As the lame
Leapt for joy

When they felt
His gentle touch. Matthew 11:2-6

And the deaf
Praised His name,

While the dumb
Could not be hushed. Matthew 15:29-31

And the blind,

Yes,
Even those
Who had no eyes

From birth John 9:1-7

Rejoiced to see
The face of He
Who healed them! Matthew 9:27-33
Luke 18:35-43

But,

The more
The twelve disciples
Watched,

And listened,

And talked

Among themselves,

The more they felt
Their faith

Was far too weak
To please Him.

Especially,
Today.

From a distance,

Jesus,

And Peter,
James,
And John,

Could see a crowd
Had gathered
Around the other nine.

But why?

*"And when they had come
To the multitude,*

A man came to Him,

*Kneeling down to Him
And saying,*

*'Lord,
Have mercy on my son,*

*For he is an epileptic
And suffers severely;*

*For he often falls
Into the fire*

And often
Into the water.

So I brought him
To Your disciples,

But they could not
Cure him.'

Then Jesus answered
And said,

'O faithless
And perverse generation,

How long
Shall I be with you?

How long
Shall I bear with you?

Bring him here to Me.'

And Jesus
Rebuked the demon,
And it came out of him;

And the child
Was cured
From that very hour.

Then the disciples
Came to Jesus privately
And said,

'Why could we not
Cast it out?'

So Jesus said to them,

'Because of your unbelief;

For assuredly,
I say to you,

If you have faith
As a mustard seed,

You will say
To this mountain,

'Move from here to there,'
And it will move;

And nothing
Will be impossible
For you.' " Matthew 17:14-21

Really?

Nothing
Impossible
With just a mustard seed?

The twelve disciples
Thought this seemed
Way too impossible

For them to acquiesce
Or believe!

Instead,

They focused on increasing
And strengthening

The thing they deemed
To be too weak,

And asked the Lord

To help them never have

A mustard seed
Of unbelief.

"And the apostles
Said to the Lord,

'Increase our faith.'

So the Lord said,

'If you have faith
As a mustard seed,

You can say
To this mulberry tree,

'Be pulled up by the roots
And be planted in the sea,'

And it would obey you.' " Luke 17:5-6

On the surface,

Jesus seemed to tell them
What He'd told them
Once before,

But if we listen in,
There is way more.

For this time,

With a simple illustration
That we all agree is true,

He takes the way
We think of faith,

And how we think

We're supposed to
Strengthen faith,

And made it
Something new.

New?

Or was it just Elijah's
Timeless message,

Dusted off
And re-introduced?

"And which of you,
Having a servant plowing
Or tending sheep,

Will say to him
When he has come in
From the field,

'Come at once
And sit down to eat!'

But will he not rather
Say to him,

'Prepare something
For my supper,

And gird yourself
And serve me
Till I have eaten and drunk,

Afterwards
You will eat and drink?' " Luke 17:7-8

"Feed me first!"

The master
  To his servant said—

The master
  To his faithful servant,

Like Elijah
  To the hungry widow said. 1 Kings 17:10-13

And what did
  His servant say?

Did he tell his master
  That he couldn't,
    Because he had to eat first?

Or that he wouldn't,
  Because he needed
    To renew his strength first?

No,
  He didn't.

And yet isn't this

Precisely what
  The twelve disciples said

When they,
  Who were the servants,

Asked their Master
  To be spiritually fed?

Jesus gently pointed out
  Whose needs

They should have focused
  On instead.

And had we asked
The same today,

This is what
He might have said.

"And which of you,
Having traveled
To your favorite place to eat,

Will say to the waiter
Who waits on your table,

'Come at once,
And sit down to eat!'

But will you not rather say,

'I want some of this,
And I want some of that,
And what is your special today?'

For everyone
Who orders knows,

That faithful waiters
Always serve the needs
Of those,

Who place an order,
First,

Before they stop to eat."

Based on :
Luke 17:7-8

Spiritually speaking,

We, too,
Must do the same.

The same as the widow,

Gaunt and sad,

Who gave a stranger
All she had.

Not waiting
Until she knew
She had enough to eat.

And not debating,
Until she knew if God
Would satisfy her needs.

This

Fundamental shift
In our priorities,

Where we seek to feed
The needs of others

First

Instead of being focused
On our own necessities,

Is the golden key
That causes Heaven's gates
To open wide,

Where the pantry
Of the Lord
Is always full,

And every shelf
Is well supplied,

From which He gives us
Everything we need

To feed the needs
Of everyone
Who sits at every table! Luke 6:38

For this
Is where the flour of faith
Comes from! 1 Corinthians 12:4-11

And this

Is where the golden oil
Of everlasting joy
Comes from! 1 Thessalonians 2:19-20

No,
Not from striving
To increase it,

But rather
From being like
A faithful waiter

Who freely
Feeds the needs
Of others *first,*

From what the Lord Himself
So freely gives us. Proverbs 11:25

This profound ability
To give so overflowing
And so endlessly

Is the secret God concealed
In the mustard seed-sized
Meal

The widow fed Elijah.

And this
Is what the Lord
Has promised to reveal

To all

Who seek
To do the same.

To all
Who seek to feed
The needs of others first,

Instead of staying focused
On their own needs first,

Or on the things
They think they need
Or must attain. Philippians 2:1-4

So is a plate
Full of patience,
Printed on the menu?

Yet *it seems like*

You only have
A mustard seed of patience
Abiding in you?

If so,

Then *don't wait*
Until you think you have
Enough to fill the order.

And *don't wait*

Until it feels like

Your faith and love
Are growing stronger.

Because it's never been about
How much the waiter
Has to have.

But rather,

It has always been about
How much his Master
Always has.

He,
Who from eternity,

Has always had
An infinite amount

And yet He often
Only gives us
Just a very small amount

To test us,

To see if we will *still seek*
To feed the needs
Of others first,

Even when it seems like,

There is not enough
For everyone
Who sits at every table.

"Increase my faith"
Is a prayer
We've often heard or said.

But Jesus
Gently pointed out
Whose needs

We really need to be
More focused on instead

When He said,

"Whoever
Desires to become great
Among you

Shall be your servant.

And whoever of you
Desires to be first
Shall be slave of all.

For even the Son of Man
Did not come
To be served,

But to serve,
And to give His life
A ransom for many." Mark 10:43-45

By the grace of God,

We, too,
Can learn to be
A faithful waiter,

And we, too,
Can learn to feed the needs
Of one another

First,

And thereby

Emulate our lowly
Servant/Savior,

Who Himself,

Always sought
To feed the needs
Of others first. Matthew 11:29 Philippians 2:5-8

For only then,
Can we ever start
To comprehend

Why the Master
Of the Universe

Will one day condescend

To set aside His royal robes
And regal crown,

And stoop
To serve the needs
Of all His loyal servants

Whom He Himself
Has seated

At His supper table.

"Blessed
Are those servants

Whom the Master,
When He comes,
Will find watching.

Assuredly,
I say to you

That He will gird Himself
And have them sit down
To eat,

And will come
And serve them." Luke 12:37

Rest

Is being a Christian
Easy?
Or hard?

Or neither one
Because it's both?

Of the three,
Which one
Is it supposed to be?

And from
Your personal experience,

Would you agree?

For centuries,

Men had twisted
And distorted
The teachings of God

Until everyone thought
The twisted teachings

Were true.

Jesus
Came to untwist it.

Because an eye for an eye
And a tooth for a tooth — Leviticus 24:20

Was deemed
More weighty a matter
Than mercy

Or forgiveness
Or turning the other cheek. — Micah 6:8; Isaiah 50:6

And sanctimonious
Public prayers

And flowing robes
And pious airs — Matthew 23; Mark 12:41-44

Had overshadowed
True humility
And sincerity

And doing good deeds
From the heart. — Proverbs 14:31; Colossians 3:12-15

But when Jesus came
To make it straight,

Those who loved it crooked
Found fault.

"Then the Pharisees
And scribes
Asked Him,

'Why do Your disciples

Not walk

According to the tradition
Of the elders,

But eat bread
With unwashed hands?'

He answered
And said to them,

'Well did Isaiah
Prophesy of you
Hypocrites,

As it is written:

'This people
Honors Me
With their lips,

But their heart
Is far from Me.

And in vain
They worship Me,

Teaching as doctrines
The commandments of men.' ' " Mark 7:5-7

In Bible times
Men taught

That pleasing God
To gain the blessing
That they sought

Was extremely difficult
And very hard.

But what about today?

Are happiness
And peace of mind

Or patience
Or the fruit of being kind
Easy?

Even though
We plead with God
To grant these very things?

Or have you ever sighed

And wondered why
Your search
For spiritual rest

Seems so laborious?

If talking the talk
Is a walk in the park,

But walking the walk
Can wear you out,

Then perhaps it is time
To redefine
What Jesus meant

When He said,

"Come unto Me,
All you who labor
And are heavy laden,

And I will give you rest.

Take My yoke
Upon you,

And learn from Me,

For I am gentle
And lowly in heart:

And you will find rest
For your souls.

For My yoke is easy,
And My burden
Is light." Matthew 11:28-30

Easy?

Some say
This is just a relative term,

And that serving Him
Is simply *easier*

Than having
A guilty conscience
Haunt us all the day.

Others
Insist the yoke is tandem,

Like a bicycle
Built for two,

Easy to ride

As long as we let the Lord
Pump the peddles
On the hills.

And while

Some of the above
Seems true,

None of the above
Sums it up,

Which is what
The Bible writer
Was alluding to

When he said,

"There remains
Therefore

A rest
For the people of God.

For he who has entered
His rest

Has himself
Also ceased
From his works

As God did
From His." Hebrews 4:9-10

"For He has spoken
In a certain place

Of the seventh day
In this way:

'And God rested
On the seventh day
From all His works.'" Hebrews 4:4

God's work?

Compared to our work?

And His rest?
Compared to our rest?

But how can we,
Who oft grow faint
And weary,

Ever learn to rest
Like He
Who never does? Isaiah 40:28

The answer is,
That *we never can*
Learn to rest like Him,

And *we never will*
Learn to rest like Him,

Until we learn
To labor like Him.

Like He
Who labored to create us. Psalm 95:1-6

For in the dawn
Of our beginning,

The very genesis

Of life on Earth
And Adam's lineage

Did the Word of God
Who made the World say, John 1:1-14

"Let there be light."

And then He stopped

To rest

And blessed
The very first day? Genesis 1:1-5

No,
He didn't.

But if not,
Why not?

Or did our Lord
And Maker,

Mankind's Savior
And Creator say, Isaiah 45:9-12 Isaiah 54:5

"Let there be air."

And then He stopped
To rest

And blessed
The second day? Genesis 1:6-8

No,
He didn't.

But once again
We have to ask,

If not,
Why not?

Or why not
Stop on the third? Genesis 1:9-13

Or hallow the fourth? Genesis 1:14-19

Or rest and bless the fifth

With all the beasts,
And birds? Genesis 1:20-25

Why
The ceaseless toil

Without a pause or break

When Jesus
Could have stopped
To celebrate,

Or commemorate,

Any day He wished?

All we need to do
To know the reason why

Is gaze into a mirror
And ask our Maker why.

For it was because
Of what He did

When everything
Was finally ready
On the sixth.

"And the LORD God
Formed man
Of the dust of the ground,

And breathed
Into his nostrils
The breath of life;

And man
Became a living soul." Genesis 2:7 KJV

And then He made
The lovely Eve.

And Adam
Deeply loved her. Genesis 2:18-23

And they both loved
The Selfless One

Whose hands
Refused to rest,

And whose heart
Could not be blessed,

Until *all*
Their earthly needs
Were fully met.

Only then,
Did the hands of Jesus
Stop to rest. Genesis 2:1-3 Isaiah 44:24

For God's rest,
The kind of rest
The Lamb of God blessed, Matthew 12:1-8 John 1:29

Is a feed-your-fellowman
Before-you-rest,
Rest.

Just like she
Who fed Elijah. 1 Kings 17:8-16

And God's rest,

The kind of rest
The Son of God
Blessed, 1 John 4:15-16, 20-21

Is a love your neighbor
As yourself
Labor of love Leviticus 19:18 Matthew 22:35-40

That constrains us

To feed the needs
Of others first
Before we stop to rest. Matthew 14:13-21

Only then

Can we ever truly
Enter into His rest. Hebrews 4:9-10

And yet if so,

Then why is wearing
His yoke

Of serving others
Said to be so easy? Matthew 11:28-29

And why
Are bearing all the burdens
That He spoke of

Deemed to be so restful
And so light? Matthew 5:38-48

It's because *we don't*
Provide the food
That feeds the multitude. Luke 9:12-17

And it's because *we don't*
Supply the seed of faith

That makes us think
It's even possible.

God does! Luke 11:9-13 Ephesians 3:14-21

All we have to do

Is freely give away
The tiny seeds of hope
That God so freely gives us.

And always seek to sow
The little seeds of happiness
That God Himself dispenses— Ecclesiastes 11:6 Hosea 10:12

Even when *it seems like*

Our faith is in decline

And hope
And happiness
Are very hard to find.

For just as surely
As we do,

We will just as surely find

That the reason why we have
An innate ability

To give so overflowing
And so endlessly John 4:6-14

Is because it doesn't
Come from within.

It comes
From God! John 3:1-8 1 John 2:28-29

And,
Because it comes
From God,

This means

That we never
Have to have
An overflowing measure

To always have enough to give
An overflowing measure
All the time.

Because for every
Seed of hope
Or happiness

That we so freely
Give away,

God will just as freely
Give us yet another,

And then another,

And then another
Mustard seeds' worth Romans 8:32

Of the very thing
We thought we never had
Enough of,

Until He overwhelms us
With the fact that

Just a mustard seeds' worth
Is *way more* than enough of
Anything we need

To always have enough
To feed the needs of others! Luke 10:25-37

This
  Is the very moment
    When we stop to marvel

At the magnitude

Of how amazing
The mustard seed miracle
Really is.

For this
Is when we finally
Start to comprehend

Why His yoke

Of serving others
Really is so easy,

And why
All the burdens
That He spoke of

Really are so restful
And so light.

Because *it's easy*

For us to always
Feel like we have

Just a mustard seed
Of faith,
Or patience,

Or peace of mind
At any given time.

And yet *it's very hard,*

For us to always

Feel like we have

An overflowing measure
All the time.

So have you ever
Felt like

You only have
A mustard seed of faith
Abiding in you?

Or has it ever
Seemed like

The measure
Of your happiness
Is so small,

That there is hardly
Any happiness at all
Residing in you?

If so,
Then that's okay!

Because He,
Whom we love to call
Our Lord and Savior,

And He,
Who also labored as
Our Maker and Creator, John 1:1-14

Has promised
He will always give us
Just exactly what we need,

And *just exactly*

When we need it, John 14:12-14

If we always seek to share it
With the very ones who need it

Before we stop to rest. Luke 12:22-34

For if we do,

Even when we think
We lack the strength to,

Then the boundless blessing
That He bound up in the rest
He promised us Isaiah 58:6-14

Will rest on us

Because our hearts
Are tightly bound

To He whose hands
Were nailed down

To the cross

Which those He loved
And labored for,
Lifted up on Calvary. Luke 23:33-34

Only then,
Did the hands of Jesus
Stop to rest.

For now He knew
That He had finally
Set us free at last

To focus on the needs
Of others first,

Just like Him,

So we could help them
Learn to labor first,
Just like Him,

Before they stop to rest. Matthew 28:18-20

"Therefore,
Since a promise remains
Of entering His rest,

Let us fear

Lest any of you
Seem to have come
Short of it . . .

For he who has entered
His rest

Has himself
Also ceased
From his works

As God did from His." Hebrews 4:1, 10

"And when Jesus
Had cried out
With a loud voice,

He said,

'Father,
Into Your hands
I commit My spirit.'

Having said this,
He breathed His last." Luke 23:46

And then our Lord and Maker
Bowed His head
And stopped to rest

On the very same day
That symbolized
The reason why

He had to wait
Until that very day

Genesis 2:1-3
Luke 23:50-56

To show us what
It really means—

To love our neighbor
As our self

Before we stop to rest.

Matthew 22:35-40
Luke 10:25-37

The Still Small Voice

Is the still small voice,
That sounds
So very near…

Always
The voice of God
The Holy Spirit,

Who whispers in our ear?

Or could it ever be
The subtle speech
Of another

Seeking to mislead us,
Or deceive us?

Jesus
Seemed not to hear
The heated talk

Of those who sought
Her execution.

But they could not demure
Nor silence

The Spirit of conviction.

"Then the scribes
And Pharisees

Brought to Him a woman
Caught in adultery.

And when they had
Set her in the midst,

They said to Him,

'Teacher,

This woman
Was caught in adultery,
In the very act.

Now Moses,
In the law,

Commanded us
That such
Should be stoned.

But what do You say?'

This they said,
Testing Him,

That they might
Have something

Of which to accuse Him.

But Jesus

Stooped down

And wrote on the ground
With His finger,

As though
He did not hear.

So when they continued
Asking Him,

He raised Himself up
And said to them,

'He who is without sin
Among you,

Let him throw a stone
At her first.'

And again
He stooped down
And wrote on the ground.

Then those who heard it,
Being convicted
By their conscience,

Went out
One by one,

Beginning with the oldest
Even to the last.

And Jesus
Was left alone,
And the woman

Standing in the midst." John 8:3-9

Both our conscience
  And every good conviction

  Are gifts of God
    To keep us from perdition. John 14:25-26 John 16:7-11

    But what if

      We will not heed His voice
        Or pay attention?

Will the still small voice
  Become a little louder,

  And then a little louder,

    Until it shouts in our ear,

      But then goes silent
        If we will not listen? Psalm 66:18 Proverbs 28:9

Or what if

  We really truly
    Want to live
      A righteous life

    But our weak will
      Can't withstand the weight
        Of strong temptations?

Will the still small voice
  Become a little
    More insistent

  And then a little
    More persistent

    Until we're so
      Sick of sinning

Or until we're so
Conscience smitten

That we finally
Can't resist it? Psalm 51:1-13

Some say

That this depicts the way
The Holy Spirit tries
To teach us.

And that by
Shouting out our sins,

And by *poking us,*
And *prodding us,*

And *shaming us*
For all our inconsistencies,

He strives to strengthen
Our resolve
To serve the Lord

Until we finally gain
The victory.

But is this
Really how the Bible says

The Holy Spirit
Tries to reach us?

By *scolding us*
If we falter or we sin? Jeremiah 31:3

Or by *deriding us*
If we stumble
Or we cave in? Hosea 11:3-4 John 3:1-8

When Satan
 Sought to find a way
  To overcome Eve,

 He did so
  By cloaking his identity

  And then by leading her
   To think that he was someone
    She could surely trust. Genesis 3:1-6

So, too,
 He still tries to do
  To this very day.

And yet whenever Satan
 Seeks to emulate

 The still small voice
  Of conviction, 1 Kings 19:11-13
John 10:27

  The very moment
   That we heed his voice

   Or start to pay attention,

    Then the father of all lies,
     Who hides behind
      His Holy Spirit guise,

     Starts to *goad us*
      And constantly *cajole us*

      To trust the Lord
       And obey.

To trust the Lord
 And obey?

But why

Would Satan ever want
To see us strive to live
A righteous life?

Because isn't he
The enemy

Of every high
And holy thought?

And doesn't he
Always seek to cause
Adversity

For everyone
Who wants to do
What Jesus taught? John 14:23-24

Yes.

But what the subtle Tempter
Hopes *we don't know*

Is how he often seeks
To hide his hatred
And his enmity

By cloaking his intentions
And his dark identity,

By sounding *almost*

Exactly like
The Holy Spirit
Speaking in our ear Isaiah 30:21

Instead of sounding
Like our evil enemy.

Because he,
 Whom we rightly call
  The Great Deceiver, knows

 That if we try
  To serve the Lord
   The way that he instructs us to 1 Timothy 4:1

  While thinking we are heeding
   What the Holy Spirit
    Says we ought to do, 1 John 3:10-15 Galatians 5:16-17

   Then we will falter,
    And become discouraged,
     And surely fail

    Because he makes us focus
     On our own needs first

     Instead of on the needs
      Of those around us.

Or,
 The Devil doesn't
  Mind at all

 If we strive
  To serve the Lord,

  As long as all we do
   Is say *we try*
    To serve the Lord,

   Because he makes us think
    That no one really
     Can obey the Lord,

    And therefore,

     He causes us to think

The deeds we do
Don't matter. James 2:14-26

This is why
The subtle Tempter

Tries so hard to imitate
The Holy Spirit's
Inner whisper. James 1:13 1 John 4:1

It's so he can make us think
That he's the Holy One
Who's sent to lead us, John 14:26 John 16:12-14

And then mislead us
Into being focused
On ourselves.

This is also how he sought
To overcome the Savior

And how he tried to cause
Our Lord to waver

In His quest
To save man.

For when the Son of God
Had fasted

For forty nights
And forty days Matthew 4:1-2

And Satan thought
He finally had a chance

To ply his wicked ways,

Then posing as an angel

Sent from God to aid Him, 2 Corinthians 11:14

He sought
  By very subtle means
    To persuade Him

  Into thinking
    We must feed
      Our own needs first

    If we ever hope
      To have the strength
        To feed the needs of others. Matthew 4:3

Jesus,
  Strongly disagreed.

  And when He pointed out
    Our duty from the Scriptures, Matthew 4:4

    He was also helping us
      To see the bigger picture.

For if we always
  Seek to feed the needs
    Of others,

  First, 1 Corinthians 10:24

    Then God has promised,
      That He will always give us
        Everything we need

      So we will always
        Have enough
          To feed their every need, Matthew 6:25-34 Luke 6:38

        Which is also how
          He feeds us,

And how He keeps us
From the talons
Of the evil Tempter. 1 Corinthians 10:13

Satan,
Still in his disguise,

Sought again
To twist the truth
To suit his subtle lies

By implying that we must
Increase the measure
Of *our own* faith first,

Or that we must improve
The greatness of *our own*
Love for God the Father first,

Before we ever try
To amplify the faith and love
Of those around us. Matthew 4:5-6

Once again,
Jesus strongly disagreed

And showed how well
He knew the meaning of
The Scriptures. Matthew 4:7

So, casting every vestige
Of his holy sounding
Masquerade aside,

Satan now tried

To terrify the Lord
And force Him to decide

To choose an easy way out.

One

That would avoid
All the pain
That saving us

Would mean
That He must suffer. Matthew 4:8-9

But how could,
The Son of Man

Bow to
The Devil's wishes
Or demands

And still be our Example ... 1 Peter 2:21

Still be He
Who from eternity

Has always sought
To feed the needs
Of others first? Isaiah 57:15 Luke 4:40

Jesus knew He couldn't,
And He knew He wouldn't,

Ever leave us
Or forsake us Hebrews 13:5

Or refuse to redeem us
With His blood. John 3:16 Romans 5:6-10

So when His evil rival Satan
Saw the Savior
Would not heed him

Nor bow the knee

By thinking He must focus
On His own needs first
And how to feed them

Then he knew
He was defeated
So he finally fled. Matthew 4:10-11

But

What the holy sounding
Wicked one

Failed to do
That day,

He still tries to do
To this very day

By making us believe
The things we hear him say

Are the promptings
And the movings
Of the Holy Spirit.

Yet there is always
Just a little catch.

Because whenever Satan
Tries to deceive us

And strives to make us think
That he's the Holy One
Who's sent to lead us, Romans 8:14

His holy sounding words
Of admonition

Always tend to make us
Focus *on our own*

Spiritual condition.

And then,
Just as soon as Satan sees
He has our full attention,

He starts to pound us
With the hammer
Of conviction

Because,

No matter
How sincere or earnest
Our petition,

He makes us think
Our faith *still seems*
Too weak

Or that our love
For God the Father
Still seems too meek.

And thus,
By causing us incessant grief
And consternation,

He tries to make us
Blame the Lord
For all his

Heartless accusations.

In the end,

Satan strives

To make us spurn

The Still Small Voice
Of conviction 1 Kings 19:11-12

By leading us to think
That God is the one

Who is always
Taunting us
With hurtful words

And harsh-sounding,
Angry accusations,

Saying,

"Surely anyone
Who really loves the Lord,
Would never feel this way."

But God
Is not the author
Of our consternation,

Nor do we ever
Need to heed

Satan's softly spoken words
Of condemnation.

For even though
We know the Holy Spirit
Often must remind us, Proverbs 1:20-30

We also know

That He will never
Chide us

Nor *deride us.*

Nor will He ever
Rub it in

Or try to make us
Feel small.

So the very next time

When you start to hear
A holy sounding
Voice of conviction

But it tends to be the one

That always *pokes you*
And *prods you*

To be absorbed
With your own
Spiritual condition,

Then let this
Be your earnest prayer
And your sincere petition.

"Thank You Lord,
For the promise
I will always have,

At least a mustard seed's worth,
Of everything I need to have.

Now please help me find someone
Who needs these very things,

And teach me how to try
To give them all away!" Proverbs 11:25

And how do we
Give them all away?

By simply seeking
To encourage or increase

The very things we think
We have the very least of

In the hearts and minds
Of others everyday! Matthew 25:31-46

Yes,
Even when,

Yea,
Especially when,

Our faith and willpower
Seem *way too weak*

To enable us to seek
To do the will of God

Or to empower us
To obey. Mark 5:1-20
2 Corinthians 12:10

Because
Now we know

That just a little tiny
Mustard seed

Of anything at all
Is all we ever need

To always have enough
To feed the needs
Of those around us! Isaiah 58:6-12
Philippians 4:13

And the Fruits
Of the Spirit

That God has promised
We will always have
Enough of are

Love,
Joy,
Peace,

Patience,
Kindness,
Goodness,

Faithfulness,
Gentleness,
And self-control. Galatians 5:22-23

God's Eternal Word
Is sure,

For if we always
Seek to give away

The little words of hope
And helpful deeds
That He so freely gives us,

Then God will just as freely
Give us

More than we can
Ever hope to give away! Malachi 3:10
Luke 6:38

So which inner voice
Will you listen to?

The one that always

Pokes you?
  And prods you?

And tries to make you think
  You need to feed
    Your own needs first?

  Or the One
    That always softly says,

    Please seek to feed
      The needs of others first,
        And emulate Me!

John 15:26-27
1 Peter 2:21-25

Seven Times

Why do certain sins
Seem so strong

That, even though we know,
The Lord has promised us
The power to defeat them,

We still seem,
Unable to prevail
Or unseat them?

And why
Does it seem

That the more we try
To understand
The reason why,

The more it only emphasizes
Why we need to know
The reason why

We must immerse ourselves
In a muddy river?

In Bible times,
Leprosy
Symbolized
Deep-seated sin. 2 Kings 5:20-27 Numbers 12

While wealth,
And status

And flowing robes
Of costly fabric Mark 12:38-40

Were all said to be
The signs that God
Had blessed you. 2 Chronicles 1:7-12 Psalm 112:1-3

"Now Naaman,

Commander of the army
Of the king of Syria,

Was a great
And honorable man
In the eyes of his master,

Because by him
The Lord had given victory
To Syria.

He was also
A mighty man of valor,
But a leper.

And the Syrians
Had gone out on raids,

And had brought back
Captive

A young girl

From the land of Israel.

She waited
On Naaman's wife.

Then she said
To her mistress,

'If only my master
Were with the prophet
Who is in Samaria!

For he would heal him
Of his leprosy.'

And Naaman went in
And told his master,
Saying,

'Thus and thus
Said the girl

Who is from
The land of Israel.'

Then the king
Of Syria said,

'Go now,
And I will send a letter
To the king of Israel.'

So he departed
And took with him
Ten talents of silver,

Six thousand
Shekels of gold,

And ten changes
Of clothing.

Then he brought the letter
To the king of Israel,
Which said,

'Now be advised,
When this letter
Comes to you,

That I have sent Naaman
My servant to you,

That you
May heal him
Of his leprosy.'

And it happened,
When the king of Israel
Read the letter,

That he tore his clothes
And said,

'Am I God,
To kill and make alive,

That this man
Sends a man to me
To heal him of his leprosy?

Therefore
Please consider,

And see how he seeks
A quarrel with me.'

So it was,
When Elisha
The man of God

Heard that the king
Of Israel
Had torn his clothes,

That he sent to the king,
Saying,

'Why have you
Torn your clothes?

Please let him
Come to me,

And he shall know
That there is a prophet
In Israel.'

Then Naaman went
With his horses
And chariot,

And he stood at the door
Of Elisha's house.

And Elisha
Sent a messenger to him,
Saying,

'Go
And wash in the Jordan
Seven times,

And your flesh
Shall be restored to you,
And you shall be clean.'

But Naaman became furious,
And went away
And said,

'Indeed,'
I said to myself,

'He will surely
Come out to me,

And stand
And call on the name
Of the Lord his God,

And wave his hand
Over the place,
And heal the leprosy.

Are not the Abanah
And the Pharpar,
The rivers of Damascus,

Better than all
The waters of Israel?

Could I not
Wash in them
And be clean?'

So he turned
And went away in a rage.

And his servants came near
And spoke to him,
And said,

'My father,

If the prophet

Had told you
To do something great,

Would you not
Have done it?

How much more then,
When he says to you,

'Wash,
And be clean?' '

So he went down
And dipped seven times
In the Jordan,

According to the saying
Of the man of God;

And his flesh
Was restored like the flesh
Of a little child,

And he was clean." 2 Kings 5:1-14

Initially,

Naaman's strategy
To conquer leprosy

Revolved around a plan
Where everyone
Was focused on himself.

First there was the king
Who knew how much
He needed Naaman.

For he knew how much

His future hinged

On Naaman's finding
Better health.

And then there were
The subjects of the king

Who also knew how much
They needed Naaman.

Because they knew
That if he died,

It could lead
To their demise

And their defeat,
At the hands of all
Their enemies.

Naaman knew too,
Just exactly what
He stood to loose

If he lost
His fight with leprosy.

And yet,
If he really knew,

Then why did he
Initially refuse

To immerse himself,
In a muddy river?

It was because
He thought

That the man of God
Should be in awe
Of his status and his wealth

And covet all the riches
That he brought

And greedily accept them
In exchange for his healing
And his health.

But God's ways,
Are not our ways, Isaiah 55:8-9

Nor does He ever
Honor those

Who are focused
On themselves. Luke 18:9-14

Even if they think
The reason *seems so pure*

That they're sure
They won't be holy
If they don't,

Seek to strengthen
Everything they think
They need to strengthen,

In their own soul first. Luke 17:5-6

But aren't we
Supposed to be

Totally focused on
Our spiritual healing

And on everything

We think we need to do

To be in better
Spiritual health?

Isn't this
The underlying reason
Why we read our Bible?

And why we meditate?
And why we pray?

Isn't it
So we can strengthen
Our faith first,

So we can overcome
The things that seem
So hard to overcome?

Or isn't it

So we can deepen
Our love for God the Father
First?

So our love for Him
Will far exceed

Our love for all
Our cherished sins?

Spiritually speaking,
In the way that Naaman
Sought to conquer leprosy,

He thought
The same thing too,

Which is why
He was so focused
On himself

And on what he thought
The Lord would surely do.

But did our Lord and Savior
Ever focus on Himself? Mark 10:35-45 Romans 15:1-7

Or did He ever say,

That we really need to be
More focused
On ourselves? Matthew 23:11-12 John 13:2-17

No,
He didn't.

Instead,
He always said
Our greatest need

Is to always focus
On the needs
Of someone else. Matthew 25:34-46

This

Is why He used
A self-centered man
With deep-seated leprosy

To help us see
The absolute necessity

Of overcoming
Deep-seated sins
And sinful tendency,

But not
By being focused
On ourselves. Jeremiah 7:3-7 Isaiah 1:16-18

Because the river
That he dipped in

Was never
Focused on itself.

Nor does *any river*
Ever cease to feed the needs
Of everybody else. Ezekiel 47:9

And nor will we,
If we *immerse* ourselves

In the spirit of the river
Seven times. Philippians 2:3-8

In the spirit
Of He who,
Like a Mighty River, Exodus 17:1-6 1 Corinthians 10:1-4

Is always focused
On the needs
Of everybody else! John 3:16-17 1 John 4:7-12

But how
Can simply seeking
To encourage others

Help us find the courage
Or discover

How to overcome the things
That seem so hard
To overcome?

Or how
  Can softly-spoken
    Words of kindness

  Help us finally put
    The things behind us

    That always seem to conquer
      And confound us
        All the time?

Simply put,

  It's because
    The change of heart
      That has to happen

    For us to want to feed
      The needs of others
        All the time

      Is the very same
        Change of heart
          That has to happen

        For us to want to heed
          The Holy Spirit

          And to serve the Lord
            With all the powers
              Of our mind.

Ezekiel 36:25-27
Matthew 22:35-40

One change of heart
  Cannot occur
    Without the other,

  For they are both
    Intertwined

And tightly
Bound together,

To the very same
Supernatural miracle

Of God's amazing grace

That softens
Hardened hearts

And makes us one
In mind and heart
With our Creator. 2 Corinthians 5:17
1 John 4:20-21

For just as surely
As we cannot wash
A table full of dirty dishes

Without *our own fingers*
Getting cleaner with it,

And neither can we help
Our neighbor wash
His muddy car

Without *our own hands*
Getting softer
In the soapy water.

So too,
With all the Lord
Has promised He will do.

Because

Neither can we stoop
To wash the feet
Of one another Luke 7:36-50

Or seek to bind the wounds
Or heal the hurts
Of one another

Without *our own hands*
Getting cleaner

And without *our own heart*
Getting softer

In the soapy water
Of the Spirit
Of He who did the same. John 13:2-14

For it wasn't
Just the act

Of Naaman dipping
In the river seven times
That healed him.

It was the fact
That it symbolized the fact,

That if we seek to feed
The needs of others first,

All the time,

Even when we only have
A mustard seed of faith

Or peace of mind, Zechariah 7:8-10

Then He who healed
Naaman's leprosy

Has promised
He will also heal

All the deep-seated sins
And sinful tendencies

That always seem
To overcome us
All the time. Isaiah 58

But,

Did God
Ever promise us

That everything
He promised us

Will happen to us
Instantly?

Or should the word
Eventually

More often
Come to mind? James 1:2-4, 12

Both!

Because sometimes,
Even deep-seated sins
Are conquered *so fast*

That we know
It had to be a miracle

Because we never could
Defeat them in the past!

But then again,

For other ordinary
Everyday sins,

The change of heart
We long for

Seem so
Imperceptible,

And so undetectable,

That Satan makes us
Want to stop
Dipping in the river

After only dipping
Six times.

He makes us

Want to stop
Seeking to encourage
Others all the time

Because the Lord doesn't seem
To heal us fast enough
To suit us all the time,

Because our deep-seated sins
Still seem to overcome us
All the time.

And, therefore,

We think we need to focus
On our own feeble faith
All the time

Instead of on
The needs of others.

By far,

The hardest part
About the part
That Naaman had to do 2 Kings 5:11-14

Was to believe
That something
So simple,

And *so opposite*
Of what he thought
We ought to do,

Could really work.

But it really did.

So too
With she who fed Elijah. 1 Kings 17:8-12

So too
When the twelve disciples
Saw the hungry multitude. Mark 8:1-10

And so too

As when they almost never
Cast their empty net
Because they *just knew*

That the Stranger
On the shore
Was surely all wet. John 21:3-6

But He wasn't.

And He still
Stands there yet,

Asking us to cast
Our empty net

Into the sea of the needs
Of those around us

To help them see
That our greatest need

Is to focus on the needs
Of those around us

Instead of being focused
On our empty net.

Because He,

From whose feet
Flows the River of Life, Revelation 22:1

Whose waters
Water the Tree of Life,

Whose leaves
Are for the healing
Of the nations Revelation 22:2

Is the very same "He"

Whose feet were nailed
To the tree
That took His life,

Which becomes to us
A Tree of Life

If we let Him heal
All our deep-seated sins
And sinful tendencies

By daily dipping
In the flood of love
That flows from Calvary

Seven times.

By daily dipping

In the Spirit
And the power

Of He who,
Like a Mighty River,

Is always focused
On the needs of others
All the time!

"And I heard a loud voice
From Heaven saying,

'Behold,
The Tabernacle of God
Is with men,

And He will dwell with them,
And they shall be His people.

God Himself
Will be with them
And be their God.

And God will wipe away
Every tear from their eyes;

There shall be
No more death,
Nor sorrow,

Nor crying.

There shall be
No more pain,

For the former things
Have passed away.' " Revelation 21:3-4

"And he showed me
A pure river,
Of water of life,

Clear as crystal,

Proceeding from
The throne of God,
And of the Lamb.

In the middle of its street,
And on either side
Of the River,

Was the Tree of Life,
Which bore twelve fruits,

Each tree,
Yielding its fruit
Every month.

The leaves of the Tree,
Were for the healing
Of the nations.

And there shall be
No more curse,

But the throne of God
And of the Lamb
Shall be in it,

And His servants
Shall serve Him …
Forever and ever." Revelation 22:1-5

And how will
We "*serve Him*"
All the time?

Simply by the way
We love and serve
One another

All the time!

By the way
We always focus
On the needs of others

"Seven times."

Just like He
Who died to save us!

*"When the Son of Man
Comes in His glory,*

*And all the holy angels
With Him,*

*Then He will sit
On the throne of His glory.*

*All the nations
Will be gathered
Before Him,*

*And He will separate them
One from another,*

*As a shepherd
Divides his sheep
From the goats.*

And He will set the sheep
On His right hand,
But the goats on the left.

Then the King will say
To those on His right hand,

'Come,
You blessed of My Father,

Inherit the kingdom
Prepared for you

From the foundation
Of the world:

For I was hungry
And you gave Me food;

I was thirsty
And you gave Me drink;

I was a stranger
And you took Me in;

I was naked
And you clothed Me;

I was sick
And you visited Me;

I was in prison
And you came to Me.'

Then the righteous
Will answer Him,
Saying,

'Lord,

When did we see You
Hungry
And feed You,

Or thirsty
And give You drink?

When did we see You
A stranger
And take You in,

Or naked
And clothe You?

Or when did we see You
Sick,

Or in prison,
And come to You?'

And the King will answer
And say to them,

'Assuredly,
I say to you,

Inasmuch as you did it
To one of the least of these
My brethren,

You did it
To Me.' " Matthew 25:31-40

Throughout all eternity,

This is what will keep
Our hearts and minds
In perfect harmony:

For everyone

Will always seek to feed
  The needs of others first
    All the time, Matthew 7:12

  Just like He who sits
    Upon His royal throne
      Before us! Revelation 21

Summary

Why did Jesus
Pay the price
For Adam's indiscretion?

Or consent to set aside
His royal crown

For a life of servitude,
And humiliation?

Was it just so He could
Focus on Himself?

Or was it

Because He was
So focused on the needs
Of someone else?

And why did He
Whose life is measured
By eternity

Agree to come to Earth
To such a lowly birth,

Where He had

To stay up late
To work all day?

And pray all night
To light the way?

And fast for forty days
And forty nights

All alone
In the wilderness?

Was it just so He could
Focus on Himself?

Or was it

Because He was
So focused on the needs
Of someone else?

If we say
It was the latter,

Then what
Does that reveal

About the kinds of things
That really matter?

The purpose of
This final chapter

Is to summarize
What every chapter
Was about.

Summary: Feed Me First

But how,
Pray tell,

Can just a mustard seed
Of patience be enough?

Or how can half an ounce
Of peace of mind suffice?

Or how

Can having hardly any
Happiness at all
Make anybody happy?

The only reason
Why it can,

Is because,

Even if we only have
An infinitesimal amount,

When we share it,

God has promised
To renew it

So we never
Run out!

This,

Is the secret He concealed
In the mustard seed-sized

Meal,

The widow fed Elijah.

And yet God has promised
To reveal it

To all who seek
To do the same.

To all

Who seek to feed the needs
Of others first,

Instead of being focused
On their own needs first,

Or on the things
They think they need
Or must attain.

Summary: Much Fruit

Some say,
That feeding others first
Sounds *way too*
Impossible.

Or that it seems
Way too implausible
To ever really work.

But is it?

Yes.

But only in
The very same sense,

That every miracle
The Lord ever did,
Or ever will do,

Is utterly impossible
For us to fabricate,

Or imitate,
Or do.

Simply put,

The ways of God
Are way beyond
Our comprehension.

And yet even though

They far exceed
What mortal minds can mention,

There is still one thing

That the God of all
Wants all His followers
To know about redemption.

And that is

The irrefutable,
Unexplainable,

"Much fruit" miracle
That changes our condition

The very moment
We believe

And serving others first
Becomes our mission.

So go ahead,
By the grace of God,
Become a fruit tree!

And seek to feed
The needs of others first,

And try to help
And bless the lives
Of others first,

Even when it *seems like,*

It's the very opposite
Of everything you think
You ought to do!

Summary: The Curse

For even if the Maker
Of the fig tree

Had only found
One little tiny fig
Clinging to its branches,

Do you think
He would have cursed it?

No,

Because it's never been
About how many figs
Are *on the tree.* Mark 12:41-44

But rather,

It has always been about
The infinite amount
The Lord can make

If He is *in the tree,*

When the tree
Seeks to feed the needs
Of others first.

And *we* are
The fig trees,
The planting of the Lord, Isaiah 61:1-3

If our deeds feed
Our neighbors need

For love and understanding. 1 Peter 3:8-9

Or if we seek to sow
A seed of patience

In those we deem to be
Impatient or demanding. Galatians 5:13-16

Notwithstanding,

The overwhelming fact
That we *feel like*
We only have

One little tiny fig
Of happiness
Clinging to our branches.

Summary: The Waiter

So is a plate
Full of patience,
Printed on the menu?

Yet *it seems like*

You only have
A mustard seed of patience
Abiding in you?

If so,

Then *don't wait*
Until you think you have
Enough to fill the order.

And *don't wait*

Until it feels like
Your faith and love
Are growing stronger.

Because it's never been about
How much the waiter
Has to have.

But rather,

It has always been about
How much his Master
Always has.

He,

Who from eternity,

Has always had
An infinite amount

And yet He often
Only gives us
Just a very small amount

To test us,

To see if we will *still seek*
To feed the needs
Of others first,

Even when it seems like,

There is not enough
For everyone
Who sits at every table.

Summary: Rest

Why is wearing
His yoke

Of serving others
Said to be so easy? Matthew 11:28-29

And why
Are bearing all the burdens
That He spoke of

Deemed to be so restful
And so light? Matthew 5:38-48

It's because *we don't*
Provide the food
That feeds the multitude. Luke 9:12-17

And it's because *we don't*
Supply the seed of faith

That makes us think
It's even possible.

God does! Luke 11:9-13
Ephesians 3:14-21

All we have to do

Is freely give away
The tiny seeds of hope
That God so freely gives us.

And always seek to sow
The little seeds of happiness
That God Himself dispenses— Ecclesiastes 11:6
Hosea 10:12

Even when *it seems like*

Our faith is in decline

And hope
And happiness
Are very hard to find.

For just as surely
As we do,

We will just as surely find

That the reason why we have
An innate ability

To give so overflowing
And so endlessly John 4:6-14

Is because it doesn't
Come from within.

It comes
From God! John 3:1-8
1 John 2:28-29

Summary: The Still Small Voice

So, casting every vestige
Of his holy sounding
Masquerade aside,

Satan now tried

To terrify the Lord
And force Him to decide

To choose an easy way out.

One

That would avoid
All the pain
That saving us

Would mean
That He must suffer. Matthew 4:8-9

But how could,
The Son of Man

Bow to
The Devil's wishes
Or demands

And still be our Example … 1 Peter 2:21

Still be He
Who from eternity

Has always sought
To feed the needs
Of others first? Isaiah 57:15
Luke 4:40

Jesus knew He couldn't,
And He knew He wouldn't,

Ever leave us
Or forsake us Hebrews 13:5

Or refuse to redeem us
With His blood. John 3:16 Romans 5:6-10

So when His evil rival Satan
Saw the Savior
Would not heed him

Nor bow the knee

By thinking He must focus
On His own needs first
And how to feed them

Then he knew
He was defeated
So he finally fled. Matthew 4:10-11

Summary: Seven Times

The twelve disciples
Just knew

That the Stranger
On the shore
Was surely all wet. John 21:3-6

But He wasn't.

And He still
Stands there yet,

Asking us to cast
Our empty net

Into the sea of the needs
Of those around us

To help them see
That our greatest need

Is to focus on the needs
Of those around us

Instead of being focused
On our empty net.

Because He,

From whose feet
Flows the River of Life, Revelation 22:1

Whose waters
Water the Tree of Life,

Whose leaves
Are for the healing
Of the nations Revelation 22:2

Is the very same "He"

Whose feet were nailed
To the tree
That took His life,

Which becomes to us
A Tree of Life

If we let Him heal
All our deep-seated sins
And sinful tendencies

By daily dipping
In the flood of love
That flows from Calvary

Seven times.

By daily dipping

In the Spirit
And the power

Of He who,
Like a Mighty River,

Is always focused
On the needs of others
All the time!

Final Thought . . .

The conclusion
Of the matter
Is this:

That even though
You may have just
Come to the end,

The very instant

You start
Experimenting with
The Mustard Seed Concept,

The book of miracles
Your life writes

Will never cease
To amaze you,

Nor will it ever end!

God bless,
As you daily seek
To better understand

How to better
Feed the needs
Of those around you!

Certified Signatures

Personalize your book,

By inviting
Those you know
To certify so,

On the following pages.

To sign
The author's book,

Download
Free resources,

Or to share
An encouraging word

With others who have
Read this book

Visit
http://certifiedso.com/others-first/

Certified So,

By Those Who Sign Below

Visit **http://certifiedso.com/others-first/**

to sign the author's book

Certified So,

By Those Who Sign Below

Visit http://certifiedso.com/others-first/

to sign the author's book

Certified So,

By Those Who Sign Below

Visit http://certifiedso.com/others-first/

to sign the author's book

Certified So,

By Those Who Sign Below

Visit **http://certifiedso.com/others-first/**

to sign the author's book

Certified So,

By Those Who Sign Below

Visit **http://certifiedso.com/others-first/**

to sign the author's book

Certified So,

By Those Who Sign Below

Visit http://certifiedso.com/others-first/

to sign the author's book

Certified So,

By Those Who Sign Below

Visit **http://certifiedso.com/others-first/**

to sign the author's book

Certified So,

By Those Who Sign Below

Visit http://certifiedso.com/others-first/

to sign the author's book

Certified So,
By Those Who Sign Below

Visit http://certifiedso.com/others-first/
to sign the author's book

Certified So,

By Those Who Sign Below

Visit **http://certifiedso.com/others-first/**

to sign the author's book

Certified So,

By Those Who Sign Below

Visit http://certifiedso.com/others-first/

to sign the author's book

Certified So,

By Those Who Sign Below

Visit **http://certifiedso.com/others-first/**

to sign the author's book

Certified So,

By Those Who Sign Below

Visit http://certifiedso.com/others-first/

to sign the author's book

Certified So,

By Those Who Sign Below

Visit http://certifiedso.com/others-first/

to sign the author's book

Certified So,

By Those Who Sign Below

Visit http://certifiedso.com/others-first/

to sign the author's book

Certified So,

By Those Who Sign Below

Visit **http://certifiedso.com/others-first/**

to sign the author's book

Certified So,

By Those Who Sign Below

Visit http://certifiedso.com/others-first/

to sign the author's book

Certified So,

By Those Who Sign Below

Visit **http://certifiedso.com/others-first/**

to sign the author's book

Certified So,

By Those Who Sign Below

Visit **http://certifiedso.com/others-first/**

to sign the author's book

Certified So,
By Those Who Sign Below

Visit **http://certifiedso.com/others-first/**

to sign the author's book

Certified So,

By Those Who Sign Below

Visit http://certifiedso.com/others-first/

to sign the author's book

Certified So,

By Those Who Sign Below

Visit http://certifiedso.com/others-first/

to sign the author's book

CPSIA information can be obtained at www.ICGtesting.com
Printed in the USA
BVOW01s0606300913

332372BV00004B/36/P

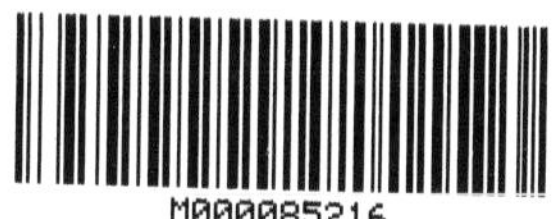

M000085216

Other Titles Available from Dorset House Publishing Co.

Becoming a Technical Leader: An Organic Problem-Solving Approach
by Gerald M. Weinberg

Data Structured Software Maintenance: The Warnier/Orr Approach
by David A. Higgins

Fundamental Concepts of Computer Science: Mathematical Foundations of Programming
by Leon S. Levy

General Principles of Systems Design
by Gerald M. Weinberg & Daniela Weinberg

Peopleware: Productive Projects and Teams
by Tom DeMarco & Timothy Lister

Practical Project Management: Restoring Quality to DP Projects and Systems
by Meilir Page-Jones

Understanding the Professional Programmer
by Gerald M. Weinberg

Rethinking Systems Analysis & Design
by Gerald M. Weinberg

The Secrets of Consulting: A Guide to Giving & Getting Advice Successfully
by Gerald M. Weinberg

Strategies for Real-Time System Specification
by Derek J. Hatley & Imtiaz A. Pirbhai

SOFTWARE PRODUCTIVITY

SOFTWARE PRODUCTIVITY

HARLAN D. MILLS

FOREWORD BY

GERALD M. WEINBERG

Dorset House Publishing
353 West 12th Street
New York, N.Y. 10014

Library of Congress Cataloging-in-Publication Data

Mills, Harlan D., 1919–
Software productivity / by Harlan D. Mills ; foreword by Gerald M. Weinberg.
p. cm.
Reprint. Originally published: Boston : Little, Brown, c1983.
Includes bibliographies and index.
ISBN 0-932633-10-2 : $25.00 (est.)
1. Electronic digital computers—Programming. I. Title.
QA76.6.M523 1988
005—dc19 88-5099
CIP

Cover Design: Jeff Faville, Faville Graphics

Copyright © 1988 by Harlan D. Mills. Published by Dorset House Publishing Co., Inc., 353 West 12th Street, New York, NY 10014.

All rights reserved. No part of this publication may be reproduced, stored in a retrieval system, or transmitted, in any form or by any means, electronic, mechanical, photocopying, recording, or otherwise, without prior written permission of the publisher.

Printed in the United States of America

Library of Congress Catalog Number 88-5099
ISBN: 0-932633-10-2

Dedication

This book is dedicated to Mr. John B. Jackson, who was President of the Federal Systems Division (FSD) of IBM during the time in which most of the articles in this book were written. Mr. Jackson provided intellectual and executive leadership for introducing an extensive Software Engineering Program into the Federal Systems Division without it losing a stride as a going business in complex systems development.

It has been my happy experience to report to a succession of legendary IBM executives during the time in question, namely Messrs. Henry J. White, Joseph M. Fox, James B. Bitonti, Albert E. Babbitt, all vice presidents of FSD, and John B. Jackson and Vincent N. Cook, presidents of FSD. (Mr. Bitonti is now IBM Vice President—Manufacturing; Mr. Jackson is now IBM Vice President—Quality.) Each has given me encouragement and freedom to look for better ways of dealing with software problems, and each of these IBM executives has made significant contributions to my own understanding of the problems of managing software development.

Foreword

In writing this foreword, I am performing an act of atonement. Years ago, when I first started to hear of Harlan Mills and his ideas, I gave them short shrift. Or, rather, I gave them no shrift at all. To shrive, the priest has to hear the confession from the sinner, not simply hear gossip about the sin. Until I met Harlan, I simply didn't bother to read any of his writings. It was an act of pure prejudice, not against Iowa farm boys or baseball fans, but against mathematicians. Or, really, against the *writings* of mathematicians.

My prejudice dates from my first geometry class, in high school. Up until that time, I had been something of a whiz kid in math, a fact which I never allowed to escape my schoolmates' attention. But geometry absolutely baffled me. For three weeks I sat open-mouthed in class while our teacher delineated proof after proof on the blackboard. How she could reason in such a straightforward, logically consistent manner was simply beyond my comprehension.

During the fourth week, as the theorems grew more complex, I began to notice her stumbling. When she did, she referred to her notes. Eventually, I caught her reasoning backwards, under her breath, from theorem to axioms. Eureka! It was all a hoax! These proofs were not methods of *reasoning,* but methods of *confirming* reasoning. They were not methods of discovery, though they were presented as if one worked from axiom through rules of inference to—oh, surprise!—a theorem.

I felt as if I had been duped, and that didn't fit well with my status as the gang's whiz kid. I resolved never again to be taken in by mathematicians and their shabby tricks. This prejudice served me in good stead through many years of college and graduate school mathematics. I never confused the proof of a theorem with the method that might have been used for discovering that theorem—a method which I knew would be anything but clean and neat.

And so, when I heard that Harlan Mills was a mathematician by origin, writing about software productivity, I scoffed. It was my loss, as I discovered when I was finally shamed into reading some of his actual work instead of some bastardized rehash. What I discovered was a thinker with a remarkable gift for exposing the origin and development of his ideas, and for taking the reader on the same intellectual voyage he himself had taken.

Of course, if the ideas had not been absolutely first-rate, the voyage would not have been worth the fare, regardless of Harlan's talents as a writer. But, as you well know, they *were* first-rate ideas—ideas that have had a profound influence on software productivity all over the world.

During the past decade or so, we have had many lesser ideas infecting the body of software productivity. Many of these ideas have spread because they are well packaged into "complete" systems of software development. Harlan's ideas, however, have always had an air of fertile incompleteness about them. To him, no problem ever seems closed, any more than his mind is closed to extensions or even contradictions of his ideas. We have all heard how software productivity is an immense problem of our time. I suppose it is the immensity of the problem that makes developers easy prey for these "complete systems of development." For myself, I like the Mills approach better.

Instead of packaging some trivial idea that is supposed to solve all problems in an unthinking way, attack the roots of the problem. Let people see your thinking process and decide for themselves how to adapt the ideas to their own environment. True, the Mills approach assumes some intelligence and attention on the part of the reader, but I can't believe that *any* improvement in software productivity is going to result from mindless mouthing of slogans.

When Harlan spoke to me about collecting his previously unpublished or inaccessible papers, I jumped at the idea. In *Software Productivity,* we have not merely the development of one significant idea, but the development of a whole set of interrelated ideas. It is no more of a "systems development package" than before—Heaven forbid. But to the intelligent, attentive reader, it is much, much more than a package could ever be. It is a chance to see into the mind of one of the profound thinkers of our industry—or of any industry. By following this chronological development of ideas, the reader's problem-solving style will be subtly changed. Mine was. I may not have learned much from those other mathematicians, but Harlan Mills has been my real teacher. You are lucky that he can now be yours.

Gerald M. Weinberg

Contents

Foreword by Gerald M. Weinberg *ix*

1. **In Retrospect** **1**

2. **Search for an Easier, Simpler Way (*1968*)** **7**

3. **The Iterative IF as a Primitive Instruction (*1967*)** **11**

4. **Programmer Productivity Through Individual Responsibility (*1968*)** **13**

5. **The Case Against GO TO Statements in PL/I (*1969*)** **27**

6. **A. *The New York Times* Thesaurus of Descriptors (*1969*)** **31**

   B. A Structural Description of *The New York Times* Thesaurus of Descriptors (*1969*) **44**

7. **Measurements of Program Complexity (*1969*)** **57**

8. **Chief Programmer Teams: Techniques and Procedures (*1970*)** **65**

9. **On the Statistical Validation of Computer Programs (*1970*)** **71**

10. **OS/360 Programming (*1970*)** **83**

11. **Top Down Programming in Large Systems (*1970*)** **91**

12. **Programming Techniques: From Private Art to Public Practice (*1970*)** **103**

13. **Mathematical Foundations for Structured Programming (*1972*)** **115**

14. **Reading Programs as a Managerial Activity (*1972*)** **179**

15. **How to Buy Quality Software (*1974*)** **185**

16. How to Write Correct Programs and Know It (*1975*) 193

17. The New Math of Computer Programming (*1975*) 215

18. Software Development (*1976*) 231

19. Software Engineering Education (*1980*) 251

20. Software Productivity in the Enterprise (*1981*) 265

Index 271

SOFTWARE PRODUCTIVITY

ARTICLE 1

In Retrospect

I joined IBM in 1964. It has been my good fortune to be in the Federal Systems Division, which has been faced with challenging problems of software development, over these years. These problems are as much managerial as technical, and during this time the ideas and discipline of software engineering have begun to emerge in visible form.

The notes and papers in this book represent a personal history of learning and growth by one person, helped by many.

First, my associates in the Federal Systems Division have been building complex real-time software systems under contract conditions. There is a major difference between programming for yourself and programming for others. There is also a major difference between "in house" software development and contract software development. The difference in each case is the need for being specific. Others never know what you didn't do for yourself; but the whole world knows what you promised and didn't do for others. These associates have been kind enough to try out many of my ideas and to provide a proving ground for the new discipline of software engineering.

Second, the university has played a central role in creating new foundations in software methodology. During this time with IBM I have also served, thanks to IBM, on the faculties of Johns Hopkins University and the University of Maryland. The interactions with faculty and students at those universities and with university people in computer science elsewhere have been most beneficial, to say the least. The major advances in the foundations of software methodology have come out of the university, not out of industry. Thanks to Edsger Dijkstra, Tony Hoare, David Parnas, David Gries, Niklaus Wirth, and others, for work in structured programming and program correctness, we now understand many deep simplicities about ideas that were formerly shrouded in the mystery and complexity of programming lore.

A Search for Productivity in Software

The underlying theme of this history has been a search for productivity in software. My approach to software has been that of a study in management, dealing with a very difficult and creative process. The first step in such an approach is to discover what is teachable, in order to be able to manage it. If it cannot be taught, it cannot be managed as an organized, coordinated activity. Since software deals with purely logical processes, it seemed clear that mathematics was the right tool to apply to the problem. In this search for teachability, it has been a pleasant surprise to find that so much of software methodology could be formulated in classical mathematics. My second surprise was to discover how closely and easily productivity grows out of manageability. With intellectual control over software development, the improvements in productivity are measured in factors, not percentages.

In 1968, I wrote an article for an IBM internal news publication (see Article 2). There was no structured programming then, but the article shows that I was looking, even then, for software productivity through mathematical development.

On first learning about structured programming from the NATO paper of Edsger Dijkstra (see reference 4, p. 101), I stated to my associates in IBM that "left to programmers, laissez faire, we could expect a productivity improvement of 50%, but if we managed it in we could expect a factor of 3." It happened just about that way; we saw both levels of improvement, resulting from different introductions of the idea in different parts of IBM. This differential in effect is typical in introducing new technology into mind-intensive work such as programming, because productivity is a result of expectations as well as capabilities. If we expect little, we get little, for many reasons. That is, managers who allow the introduction of new technology to see how it comes out invariably get less out of it than managers who develop convictions that major improvements are possible. In the latter case, managers become actively involved with "making it happen," rather than simply passively "letting it happen."

My search for teachability and intellectual control has turned to mathematics and other hard science areas because without such leverage, one is reduced to being more clever than one's predecessors. While I might hold my own in being as clever as a randomly selected predecessor, that is not good enough. One needs to better the best ideas of all predecessors, because those best ideas to date will already have been tried and used.

But once this mathematical leverage is found, paradoxically, the ideas must be translated back into the context of the subject for teaching. I have found that this translation has its own pitfalls. The more natural one makes the final idea, the more the danger of viewing and discussing it on a common sense basis. A striking illustration of this pitfall recurred in my discovery that the individual statements of a structured program could be enumerated in a special way, so that no statement had to depend for its correctness on statements yet to be enumerated. I discovered this by thinking about computability theory and about problems that could be solved without ever solving sets of simultaneous equations (solving simultaneous interface problems in program integration). I called the translation into programming context "top down programming." It was the result of specific mathematical rigor in application to programming. In fact, it is valid only for digital computers, and not for analog computers.

Other Views and Interpretations

To my surprise, after my writing about it, there occurred many discussions of "top down programming" in conferences and magazines, based entirely on common sense arguments about the name, that ignored completely the computability theory I had in mind. For example, it was argued that "the user is the top of the system," that "the job control interpreter is the top of the system," and on and on. Since there was no mathematical rigor to inhibit these discussions, some became quite vehement. Now the virtue of the top down definition from the computability theory was that we had a built-in integration process, which was carried out during, rather than at the end of, the programming process. These various common sense definitions did not share this virtue, and people who used them did not get its benefits. But this did not stop the chorus of people who invented their own convenient meanings for the term rather than taking the trouble to find out the idea behind it. As a result, an astonishing number of people in software still view top down programming as a "way of looking at things," rather than as a rigorous mathematics idea applied to programming, and they get only superficial benefits from the idea.

Pursued with mathematical rigor, top down programming dictated that the job control code had to be written first, rather than last as had been universally done previously. It dictated that the code to open files had to be written before the code to access these files. It meant that we could reduce programming errors to a matter of human fallibility, while the traditional bottom up integration contained not only human fallibility but mathematical noncomputability to contend with. This is because debugging a system with interface errors requires solving simultaneous interface equations, for which no finite procedures exist and which can be done only approximately and never completely reliably.

As a result of this mathematically discovered idea, people who understood it for what it was, rather than inventing some common sense meaning for it, indeed experienced a dramatic improvement in the integration process. There was simply no integration crunch in the last phase of software development. In fact, my principal criterion for judging whether top down programming was actually used is just this absence of any difficulty at integration. The proof of the pudding is in the eating!

The chorus of contending interpretations of the term "top down programming" was exceeded in diversity only by that for the term "chief programmer team." The chief programmer team was conceived in the industrial engineering sense as a work-structuring activity to divide up the work rather than to divide up the product. Work structuring for a creative process is a deep problem of the process, work psychology, industrial method, and management principles. The chief programmer team had many considerations and explicit checks and balances built into it. But that did not stop many people from inventing their own ideas for the term. In spite of my original criterion that a chief programmer be both a good design level programmer and a good manager, particularly of schedule and budget, chief programmers of all categories from prima donnas (whom we don't know what to do with) to clerical administrators (whom we don't know what to do with) appeared in common sense rationalizations, which conveniently ignored the central issues of creativity and intellectual control that drive the chief programmer team idea. Small wonder that such chief programmer teams did not always work out well, and some led to real disaster. It is the old problem of silk purses and sows' ears.

Methodology and Management

My search for productivity in software has uncovered no magic, no panaceas. There are remarkable improvements in productivity possible over today's accepted levels. But they require sound methodology and sound management. Mastering the methodology requires an intellectual commitment of several years. If it were easier, everybody would be doing it already. The management is as necessary as the methodology, to focus potential for productivity into realized productivity, in ways we illustrate below.

The notes and papers in this book represent the original ideas for many terms the industry has begun to use. I am happy that people are using the terms. I will be even happier when they begin using the ideas.

ARTICLE

2

Search for an Easier, Simpler Way

(1968)

A major objective of the mathematics consultant in the Federal Systems Center is to discover ways of increasing programmer productivity by finding new technical dimensions in computer programming. The origins of these new technical dimensions must be logical and mathematical.

The idea of mathematics is to make life easier, to find simpler ways of doing things. A mathematics theorem is elegant, not because it is complicated or hard to understand, but because it says more with less wasted motion. In this way, mathematics can be a source of great power in organizing ideas and describing processes.

We need this kind of power in computer programming to handle more detail with less effort. However, it is easy to mix up the simplicity that comes from a deep analysis with a simple-minded analysis, which leads to hopeless complexities. Finding the key simplicities in a data processing problem is a deep problem not often resolved by a simple-minded approach. But these simplicities, found before the detailed programming begins, spell the difference between a program completed quickly and cleanly and one difficult to finish and even more difficult to debug.

Just getting a computer program written and running to solve a data processing problem is much like getting the ball in all 18 holes on a golf course. That's a good start—but just barely a start on the problem. In golf, the next questions are easy to ask, such as "How many strokes did it take?" But in programming, things are much more difficult. The first thing

Reprinted with permission from International Business Machines Corporation.

we don't know is "What is par? How big is the programming job?" We can ask how long it took. And we can ask some more questions, such as:

1. Does the program run correctly; is there good evidence in the form of program clarity and/or systematic testing to support this?
2. Does it run effectively in terms of time and resources; are there good arguments to say the time and resource requirements are near optimal?
3. Can the program take care of itself faced with incorrect data or control information; can it identify and signal diagnostics or suggestions to operators or users?
4. Is the program documented well enough for others to understand what it does; is it documentable at all in terms of structure and modularity in the overall program?
5. Can the program be maintained; can it be updated through equipment changes that may arise, through bugs found later, maintained through longer periods of time when no one is devoting full time to it?
6. Can the program be modified, added on to, or incorporated into programs of larger dimensions as new ideas in the subject matter come to light; or is it destined to become a dead program which no one understands or uses?

The foregoing questions reflect our ignorance more than our wisdom. They inquire, piecemeal and haphazardly, about our intuitive hopes and fears for the program, rather than about a systematic set of properties which defines the value of the program.

Computer programming is less than a generation old, and has nooks and crannies galore, compared with a subject like geometry. Yet it took many generations of brilliant minds to evolve geometry into a well organized subject—enough to be of value to a land surveyor, for example. Scientific discovery goes at a faster pace today, but we are still far from bedrock in computer programming and far from a well organized set of principles and techniques.

At the moment, it appears that this bedrock may eventually consist of the unification of two quite distinct branches of information theory into a single body.

There is a statistical theory of information, embodied in the work of Claude Shannon and others, that provides quantitative measures of information in data transmission and storage processes. These measures can be applied to computer programming in two ways rather directly. First the information content of a programming language can be studied in much the same way that natural languages are treated; second, the information content of executing programs can be studied in ways similar to the way stochastic control processes are regarded.

There is also another older theory of information, more qualitative in character, that deals with matters of syntax and semantics in messages with rational meanings. This branch seeks to identify what is stable (semantics) in patterns of information, for analysis and exploitation. In current programming practices, these ideas are found in such diverse areas as syntax-directed compilers and table-driven file processors.

It seems more and more evident that neither of these branches can be a sufficient foundation for computer programming in itself. But their union, with elaborations appropriate and peculiar to the subject of computer programming, gives promise of getting closer to fundamental questions such as:

1. What is par?
2. Are there basic limitations in program efficiencies and capabilities based on the logic of computer programming itself, regardless of the ingenuity of programmers?
3. What is a complete set of questions to ask about a program to evaluate its worth?

It is typical in scientific development to find progress primarily through finding the right questions to ask, and computer programming will be no exception. We can expect these three questions to be modified and sharpened in unexpected ways as the right ideas come to light.

ARTICLE 3

The Iterative IF as a Primitive Instruction

(1967)

We consider the problem of formulating high-level programming instructions in primitive forms (recognizing that it is logically ill defined but pragmatically of first importance). Our main observation is that we can define a statement called Iterative IF (IIF) to serve as an easy building block (with statement blocking and assignment statements) to both IF-THEN-ELSE and DO (FOR) compound statements. This, coupled with the further observation that programming can be accomplished in a reasonable way with *no statement labels* (and no GO TO statements), leads to a high-level programming language with only two instructions: assignment and Iterative IF.

The Iterative IF (IIF) statement is of the form

IIF E;

where E is a logical valued expression and means: if expression E is true, execute the maximal syntactical block immediately following this statement, and *then* return to this IIF statement for reexecution. For example, using Algol delimiters, the sequence

```
IIF X < 10;
BEGIN . . . END;
```

would execute the BEGIN . . . END block repeatedly as long as $X < 10$ (forever, if $X < 10$ to begin with and X is not altered in the block). In order to get a DO looping capability, we add two assignment statements,

```
X = 1;
IIF X < 10;
BEGIN; X = X + 1; . . . END;
```

and we have the effect of DO $X = 1$ TO 10. In order to get an IF-THEN capability we can do as follows:

```
B = true;
IFF B and X < 10;
BEGIN; B = false; . . . , END;.
```

From there it is easy to get to IF-THEN-ELSE.

ARTICLE 4

Programmer Productivity Through Individual Responsibility

(1968)

Abstract

The following begins to articulate a working hypothesis for regarding programming in IBM as an individual, rather than a team, activity. It recognizes that software support systems, such as OS/360, now allow one dedicated person to address major programming systems presently assigned to teams of about 10 to 30 people.

The major question is not whether one-man projects can be productive, but whether they can be managed and organized into the IBM framework. There seems to be little doubt that they can and they should be.

Introduction

It may become possible to attack the whole spectrum of computer programming problems of the Division and the Corporation by shifting from a team approach to an individual approach in designing and producing programming systems. In this approach, a single individual is *solely* responsible, in total and in complete detail, for developing a major programming system.

Objectives that may be achievable in productivity, given as factors of improvement over present levels using the team approach, are:

Scientific Systems	10–50
Command/Commercial Systems	5–20
Software Systems Programming	2–10

These varying factors reflect the varying degrees to which higher-level programming languages can assume detailed responsibilities in the production of programs in various areas.

The basis for such productivity is the introduction of a new IBMer, an *Individual Programmer,* of highest professional qualifications, comparable in ability and training to professionals in such other fields as medicine, law, and university teaching, performing as an individual on a career level. New ingredients that may make this productivity possible are:

1. A new concept of "deep immersion" by an Individual Programmer into a data processing problem over a period of several months.
2. A more precise distinction between systems analysis and programming, which permits the programming operation to be "clean and quick."
3. The software tools of OS/360, PL/I, and so on, which can be used by Individual Programmers to handle details in wholesale lots.

Historical Background

It is easy to see why the team approach to programming came about, out of necessity, in the growth of the data processing industry. Large and complex systems, such as SAGE, space tracking, and others, were tackled with very primitive programming tools. As an aside, there is the story of the fellow at the dude ranch who had never ridden a horse. "Fine," said the foreman, "we've got a horse that's never been ridden, so you can start out together!" So it was in data processing. With hardware of unprecedented capability, grown up practically overnight, the collection of engineers and others who were the first programmers started out simultaneously to learn how to build complex systems and to learn how to build the tools with which to build the systems.

Thus programmers started out with tremendous amounts of detail to handle and no theoretical basis with which to handle it. No wonder there was an inherent "safety in numbers." But prophetically, in the experience of many, this safety in numbers lay not in the combined efforts of many people, but in the fact that there was more chance, with many people, of finding a few who would do the bulk of the job.

It is also easy to forget how young and immature computer science is, particularly in programming theory, and how rapidly it is growing. For example, the FORTRAN compiler appeared in 1957, culminating a few earlier efforts in the direction of high-level programming languages. And yet, the first syntax-directed compiler ideas did not appear until 1960, after FORTRAN rather than before. Even now, it is clear that we are far from bedrock ideas in programming languages and their translation. For example, PL/I, by far the best we have as a general purpose implemented language, is an ad hoc hodgepodge whose origins are exterior pragmatics rather than any deep theoretical synthesis of user needs and computing realities. Matters in data organization and structure are even farther behind programming languages.

This does not mean there is not a lot being said and written about programming theory. There is. But it is written in an amorphous environment, in terms of various specifics, precisely because no basic structure for literature in the subject has really emerged. As a result, there is much chaff surrounding most grains of wheat, and much reinventing of wheels, and so on.

Because of this, it is difficult to keep up with the literature, which is expanding rapidly and is not very well structured. It is easy to see how computer science, such as it is, can "grow past" a manager in the industry, for these very reasons. A bright programmer ten years ago, in the days of assemblers and loaders, who became a manager shortly after, not only has had to add new facts and techniques to stay current, as most disciplines require, but has also had to add whole new categories of subject matter to his or her thinking, for example, mathematical linguistics and library management.

But the fact is that, as embryonic and as poorly structured as they may be, there are new techniques in computer science now, not at all visible at the beginning, which can allow people to handle detail in wholesale lots. The chief and most obvious of these techniques are in the high-level programming languages, best embodied today in PL/I, and in the operating systems facilities, such as in OS/360. But there are additional new capabilities at a deeper theoretical level that are just beginning to emerge, based on syntax processing and the decomposition of syntax and semantics in data processing operations. The syntax-directed compiler embodies the latter capability in the support of a high-level programming language.

It is these theoretical capabilities, as they are used, that will permit the Individual Programmer, as a professional, to carry out complete programming projects, which are now addressed by teams.

Empirical Evidence

The validity of the individual approach will finally depend simply on whether it works. It does not take much looking around to find evidence that it can work. Ordinarily, however, this evidence is examined with a rather different hypothesis in mind.

The evidence is that on many occasions, highly motivated individuals, plus favorable circumstances in problem formulation, machine availability, and so on, have turned in performances that were astonishing when compared with what the industry has had to settle for as normal—up to two orders of magnitude higher in productivity.

If the question is "Can we get the average programmer to do this?", then these performances are somewhat irrelevent because, by definition, average programmers are not highly motivated, nor do they have favorable circumstances to work under.

But that is the wrong question for our purposes. A skilled heart surgeon is not an average person, nor is a life master in bridge. In their own ways, they are dedicated people. And we know that people of talent and vision are willing to dedicate themselves to ideas they believe in.

The reason the foregoing question comes up in an organizational content is an assumption made ceteris parabis about the number of programmers we need. It is tacitly assumed that we need more and more programmers, and hence most of them will fall in the average category. It is this assumption that is challenged here.

If the objectives in productivity are achievable through professional development and personal dedication, as outlined in more detail below, then the Division and the Corporation will require remarkably few computer programmers to accomplish the same level of effort as we do now. Therefore these programmers will not be drawn from the pool of average programmers at all, but from the top 10 or 20%.

So the burden of the evidence is that a few programmers, if capable and motivated, can do the work of many. The important questions are "Can IBM ask them to?" and "Can IBM depend on them to do it?" These are addressed next.

The answer to both questions is "Yes, indeed!"

The Individual Programmer

We sketch out, briefly, a portrait of an Individual Programmer: his or her mode of working, professional growth process, motivations, and relations with the company. The person is fictional, practically out of necessity. People with the requisite capabilities and latent motivations exist in the company, possibly as many as 100 or so. But the conditions for pursuing the career outlined here are not present in the company. Many of these people will be in senior technical staff positions, others in technical managerial positions because they can now get more recognition there.

There is one thing to note at the start: the title "Individual Programmer" is used to be descriptive. For job satisfaction, prestige, and so forth, a better title might be selected, such as "System Architect," "Programming Architect," "System Definer," or something along those lines. We want this title to describe an important position.

An Individual Programmer takes on a programming project that we would currently assign to a team of up to 10–30 people (or more or less, depending on the circumstances). The point is that we assign to one person a very large responsibility. (The person will grow into this, as we develop below, through smaller assignments.) This Individual Programmer will be solely responsible for the program or programming system required, in overall conception and in complete detail. Help will be available in the form of personal services such as secretarial, keypunching, and data collection, and of consulting services with experts in programming theory, software services, and the subject matter of the programming problem. But the Individual Programmer will not delegate any of the program design or any of the detailed coding to anyone. Some of the consultants will be other Individual Programmers "between jobs," as we discuss below.

The bases for assigning a large problem and expecting the productivity are:

1. *Deeper theoretical capabilities for solving data processing problems.* The Individual Programmer will have subject matter knowledge, and expert consulting help as a backup. With a thorough knowledge of the software support and consulting in that area, the Individual Programmer will work directly with the customer and will solve any disparity *between* customer needs and data processing realities.

2. *Better use of software support tools, in programming languages and library maintenance and utilization.* Knowing the full scope of software support possible, the Individual Programmer will build from, rather than reinvent, capabilities that may be needed and will adapt data processing needs to existing capabilities through an overall view of the programming operation.

3. *Decreased intermediate specifications between the data processing problem and its solution in programming languages.* The Individual Programmer is a professional and works with the customer on a level of

respect and trust to solve the data processing problem without entangling the customer in the details of the solution. This is not to imply any mystery in the way the Individual Programmer works, but to recognize that programming languages, more and more, are themselves the best languages to use in writing specifications for a data processing system.

4. *Decreased internal communication problems in producing programming systems.* This is the most obvious advantage of an Individual Programmer over a team of programmers, and an important one.

5. *Intense motivation and dedication over the period of time required to complete the project.* The Individual Programmer, like any other professional, is capable of a sustained level of motivation and dedication in carrying out a project. This motivation arises from the opportunity to create a programming system of value to customers and peers.

Systems Analysis and Programming

It is important, in understanding the responsibility of an Individual Programmer, to make a careful distinction between systems analysis, operations research, and other activities that may well precede the programming of a data processing system. We identify systems analysts from programmers today in concept. But a programming project often has large ingredients of systems analysis in it, and this fact confuses and confounds managerial considerations in carrying out such projects.

The reason for making a careful distinction is this: In the programming operation, some major problems are communication and the maintaining of detailed coherence throughout the system. The Individual Programmer has a tremendous advantage over a team in this aspect, but even so, time is still of the essence in bringing the project to a successful conclusion. That is, the programming must be carried out in a time span as short as possible, even though it may be several months, in order to maintain this coherence as rigorously as possible. If, however, the systems analysis is going on concurrently with the programming, the whole effort gets diluted and extended in time to the detriment of the programming itself.

As a result of these considerations, an important managerial distinction in overall systems development is the identification of a boundary between systems analysis and programming. The Individual Programmer should come into the overall development at that point, so that the programming operation can be relatively clean and quick. Of course, the same person may well function first as a systems analyst and then as a programmer, but these separate roles should still be identified.

It is frequently—and, in fact, should usually be—the case that the systems analysis effort takes more time than the programming effort. Determining *what* the data processing system should do requires subject matter creativity, whereas determining *how* the data processing system should do this "what" involves creativity in programming itself. The Individual Programmer should know the subject matter in order to guarantee the integrity and relevance of the data processing system in that subject matter. But the Individual Programmer should engage in little creative thinking about the subject matter itself while programming. Otherwise, the time advantage of a quick and clean programming effort will be lost.

In summary, the systems analysis activity is essentially inductive—a gathering together of the data requirements, the techniques and algorithms for processing it, and the way the results should be interpreted. It is an extroverted activity, involving drawing out of a customer problem area a solution in terms of a general systems design, independent of machine considerations in most cases. This solution is couched in English, mathematics, and so on, for communication between people; and the rigor called for is from the subject matter, not the details of the communication, because people have very elaborate error-correcting and feedback capabilities in these processes. As a result, the systems analysis activity can be carried out somewhat leisurely with problems "lying fallow" in people's minds, unless customer time requirements dictate otherwise, without particularly jeopardizing the activity itself.

However, the programming activity is more deductive in character, beginning with the results of systems analysis as its "axioms" and determining the most effective way for realizing these requirements in a data processing system. It is an introverted activity, by and large, involving handling the complete detail required in designing and implementing the data processing system. This solution is in programming languages, and the rigor called for is in reflecting the system requirements in these programming languages. But unlike systems analysis, time is indeed of the essence in completing the programming operation, in order to maintain rigor and coherence in the complete detail demanded by machines and their programming languages.

We note that the description of systems analysis as extroverted and programming as introverted refers to the work processes and not to customer relationships. There are still many decisions to be made between the customer and the Individual Programmer. To stay within reasonable bounds, these decisions should primarily involve how the customer interfaces with the data processing system—control sequences, output formats, etc.—rather than the algorithms and techniques of processing the data. This is not to say that exceptions are not possible; the Individual Programmer, as a person, will have the capability of addressing the system he or she is programming on a much wider basis. Rather, these bounds represent a voluntary discipline on all parties concerned, which can make the whole process of system development more effective.

Will the Individual Programmer Be Responsive to Customers?

One question that might arise is the responsiveness of an Individual Programmer to customer needs. Will such a person program what he or she "thinks best" for the customer, only later to have it turn out not to solve the customer's data processing problem in the best way?

On a little reflection it seems that the answer is that this will be far less of a problem for an Individual Programmer than for a team. There are two main reasons for this: responsibility and capability.

First, the Individual Programmer is completely responsible for the programming system, and knows it. If the system subsequently does not satisfy the customer, it is a reflection on the Individual Programmer, who knows that, too.

Second, the Individual Programmer is more capable of being responsive to a customer than a team is. Frequently, because of communications problems and compartmentalization, a team manager simply does not know whether a new customer request can be accommodated. Even if it can, the manager may hesitate, wanting to keep the team integration problems under control. An Individual Programmer has no such inhibitions. An Individual Programmer is the complete master of the situation.

It should be characteristic of Individual Programmers to be extremely responsive to customers—to interface at a professional level, which includes finding out what is in customers' minds as well as what they say. A frequent complaint in team programming is that "the customer doesn't know what he wants," which is all too often an admission that the team has not found out what the customer wants. Frequently, for example, customers cannot really be expected to know what they want until they have seen some system output or tried to use system control procedures that may be proposed. An Individual Programmer could be expected to show lots of output to such customers, having the capability to modify a solution according to the customer's problem.

Of course, this capability for "turning on a dime" in the development of a system is not necessarily present in all people. People who do not have it should not be Individual Programmers, just as some people should not be heart surgeons.

It is also worth noting that another reason that customers may seem to keep "changing their minds" is that the program development cycle takes so long that changes in personnel occur or new ideas arise in the subject matter. This program development cycle should be shorter for an Individual Programmer than a team.

Still another reason, of course, for team difficulties, is that different team members interpret what they hear differently when the customer was saying the same thing all along.

Can Individual Programmers Be Motivated Highly Enough?

With just a moment's thought, this can be seen to be no problem when there is any reasonable long-range layout of assignments. First, the Individual Programmer has the opportunity to be a very important person, to make his or her life count. The primary motivation is in the work itself. Anyone who is not intensely interested in the work, will not have made it to this point anyway. The Individual Programmer should be paid well—at the top of the scale for individual technical workers. At the moment, comparing the cost with that of team programming, one might justify rather astronomical salaries, but this is not a realistic approach. For with recognition of the possibilities to be an Individual Programmer, conditions of the labor market will prevail—even as for heart surgeons. At the present time, a range of $20,000 to $40,000 would seem reasonable (young people working into this range, and senior people of merit leveling off toward the top). Primarily, this is "sincerity" and "proud" money for an Individual Programmer.

However, the most important aspect for an Individual Programmer—motivation—can also be converted into a major asset for the company: in assignments "between customer jobs."

An individual assignment for an Individual Programmer should usually amount to three to nine months. A year may be a little long, though not out of the question, and shorter assignments ought to be given to more junior people coming up. These assignments will be intense and demanding and should be interspersed with other assignments involving less pressure.

One part-time assignment that should be nearly automatic is the maintenance of the programming system just completed. This gives the customer the best qualified person to handle that phase of the job. It also gives the Individual Programmer feedback on the value of the work he or she has just done. This ought to be especially valuable for younger people, in their growth into larger and larger jobs.

But the main assignment "between jobs" ought to be in research and tool building, for oneself and other Individual Programmers in future jobs. There are two main reasons why this can be of particular value to the company.

First, the Individual Programmers are the best programmers around, and they are equipped to generate tools—which, after all, are just other programming systems. We are remarkably fortunate in programming. Heart surgeons do not themselves use heart surgery to build tools for further heart surgery, such as artificial valves and pumps. But it is programmers who build programming tools by programming—such as compilers, for example.

Second, the Individual Programmers will know better than anyone else what tools are needed "in the field," for they have been there and are going back. In this connection, Individual Programmers will go back to the field for the same reason that people climb mountains—"because it's there!" They will be glad for the rest and the time to reflect and build theory and tools, but if they have the talent required, they will also have the restlessness that will not let them vegetate.

Is Management Exposure Tolerable in One-Man Projects?

This question, like the previous two, can be answered more easily than might be apparent at first glance. A good case can be made for the idea that management exposure can be made less in a one-man project than in a team project. Superficially, it would seem that the danger of losing someone in a team project would be less severe than of losing the person in a one-man project. But a little thinking shows that this need not be the case. There are two reasons.

First, the Individual Programmer is the antithesis of the "mad scientist," who is producing a program that works, only no one else can figure out how. Instead, Individual Programmers are engaged in programming problems of considerable substance; they must work systematically and maintain well-documented trails for their own use in completing their own projects. They will also be using major software tools in library management, in automatic documentation, in job control, and in high-level source programming languages. All these tools, used in common by Individual Programmers in their projects, also impose, in return, considerable built-in discipline. Thus an Individual Programmer leaves a trail of documentation in a form familiar to other Individual Programmers.

One of the services that should be supplied jointly to management and to an Individual Programmer in a project is a Design Review Team to which the Individual Programmer can explain the design and progress for his or her own peace of mind about not overlooking things, for instance. This Team should have at least one other Individual Programmer of equal capability who is between jobs and is designated as "backup" for this job. If something happens to the first Individual Programmer, the backup should be able to step in with a minimum of disruption.

Second, it turns out that the backup capability assumed in the team approach is often illusory—for the same reasons as the communications problems that arise in teams. When someone is lost in a compartmentalized project, the effect is often harder to counteract than when going into a project that exists as an organic whole, because decisions at interface points have been based on breaking up the project more than on any inherent properties of the problem.

Very Large Programming Projects

The majority of today's projects could be handled by a single person as an Individual Programmer, but a few will require more than one, such as the Houston RTCC, OS/360, or a large command/control system. In this case, several Individual Programmers would jointly carry out the project, not as a team, but as a set of major subsystem developers that interface in a predetermined way with one another. For example, in an operating system an Individual Programmer may take on a language translator or a data management processor that operates as an ordinary applications processor in the operating system.

In another place the idea of developing software support systems through building on a Kernel System is discussed. This technique of evolving operating systems to satisfy individual installations is especially suited to the use of Individual Programmers.

Major applications systems in such areas as defense and space, without exception, have subsystem structures that can be used to demarcate parts of a total system for assignment to Individual Programmers. In any such system there needs to be a chief Individual Programmer who defines the system in its entirety and identifies the inputs and outputs required from the subsystem, but he should behave in every way as another Individual Programmer and not as a team leader in the ordinary sense.

A Community of Individual Programmers

The foregoing has sketched out characteristics of Individual Programmers, and how such people might interact collectively as a Community of Individual Programmers. In summary, such a Community might present the following kind of picture.

Imagine a group of some 15–50 Individual Programmers as a stable operation, addressed to some general area of data processing, such as Command Systems, Space Computation, or Financial Operations. The group may possibly be further divided into subcategories for management purposes. At any point in time, about half of the Individual Programmers will be in active jobs, each interfacing and building a programming system for a customer. The other half will be involved with maintenance of previous jobs, consulting in active jobs, serving as backups, researching new ideas in programming theory, and carrying out tool building jobs.

There will also be an additional group of young candidates to be Individual Programmers, acting very much like the regular Individual Programmers, but working on job assignments of smaller scope and time periods. They are growing into Individual Programmers this way, through a process of internship.

It is an honor to be one of these candidates, just as it is an honor to graduate from medical school. Candidates have at least a Master's equivalent in a subject of interest to the Community. They also have a Ph.D. equivalent by today's standards in computer science and already know how to program and design programs. The candidacy is to find out whether they can maintain their level of concentration over the length of time needed to complete major programming projects.

There is also a larger Community of Individual Programmers at the company level. The tool building going on in the various subject communities is coordinated at this larger level, and the tools are disseminated. Among a group of dedicated professionals, secure in their own opinion of themselves, there is not much room for a "not invented here" attitude. They want all the tools they can lay their hands on and should not be competing among themselves in that area.

The management of this Community of Individual Programmers has some unexpected simplicities in it, compared with team operations. In team operations there is always the problem of sorting out interrelated individual performances. This is not much of a problem with an Individual Programmer. You find out whether the customer likes the system—it is one person's system and no one else's. There is also less of a problem in promoting candidates. They are learning and working on customer systems, too, all by themselves, but smaller systems.

Can IBM Use Individual Programmers Effectively?

There seems to be little question that IBM can, indeed, ask for and count on Individual Programmers at this time and build effective Communities of Individual Programmers within the next three to five years. A more careful estimate should be made, but it seems that on the basis of a constant level of work, a factor of at least two to five could be taken out of the programmer categories in the company, with somewhat less reduction in costs because of the higher level of personnel involved.

One question that arises is "What happens to all the programmers we have?" The answer is easy. The good ones are converted into Individual Programmers. The rest are absorbed into other operations of the company, in its growth, where their programming experience will serve them in good stead for other jobs.

Another question is "Can IBM expect Individual Programmers to take on the assignments required?" We do not really know how difficult programming is, because it is part of such a young industry. But it is apparent that isolated people can take on the kind of assignments we need; it has happened in programming, already in at least tens of cases, and possibly hundreds—for example, the ALGOL compiler that Edgar Irons wrote by himself in one year and the one-man PL360 compiler at Stanford. And in this connection the dedication required seems to be no more than many IBMers are already putting out in engineering, manufacturing, marketing, and management (including the management of programming).

ARTICLE

5

The Case Against GO TO Statements in PL/I

(1969)

It is not possible to program in a sensible way without GO TO's in FORTRAN or COBOL. But it is possible in ALGOL or PL/I. The difference is in alternative ways available for controlling branching. This note is to point out that the new language technology in programming has moved out from under the GO TO and makes it of dubious value for use at all in PL/I. It also points out a new possibility in PL/I: that programmers can and should read programs written by others, not in traumatic emergencies, but as a matter of normal procedure in the programming process.

In the early days of programming, when programs were written directly in machine code or, at most, in Assembly language, the branch statement was a very simple machine step to execute and found its way into early programming languages through the GO TO statement, which translated very readily into the branch statements. While programming languages have increased in complexity and power, the GO TO statement has remained conceptually the same in the minds of programmers. However, these programming languages now provide for blocking and nesting of program statements and for the delayed dynamic binding of variables. These capabilities have introduced serious side effects for the GO TO statement in compilers.

A modern language, such as PL/I or ALGOL, has a block structure, for example, BEGIN. . . END, DO. . . END, to permit the grouping of statements into compound statements in the language, and it permits new ways of control logic that can eliminate GO TO statements entirely. At first glance this may seem surprising or may seem trivial by way of duplicating sections of code throughout a program. But this is not the case. PL/I programs can be written with a very minimum of code duplication, excessive CALLS, and awkwardness by using IF-THEN-ELSE, simple and iterative DO, and ON statements in place of GO TO's. In particular, the DO-WHILE loop, where the WHILE condition is a truth value turned off within the loop at the proper time, is a convenient way of handling typical control logic otherwise calling for GO TO's. For example, a program that reads data, does a computation, prints results, then reads data, and so on, while data remains to be read in, can be organized as a single DO-WHILE group, preceded by an ON ENDFILE statement to turn the WHILE condition to false.

Similarly, IF-THEN-ELSE, where the THEN and ELSE clauses may be DO groups or BEGIN blocks, can be used in various combinations to eliminate GO TO's. The IF conditions for branching must frequently be altered, but usually reorganizing such branching conditions adds to program clarity and control simplicity in itself. ON statements with BEGIN blocks can be used to handle interrupt conditions conveniently.

The foregoing findings are empirical. It might not be obvious, even if formal theorems were available, that GO TO's could be eliminated in everyday PL/I programming without its being excessively awkward or redundant. But some experience and trying soon uncover the fact that it is quite easy to do; in fact, the most difficult thing is to simply decide to do it in the first place.

There are, however, much deeper reasons than programming style or taste for doing without GO TO's in programming in a modern language. No statement in programming so neatly scrambles syntax and semantics as one such as "GO TO LL"; it is easy to identify its syntactic type as a GO TO statement, but the "LL" is a value that permits the control logic of the statement to lead anywhere. Five reasons why GO TO's are not good practice in PL/I are explained.

1. *The Readability of Programs.* Programs that are written without GO TO's can be read by others from top to bottom without requiring any mental gymnastics or short-term memory feats on the part of the readers. The only way for control to move out of the direct line of code is through the IF-THEN-ELSE, DO, CALL, or ON statements, each of which is easily understood and visualized in reading code. In addition to writing without GO TO's, when BEGIN, DO groups, IF-THEN-ELSE statements, and such are indented in a uniform way and every BEGIN or DO has its own explicit END statement, then it becomes particularly

easy to see the flow of control just from the typographical form of the program itself.

2. *The Complexities of Compiling.* In a compiler that deals only with static code and no dynamic block structure or binding of variables, the GO TO is exceptionally easy to implement. However, in PL/I, the GO TO is one of the most difficult statements to implement in the language. When the GO TO is given, there must be a search for the label in the block containing the GO TO. If the label is found, this is the simplest case, and the branch can be made directly. However, if the label is not found, then it must be searched for in the next outer block, if any, that includes the current block. This means undoing the variable binding and other dynamic conditions associated with the inner block in advance of transferring to a label outside it. If the label is not found in that block, the search must be continued to further outer blocks, if any, until either successful or not. If it is not successful, then one typically must get back into the inner block in order to produce appropriate diagnostics or other action, as called for. The complexity of handling the GO TO statement is in sharp contrast to that required for DO groups or IF-THEN-ELSE statements, which involve no dynamic blocks or binding of variables in themselves.

3. *The Simplicities of Documentation.* A future use of program syntax of potential major benefit is in the automatic organization of documentation files and the generation of appropriate questions about program structure and content to the originating programmers. The absence of GO TO's makes the control semantics of the program transparent to the syntax, so that the structure of documentation files and the interrogation of programmers about their programs become correspondingly simpler.

4. *The Optimization of GO TO–Free Code.* The optimization of machine code from compilers always begins with the determination of basic blocks, that is, blocks of straightline code in the program to be executed, and the directed control graph that connects these basic blocks. The directed control graph can be arbitrarily complex and can itself tax any optimization analysis. In contrast, a PL/I program with no GO TO statements has the property that its basic blocks are now transparent to the syntax, for the basic blocks are typographical segments of code, delimited by IF, BEGIN, DO, and ON statements. For example, when execution reaches an IF statement, it is known at that point that the execution will go to either the THEN unit or the ELSE unit and nowhere else. Thus, for example, a register-loading strategy should load either the registers of the THEN unit or the ELSE unit, but never some of each.

5. *The Loading and Execution of GO TO–Free Code.* When the basic blocks and other executable program segments are transparent to the syntax, then it becomes possible for the loading and execution control programs to allocate core and bring in code on the basis of syntactic structure. For example, core can be allocated to DO groups, BEGIN blocks, and so on, rather than simply to a given number of bytes of machine code.

In the same way that GO TO's can be eliminated, one can also eliminate RETURN statements with control always going through the final END statement of a procedure in PL/I. In procedures that have no parameters and declare no variables (for example, one that is included in another procedure) it is possible to replace the PROCEDURE statement by a DO statement and to include the resulting DO statement in-line (replace the CALL of the procedure by the macro process or %INCLUDE statement) with the same computational effect. As a result, one has a way of maintaining a "design system" highly modularized with various capabilities for maintenance and debugging, and then of converting this automatically into a monolithic, but faster running "production system."

The foregoing is a realistic possibility because of the way programming modularity usually comes about. It is frequent in programming that procedures fall into one of two distinct classes. The first class is one in which a common action is performed many times in the course of a program, for example, a SINE routine, and the objective is to provide the code only once. It is natural in this class to pass parameters explicitly and to make the subroutine completely independent of any other data in the calling program. A second class arises from the desire of a programmer to achieve general modularity in a system and to identify certain system activities for his or her own convenience as separate procedures. But it is typical that the communication between such procedures and the calling program is broader, not necessarily through parameters, but more likely through external data or included data. It is also usual that such a procedure is not called so many times, but quite often only once, or at most twice. It is this second category that lends itself to the foregoing treatment and permits the elimination of prologue/epilogue processing through in-line DO statements.

ARTICLE 6

The New York Times Thesaurus of Descriptors

(1969)

Abstract

The documents making up this article consist of: first, the Foreword and Introduction to *The New York Times Thesaurus of Descriptors,* republished here with the kind permission of The New York Times Company; and second, a working document called "A Structural Description of The New York Times Thesaurus of Descriptors." The second document was written over the four-day period from July 22 to July 25, 1969, and is based on the first document. It is a sample of an applications programmer at work, trying to reduce a complex applications problem to simple terms by methods of computer science. In this case *The New York Times Thesaurus of Descriptors* is described by a formal grammar (a running tutorial for understanding the grammar is given as well). Then the grammar is used in a critical way for defining the interface between program designer, system manager, and system user for file maintenance and on-line retrieval operations. The working document illustrates an attempt at communication between a program designer and an intelligent client. In this case it is remarkable that the BNF (Backus Naur Form of describing formal grammars) for the New York Times Thesaurus is so clean (cleaner than most programming languages), which goes to show that intelligence and taste are the best tools possible, whether the designers of the language know formal methods or not.

PART A
The New York Times Thesaurus of Descriptors

Foreword

The project to devise a thesaurus as an aid in processing and searching information from newspaper files was undertaken as part of an effort by The New York Times to coordinate all its information facilities. It grew out of preparations for the application of computer technology to the production of The New York Times Index. The vocabulary and structure of the Thesaurus are therefore based largely on those of the Index, but include many additional terms from the subject card file of The Times clipping "morgue" and from the vertical file catalogue of The Times Editorial Reference Library.

The following works were consulted in designing the format of the Thesaurus: The *ASTIA Thesaurus of Descriptors,* 2nd edition, December, 1962; the Department of Defense *Manual for Building a Technical Thesaurus,* Project LEX, Office of Naval Research, April, 1966; and the Engineers Joint Council's *Guide for Source Indexing and Abstracting of the Engineering Literature,* February, 1967. The *Subject Headings Used in the Dictionary Catalog of the Library of Congress,* 7th edition, 1966, was consulted in solving certain problems of terminology.

The work is a cooperative effort of the staff of The New York Times Index under the general direction of Dr. John Rothman, editor. The huge task of compiling and annotating the entries was handled by the following staff members:

Robert A. Barzilay, coordinator
Marvin M. Aledort
William F. Marshall
Robert S. Olsen
Daniel Pinzow
Susan L. Pinzow
George D. Trent

The job of final editing was shared by Dr. Rothman and Thomas R. Royston, assistant editor.

Computer programming and operations were done by Central Media Bureau, Inc., of New York.

© 1969 by The New York Times Company. Reprinted by permission.

About The Second Edition

Within a few months after publication of the Thesaurus, enough corrections and additions had accumulated to make it advisable to publish a complete revision rather than the individual pages with changes originally planned.

In all, almost a thousand changes were made by the time this Second Edition was ready for its final computer run. Many of them were based on suggestions received from Thesaurus users.

The physical format has also been improved. This edition is printed on heavier paper, which will turn more easily and be more resistant to tearing. In addition, continuation headings have been added where required.

The active interest of Thesaurus users has helped make this new edition a more useful reference tool. Your comments will always be welcome and sincerely appreciated.

Introduction

The word "thesaurus" derives from a Greek word meaning "treasure." As applied to the conventional dictionary of synonyms and antonyms, such as Roget's, it is most apt; such a thesaurus is indeed a treasure, displaying the riches, the fullness and diversity of the language.

The kind of thesaurus that has evolved in the last decade or two in the field of information processing and retrieval is not a treasure so much as the key to one. The riches lie in a file of information—a collection of books or pamphlets or reports or photographs or newspapers—and the thesaurus is a means for their exploitation. A thesaurus of this kind is a device for ordering and controlling the file, so that new items may be added consistently to related items, and so that all relevant items are made readily and quickly accessible.

The New York Times Thesaurus of Descriptors is a structured vocabulary of terms designed to guide information specialists in processing and organizing materials from newspapers and other works dealing with current events and public affairs, and to guide users in searching collections of such materials. Because it covers the same vast variety of subject matter as the daily press, it will prove a valuable tool, we trust, not only for newspaper libraries but also for general reference libraries, for educational institutions, for government agencies, for business and financial organizations—in short, for any organization that collects, stores and uses information on the events of today and yesterday.

The Thesaurus consists of terms (descriptors), in a single alphabetical sequence, which denote the diverse subjects that may be found in the collection. For each descriptor, some or all of the following data are given, in the order indicated:

1. Qualifying Terms
2. Scope Notes
3. "See" or "See also" References (listed alphabetically)
4. "Refer from" References (listed alphabetically)
5. Subheadings (listed alphabetically).

These are designed to define descriptors and to correlate them with one another.

A model page appears on page 35. The remainder of the introduction explains the various features of the Thesaurus in detail and discusses the major principles of organizing such a file of information. It also includes some general guidelines for certain types of material (for example, foreign names and corporation names) that are not covered item by item in the Thesaurus itself. A brief index to the contents of the introduction follows:

1. Descriptors

Descriptors are primarily subject headings. Geographic names, personal names, names of companies, institutions and organizations, and other proper names are included only when they require the use of qualifying terms, scope notes, a regular pattern of cross references, or a regular pattern of subdivisions.

The Thesaurus does not include a descriptor for each individual member of a family. There would be little purpose in listing every item of furniture, every kind of weapon, or every kind of animal, vegetable or mineral. Descriptors are given for typical items and for those requiring any special or unusual handling; and these will serve, it is hoped, as models for any similar items that are not listed.

Synonyms. Preferences between synonymous or nearly synonymous terms are indicated by "see" references (AVIATION. See Aeronautics).

Non-Standard Terms and Recent Coinages. Descriptors include terms current in the news (such as BLACK Power or BRAIN Drain) even though they are not found in standard library catalogues or dictionaries. Descriptors do not include brand names or trademarks, technical terms not nor-

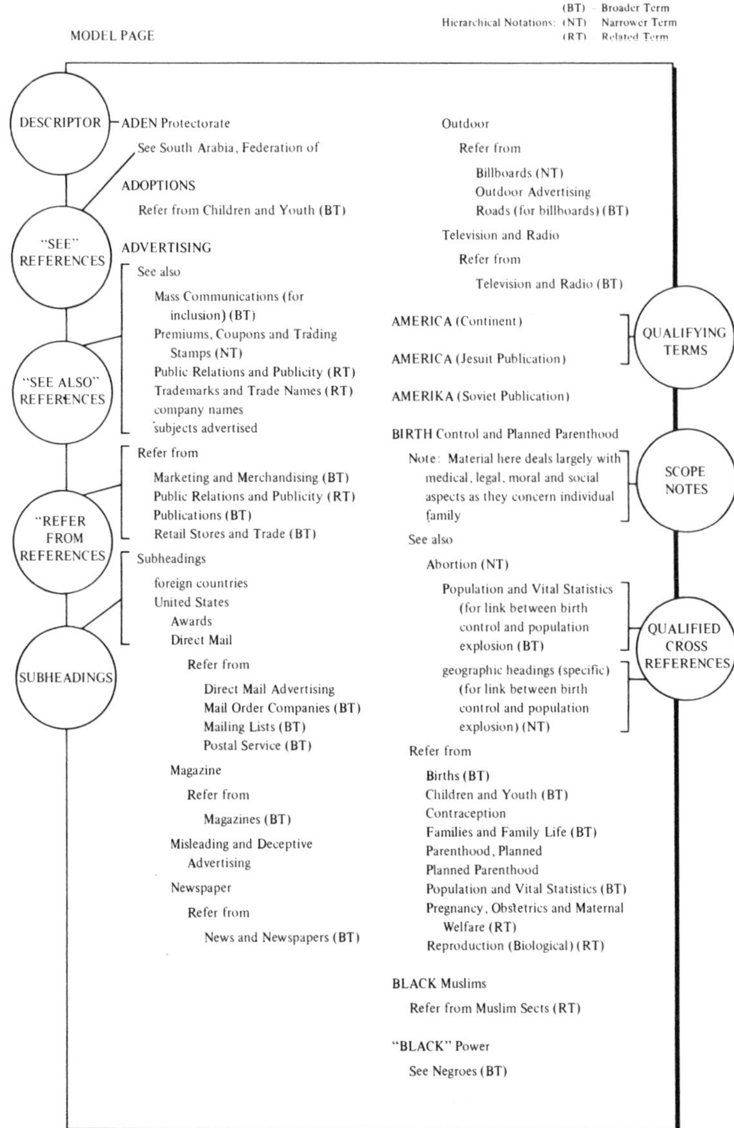

mally used in newspaper articles, slang words, and terms used exclusively in professional jargon. When colloquialisms, slogans or unusual coinages are used as descriptors, they usually appear in quotation marks. Archaic or obsolete terms are included when this is considered helpful.

MODEL PAGE
Hierarchical Notations: (BT) Broader Term
(NT) Narrower Term
(RT) Related Term
DESCRIPTOR
"SEE" REFERENCES
"SEE ALSO" REFERENCES
"REFER FROM REFERENCES
SUBHEADINGS
QUALIFYING TERMS
SCOPE NOTES
QUALIFIED CROSS REFERENCES
ADEN Protectorate
See South Arabia, Federation of
ADOPTIONS
Refer from Children and Youth (BT)
ADVERTISING
See also
Mass Communications (for inclusion) (BT)
Premiums, Coupons and Trading Stamps (NT)
Public Relations and Publicity (RT)
Trademarks and Trade Names (RT)
company names
subjects advertised
Refer from
Marketing and Merchandising (BT)
Public Relations and Publicity (RT)
Publications (BT)
Retail Stores and Trade (BT)
Subheadings
foreign countries
United States
Awards
Direct Mail
Refer from
Direct Mail Advertising
Mail Order Companies (BT)
Mailing Lists (BT)
Postal Service (BT)
Magazine
Refer from
Magazines (BT)
Misleading and Deceptive Advertising
Newspaper
Refer from
News and Newspapers (BT)
Outdoor
Refer from
Billboards (NT)
Outdoor Advertising
Roads (for billboards) (BT)
Television and Radio
Refer from
Television and Radio (BT)
AMERICA (Continent)
AMERICA (Jesuit Publication)
AMERIKA (Soviet Publication)
BIRTH Control and Planned Parenthood
Note: Material here deals largely with medical, legal, moral and social aspects as they concern individual family
See also
Abortion (NT)
Population and Vital Statistics (for link between birth control and population explosion (BT)
geographic headings (specific) (for link between birth control and population explosion) (NT)
Refer from
Births (BT)
Children and Youth (BT)
Contraception
Families and Family Life (BT)
Parenthood, Planned
Planned Parenthood
Population and Vital Statistics (BT)
Pregnancy, Obstetrics and Maternal Welfare (RT)
Reproduction (Biological) (RT)
BLACK Muslims
Refer from Muslim Sects (RT)
"BLACK" Power
See Negroes (BT)

Abbreviations and Acronyms. Abbreviations and acronyms are used as descriptors, usually with "see" references to the name spelled out (NATO.

See North Atlantic Treaty Organization). The practice may be reversed when the abbreviation is much better known and more widely used than the term it represents (DICHLORO-Diphenyl-Trichloroethane. See DDT). No attempt has been made to compile an exhaustive list of abbreviations and acronyms.

Alphabetization. To give a complete description of the alphabetization scheme followed in the Thesaurus would go far beyond the scope of this introduction; but the following are the major rules applied in alphabetizing entries here, and recommended: word-by-word order rather than letter-by-letter (AIR Pollution before AIRLINES); abbreviations filed as words (NATO between NATIONAL and NATURE); inverted headings filed before uninverted headings (NEW York, State University of, before NEW York Airways); homographs filed in the order of person, place, thing (BROOKLYN, William; BROOKLYN, NY; BROOKLYN Bridge) or in the alphabetical order of qualifying terms (MERCURY (Metal); MERCURY (Planet)); numbers filed as though spelled out (20th Century as TWENTIETH Century), except where the numerical order is clearly preferable (HENRY VII before HENRY VIII); and compound terms filed as though two words (REAL-Time before REALISM), except when the first component is a prefix (TRANS World after TRANSIT) or a term of direction (SOUTH-West) after SOUTHERN).

Specificity. In general, files of information must be so organized as to bring together all items relevant to a given inquiry and yet permit prompt access to any single, specific item. In this Thesaurus, the choice of descriptors and their degree of specificity reflect the vocabulary and scope of current journalistic writing and seek to anticipate the needs of users who consult files of newspapers, magazines, pamphlets, reports and the like for information. When the amount of material on a subject is large (for example, AERONAUTICS), separate descriptors for specific aspects are advisable (AIRLINES, AIRPLANES, AIRPORTS, etc.). When the amount of material is relatively small and should not be scattered, or when its separate aspects are not readily segregated, the use of a more comprehensive descriptor is advised. (For example, the descriptor PLASTICS is used for all kinds of plastic materials, since these are rarely differentiated in newspaper stories; obviously, such a comprehensive descriptor would be inadequate for the literature of organic chemistry.)

Generics. Because the subject fields in current events tend to overlap widely and terms are often vague and imprecise in meaning, a hierarchical or classed arrangement of descriptors was impossible to achieve. Where feasible, hierarchical relationships between descriptors are indicated by means of "broader term" (BT) and "narrower term" (NT) notations in cross references.

Geographic vs. Subject Terms. The problem of whether to organize a file by subject or by place is one of the most difficult confronting a librarian (HOUSING—New York City or NEW York City—Housing?). Except in mechanized coordinate files, the effort and expense required for complete duplication are prohibitive, and a choice between the two approaches must be made. Our preference for the subject approach is reflected in the Thesaurus. It is based on the fact that most news developments have regional rather than uniquely local significance. Much of the political and economic news deals with broad geographical areas; cities throughout the world have similar traffic, air pollution, water supply and slum housing problems; and so forth. Hence, geographic terms are used mostly for general descriptions and for general material on the economics, politics, defenses, population, history and customs of an area; in short, for material too broad to fit under subject descriptors. Organizational material on specific government agencies (formation, budget, personnel) is covered under geographic terms; their activities are covered under appropriate subjects. Names of government agencies (except for international and American interstate agencies) are not given as descriptors. An attempt has been made to provide a list of United States (Federal) agencies (as subheadings under UNITED States), but because their names change frequently and the status of some is now in doubt, the list may not be complete and is subject to frequent revision.

Word Order in Multiple-Word Descriptors. For most subject descriptors consisting of more than one word, the natural word order is preferred and given here (AIR Pollution; not POLLUTION, Air). For personal names, the last name is always given first (JOHNSON, Lyndon Baines). For foreign personal names, determination of the correct "last name" is often troublesome; see the next section for some general rules. Geographic names usually invert from and are alphabetized under the proper-name element (PHILIPPINES, Republic of the; not REPUBLIC of the Phillipines). Company names should be in natural word order (NATIONAL Broadcasting Company; not BROADCASTING Company, National) except when inversion from a proper-name element is clearly preferable (MACY, R. H., & Co.; not R. H. Macy & Co.) (for dubious cases, the stock market tables often provide a useful guide). Names of schools, universities and museums should generally be in natural word order (MASSACHUSETTS Institute of Technology), but there are some obvious exceptions (CHICAGO, University of; not UNIVERSITY of Chicago). Names of business, trade, civic and professional associations, labor unions, foundations and certain other organizations should invert from an appropriate subject term or personal name (KANSAS City, Chamber of Commerce of; ADVERTISING Agencies, American Association of; CIVIL Liberties Union, American; LONGSHOREMEN'S Association, International; SLOAN, Alfred P., Foundation). It is often helpful to use inversions of word order to bring together, in the same alphabetical location, all organizations concerned with the same subject that use the descriptor for this subject as part of their names (for example, all organizations whose names contain the word EDUCATION). When the inversion is not obvious, or when there is a choice between two or more possible inversions, alternatives should be covered by "see" references to the preferred version (BROADCASTERS, National Association of Educational. See Educational Broadcasters, National Association of). Some "see" references of this type are included in the Thesaurus, especially under common words such as American, General, or International.

Foreign Names. Foreign names present problems both in determining the proper word order and in determining proper spelling for transliterations. Authoritative reference works such as *Who's Who* should be consulted, but even these are not always in agreement, and, of course, they cover only a limited number of names. Helpful advice can be obtained from information officers of foreign consulates, trade missions and delegations to the United Nations and other international organizations. The following rules are offered as a general guide, but they are not exhaustive, and there are many exceptions.

a. British names including two "last" names (Anthony Wedgwood Benn) usually invert from the second of these (BENN, Anthony Wedgwood).

b. Spanish names including two "last" names (Eduardo Frei Montalva) usually invert from the first of these (FREI Montalva, Eduardo).

c. European and Latin-American names containing a partitive (de, di, van, von) usually invert from the name following the partitive (GAULLE, Charles de; HASSEL, Kai-Uwe von).

d. Names containing a definite article usually invert from the article if they are French, Italian, Spanish or Portuguese (LA Guardia, Ernesto de) and from the name following the article if they are German or Dutch (HEIDE, Gottfried von der).

e. Arabic names containing a partitive (al, el, ben, ibn) usually invert from the name following the partitive (ATTASSI, Fadhil al; BELLA, Ahmed ben).

f. Chinese, Indochinese and Korean names invert from the last element if they have been Westernized (PARK, Chung He), but run uninverted if not (MAO Tse-tung; NGUYEN Cao Ky). (If such names become popularly known in an incorrect form, such as "Premier Ky" instead of "Premier

Nguyen Cao Ky," appropriate "see" references should be run from the incorrect form to the correct form.)

g. When foreign names may be transliterated in several different ways, the preferred transliteration should be determined, if possible, and "see" references to it should be run from alternate transliterations. Among the more common instances are the following: In Arabic names, use ai instead of ei (FAISAL, not FEISAL) and use kh instead of q as the first letter (KHALIDI, not QALIDI). In Russian names, use of ch instead of tch or tsch (CHERNISHEV, not TCHERNISHEV or TSCHERNISHEV) and use v instead of ff as the last letter (SUVOROV, not SUVOROFF). In Greek names, use k instead of c or ch as the initial letter (KARAMANLIS, not CARAMANLIS; KRYSOSTOMOS, not CHRYSOSTOMOS). However, names for which the alternate transliteration is well established (TCHAIKOVSKY, PROKOFIEFF, CONSTANTINE) should be retained thus.

Corporation Divisions and Subsidiaries. The question of whether to establish separate descriptors for corporate divisions and subsidiaries, or to carry material about them under the name of the parent company, poses another major problem. In general, separate descriptors should be established for subsidiaries that issue their own stock, have well-known names distinct from those of the parent company, or have otherwise a separate identity (CHEVROLET Division of General Motors Corp.; IBM World Trade Corp.), and then the parent company should be linked to the subsidiary by a "see also" reference. When the subsidiaries do not have a clearly distinct identity, it is advisable to carry material about them under the name of the parent company, especially when the material does not consistently identify them by name. For example, it is virtually impossible to use separate descriptors for the overseas operating units of the major international oil companies. These are referred to sometimes by their own names (ESSO Libya Ltd.) and sometimes merely as units of the parent company (Standard Oil of New Jersey's Libyan affiliate), and there may be no way of determining whether the same unit or two different units are involved. Even when the distinction can be made, it may be better to keep material about the company together under one name than to scatter it among several names, some of which may be quite unfamiliar to the users.

Religious Denominations. When the amount of material is relatively small, material on branches, regional bodies and other agencies of a denomination is carried under the collective name of the denomination, and not under separate descriptors. (For example: Greek Orthodox Church under ORTHODOX Churches; Southern Baptist Convention under BAPTIST Churches.) Individual congregations and parishes, if not intersectarian, should also be included under the name of the denomination, rather than given separate descriptors; but the names of well-known churches (such as St. Patrick's Cathedral in New York) should be covered by "see" references to the name of the denomination.

2. Qualifying Terms

Qualifying terms are parenthetical expressions given after certain descriptors to distinguish between homographs. For example:

MERCURY (Metal)
MERCURY (Planet)

Qualifying terms may also be used to resolve other contextual ambiguities in some descriptors. For example:

FIFTH Amendment (U.S. Constitution)

3. Scope Notes

Scope notes are notes appearing after certain descriptors to define or describe the range of subject matter encompassed by the descriptor. For example:

DRUG Addiction, Abuse and Traffic.
Note: Material here includes narcotics, stimulants, hallucinatory drugs and others deemed socially undesirable.

Scope notes may be used at subheadings for the same purpose, and may also be used to describe the system of subdividing material under certain descriptors.

4. Cross References

Cross references serve as substitutes for multiple entries and as guides between descriptors encompassing related material. They are also used at subheadings as required.

Contrary to usual library practice, cross references have not usually been established between related descriptors that are immediately adjacent in the alphabet. (For example, there is no cross reference from ARMORED Vehicles to ARMORED Car Services.) It was felt that the connection between such adjacent descriptors is self-evident and that cross references there would be superfluous.

See References. "See" references guide from descriptors not used for "entries" in the system to equivalent descriptors used in preference. They are used mainly between synonyms (AVIATION. See Aeronautics), and when material denoted by one descriptor is subsumed under another (ORCHESTRAS. See Music).

See Also References. "See also" references guide from descriptors used for certain "entries" in the system to other descriptors where related material is entered. They may lead from more general, broader terms to more specific, narrower terms (REAL Estate. See also Housing), or vice versa (THEATER. See also Amusements). They may also lead from one descriptor to another on the same hierarchical level which may cover tangential topics or different aspects of the same topic (ROADS. See also Traffic).

Refer from References. "Refer from" references are the inverse of "see" and "see also" references. They show all the descriptors linked by "see" and "see also" references to the descriptor consulted (AERONAUTICS. Refer from Aviation).

Qualified Cross References. Numerous "see," "see also" and "refer from" references are followed by parenthetical expressions defining the particular aspect of a topic covered by the cross reference, as in DOGS. See also Blindness and the Blind (for seeing-eye dogs).

Hierarchical Notations. Many cross references are annotated to show hierarchical relationships, as follows: (NT) when the reference leads from a broader term to a narrower term (REAL Estate. See also Housing); (BT) when the reference leads from a narrower term to a broader term (THEATER. See also Amusements); and (RT) when the reference leads from one term to another on the same hierarchical level for related material (ROADS. See also Traffic). The use of these notations could not be sustained throughout the Thesaurus, however, because the subject fields covered in newspapers and other current-events publications tend to overlap widely and the vocabulary is extremely varied, complex and often imprecise; and hierarchical relationships could therefore not always be determined. (For example, CRIME and Criminals. See also Courts—which of these is the narrower descriptor, and which the broader?) In many cases, the question of hierarchy was moot, and the choice was finally governed by the descriptor from which the cross reference runs. (For example: HOUSING. See also Zoning is annotated (NT), even though zoning encompasses all kinds of land uses, because the cross reference is intended to cover a specific aspect of housing, namely, residential zoning.) Also, no attempt has been made to include cross references from all specific descriptors in a given subject field to the broad descriptor denoting the field as a whole. (For example, no broader-term cross references have been made from the many specific agricultural products, such as GRAIN, to the descriptor AGRICULTURE and Agricultural Products.)

5. Subheadings

The Thesaurus lists suggested subheadings for descriptors encompassing a large amount of material. Where a category of subheadings consists of names of individual components (for example, names of countries, of states, or of motion pictures), only the category is given, not an inclusive list of all components.

With few exceptions, subheadings are limited to two hierarchical levels (main subheadings and sub-subheadings). Further subdivision is usually not advisable; it makes the heading structure too complex and too difficult to search. When the need for further subdivision arises, it is usually an indication that the main heading (descriptor) is too broad, and that, instead of subdividing it further, narrower descriptors should be established.

Most descriptors lend themselves to both geographic and subject subdivisions. However, it is usually not advisable to mix geographic and subject subheadings at the same level (if under EDUCATION, for example, both Elementary and California are used as subheadings at the same level, which one would be used for material on elementary schools in California?). The nature of the material and the interests of the users should determine whether subdivisions should be geographical or by subject.

Subheadings may appear with qualifying terms, scope notes and cross references, just like descriptors.

6. Orientation and Format

Since the Thesaurus is based on the vocabulary used in processing information from The New York Times, it necessarily reflects the fact that The Times is published in New York. Thus, the descriptors NEW York City and NEW York State have subheadings not given for other cities and states, and New York City and New York State are used as subheadings under many descriptors that have no other city and state names as subheadings. Similarly, descriptors for local institutions (such as COLUMBIA

University or NEW York Times) are shown with a detailed structure not given for similar institutions elsewhere. However, the structure outlined under NEW York City, NEW York State and some local institutions may be easily applied to other cities and states and their institutions in processing local newspapers and other collections there.

In this context, it should be pointed out also that the detailed structure shown under PRESIDENTIAL Election of 1968 applies to the election in any current Presidential election year. Similarly, the structure shown under JOHNSON, Lyndon Baines, applies to any President and may be applied, with any necessary modifications, to governors, mayors, heads of foreign governments and other prominent figures.

Generally, the Thesaurus is intended, as its subtitle states, as a guide in processing and searching materials rather than as a body of firm and strict rules. Deviations from the guidelines set forth here should be made as the nature of the materials processed and the interests of their users require. In processing newspapers and other current events materials for information retrieval, flexibility is mandatory, and therefore frequent changes in the Thesaurus are envisaged. These changes may be initiated by us, or they may be made by individual users to cope with their specific problems and meet their specific needs.

It is for these reasons that the Thesaurus has been issued in looseleaf form. Even-numbered pages have been left blank to enable users to write their own notes at will opposite the appropriate Thesaurus material. Changes initiated by us will be on individual pages to be substituted or inserted. The looseleaf format permits users to insert separate sheets with their own material as desired.

PART B
A Structural Description of The New York Times Thesaurus of Descriptors

An important objective of the New York Times is contained on page 13 of the Introduction to *The New York Times Thesaurus of Descriptors.*

> Generally, the Thesaurus is intended, as its subtitle states, as a guide in processing and searching materials rather than as a body of firm and strict rules. Deviations from the guidelines set forth here should be made as the nature of the materials processed and the interests of their users require. In processing newspapers and other current events materials for information retrieval, flexibility is mandatory, and therefore frequent changes in the Thesaurus are envisaged. These changes may be initiated by us, or they may be made by individual users to cope with their specific problems and meet their specific needs.

In order to provide the kind of flexibility desired in on-line files, it is important that the computer programs not be based on a set of implicit or hidden assumption about how the Thesaurus is handled at the present time. For this reason a structural description of the Thesaurus is developed here to promote future flexibility and growth through a commonly understood interface between the designers of the Thesaurus and the programmers.

The final definition for a thesaurus, when pursued through all the intermediate definitions below, reduces to a (gigantic) natural language sequence, accessible and alphabetized on the basis of certain subsequences —Descriptors, See also References, and so on. It is just that.

How this large character string is to be formatted and stored in a computing system (with auxiliary directories, pointers, counts, separator characters, and so on) is a matter of programming strategy and tactics. It is an important matter, but designers of the Thesaurus need not get tangled up with it. Rather, they need only be concerned with the Thesaurus in its external form, as a structured natural language sequence that can be queried on and added to or deleted from, with certain automatic cross-referencing facilities carried out thereby.

Thus the important question for the designer is "Is this the structure I want for the Thesaurus?" in contrast to questions of content, criteria for placing content, and such. The objective of the following description is to permit the designer to examine that question with confidence and precision. The tools may seem a little formal and formidable at first glance.

But it is believed that concern will disappear with a little familiarity. The purpose is not to obscure, but to make analyses more precise and comprehensive—so that the designer can see the Thesaurus structure per se.

In this connection, the description developed below is somewhat more general than the present Thesaurus structure. It frequently happens that the simplification and unification desirable for automatic processing come only with a certain degree of generalization. And it frequently happens that more flexibility, rather than less, accompanies such generalization. Not all the flexibility inherent in the proposed file structure is used in present Thesaurus activities, and it is never expected that all of it will be used. But it is there to use and, more importantly, known to be there.

The Structural Description

The structural description for the Thesaurus will be given through a series of syntactic definitions (or "syntactic equations"), each of which expands a Thesaurus term (a generic form for a part of the Thesaurus) that is being defined into one or more patterns using simpler and more basic parts. Any term so defined is ultimately expanded thereby into natural language text, which is the unspecified primitive for the Thesaurus. As noted, the description concerns itself only with the structure of the Thesaurus and not with its contents.

The syntactic terms, or entities, used in the description are given in Table 6-1, first as natural language terms and then in a briefer symbolic form that will be used for convenience later. Notice that the Thesaurus terms are in three categories. First, there is a primitive term from which the Thesaurus is ultimately constructed, which is simply natural language text. All subsequent terms are eventually decomposable into this natural language text; this is the responsibility of the designers of the Thesaurus. Second, there is a set of terms used by The New York Times that are intended to be used in the structural description exactly as the Times personnel mean them. Finally, there is a set of additional terms (that will be defined by syntactic equations), which serve as intermediate syntactic entities between some of the lower- and higher-level terms used by The New York Times. These intermediate entities are, in fact, known in various forms to Times personnel as well; the reason for treating them more rigorously is to improve on the precision possible over natural language descriptions.

The syntactic equations of the descriptions are given (and numbered) in Table 6-2, and a brief word of explanation is in order so that the equations in Table 6-2 can be understood. Each equation consists of

TABLE 6-1. *Thesaurus Terms*

	Syntactic Entity
Primitive Term	
Natural Language Text	<TEXT>
New York Times Terms	
Descriptor	<TERM>
Qualifying Term	<QT>
Scope Note	<SN>
Hierarchical Notation	<HN>
See Reference	<SR>
See also Reference	<SAR>
Refer from Reference	<RFR>
Subheading	<SUBH>
New York Times Thesaurus of Descriptors	<THESAURUS>
Additional Terms (defined by equations in Table 6-2.)	
Text List	<TL>
Qualifying Terms List	<QTL>
Term Extension	<TE>
Term Extension List	<TEL>
Term Structure	<TS>
Term Structure List	<TSL>

a "left-hand side" and a "right-hand side." The left-hand side consists of the syntactic entity being defined by that equation. The right-hand side is its definition.

There are two major ways in which a definition is made in Table 6-2. The first way is through an *informal definition,* given in natural language *between asterisks.* This kind of definition may be used when no ambiguities or misunderstandings are likely. In any case, at least one term (a primitive term such as the first one in Table 6-2) must be defined in some informal way, or else the whole system of definitions will be circular. The second method of definition is by *syntactic formula,* which expresses one or more possible patterns of terms, using some notation, which we describe next.

Note that each syntactic entity in Table 6-1 begins and ends with an angle bracket (<, >), which seems to enclose a meaningful acronym or word. In fact, the whole string, including the angle brackets, is to be regarded as a single symbol, and the internal sequence of characters is of mnemonic significance only. In addition to the angle brackets (which are used to construct multiple-character symbols thereby), we also use as metasymbols equals (=), comma (,), square brackets ([,]), and braces

TABLE 6-2. *Thesaurus Equations*

1	<TEXT> = *Natural Language Text*
2	<TERM> = <TEXT>
3	<QT> = (<TEXT>)
4	<SN> = Note: <TEXT>
5	<HN> = {(BT), (NT), (RT)}
6	<SR> = See [<TEL>] [<TL>]
7	<SAR> = See also [<TEL>] [<TL>]
8	<RFR> = Refer from <TEL>
9	<SUBH> = Subheadings [<TSL>] [<TL>]
10	<THESAURUS> = <TSL>
11	<TL> = *Alphabetized list of <TEXT> items*
12	<QTL> = *List of <QT> items*
13	<TE> = <TERM> [<QTL>] [<SN>] [<HN>]
14	<TEL> = *Alphabetized list of <TE> items*
15	<TS> = <TE> [{<SR>, <SAR>}] [<RFR>] [<SUBH>]
16	<TSL> = *Alphabetized list of <TS> items*

({, }). The equals has already been informally explained above, in the definition of syntactic equation. The comma is used merely to separate items in a list. The square brackets are used to enclose an item; they mean that the appearance of that item is optional, that is, it may or may not appear in the pattern given by the formula. The braces are used to enclose a list and mean that precisely one item of the list must be used in the pattern. Natural language text appearing by itself, that is, not within angle brackets or asterisks, stands for itself. For reasons that are apparent with a little reflection, such occurrences of natural language are called syntactic constants. (The expression "See also" is a frequently recurring syntactic constant in the Thesaurus, for example.) The formula of a right-hand side of a syntactic equation can thus vary, by the use of brackets and braces, over several forms; the meaning of the syntactic equation is that the syntactic entity on the left-hand side is defined as any and all forms on the right-hand side that are possible.

To illustrate these ideas, note that Equation 4 of Table 6-2 states that <SN> (i.e., Scope Note) consists of the five characters, Note:, followed by the syntactic entity, <TEXT>, which by Equation 1 is simply natural language text. That is, Equation 4 sets up the *syntactic constant* "Note:" as the opening five characters of a Scope Note, followed by the *syntactic variable* <TEXT>, which stands for any text (sense or nonsense) desired. The first four syntactic equations can be translated back into the descriptions in the reference very readily. Note that <QT> (Qualifying Term) is placed between parentheses in Equation 3. Equation

5 illustrates the use of braces. The entity <HN> (Hierarchical Notation) is one of the three strings of four characters "(BT)," "(NT)," or "(RT)." Just to check understanding, note that an equivalent form of Equation 5 is

$$< HN > = (\{BT, NT, RT\})$$

or even

$$< HN > = (\{B,N,R\}T).$$

Table 6-2 is a reference table rather than an exposition table. Its virtues are its conciseness and precision in defining the Thesaurus structure. But the equations leading up to Equation 10, for <THESAURUS>, take a little more examination and explanation, which we go into next. The motivation for so doing is that, once understood, Table 6-2 is a complete and authoritative map of the structure of the Thesaurus.

More on Table 6-2

The idea leading up through the higher-level entities in Table 6-2, to <THESAURUS>, can be illustrated by examining several instances of a <SAR>—a "See also Reference." We note that a <SAR> consists of the phrase "See also," followed by one or more References to Descriptors. However, along with the Descriptors may or may not come a list of <QT> (Qualifying Term) items, a <SN> (Scope Note), and a <HN> (Hierarchical Notation). We build up these possibilities in Equation 13 (using Equation 12 first to define a list of <QT> items, in contrast to a single <QT>). Now with each single Reference defined by Equation 13 as <TE> we use Equation 14 to define an alphabetized list of such References, naming it <TEL>. Also, since some References may be to nondescriptors ("See also foreign countries"), we also build an alphabetized list of such References, naming it <TL>. Now, finally, we can form <SAR> in Equation 7, as the syntactic constant "See also" followed (optionally) by a list of Descriptor References and/or a list of nondescriptor references.

We used the expansion (or synthesis) of Equation 7 to illustrate a similar process for Equations 6 and 8. Equation 9, defining Subheadings, is a little more complex and uses what is known as a "syntactic recursion" in its definition. First, we define the structure possible under a "main heading" of the Thesaurus as <TS> (Term Structure) in Equation 15. It is a <TE>, already defined, followed (all optionally) by either or neither of <SR> or <SAR>, by <RFR>, and by <SUBH>. Next we note that a Subheading can be defined in this way itself if we realize two crucial points:

1. The options available include all possibilities in Subheadings, and then some—we can choose to ignore the additional possibilities if we please.
2. The relation of being a subheading (to a heading) can be relative rather than absolute, so that, for example, a <SUBH> under a <SUBH> (that is, in its syntactic expansion) is an (absolute) subsubheading.

Thus the right-hand side of Equation 9, which defines <SUBH>, when expanded through Equations 16 and 15, in turn, includes an item <SUBH>, which is the entity being defined. This is thereby called a recursive definition.

In more abstract topics there are inherent theoretical difficulties with recursive definitions, but there are no practical ones here. What Equations 9, 15, and 16 say, together, is that any number of "subhead nestings" are possible in the structural description—and this is an instance of the generality of this description. In practice, the user will create only a given number of such nestings. The lowest Subheading in the nesting will have the term <SUBH> missing on the right-hand side of Equation 15 (the whole term [<SUBH>] is optional). Thus the full expansion of Equation 9 (or Equation 15) in a realized file will always terminate.

It may now be somewhat of a surprise at first glance, but in defining a <TSL> in Equation 16, originally conceived to be the list of Term Structures that may be contained in a Subheading, we have indeed defined the Thesaurus, and Equation 10 merely records this fact. The number of characters and entries may be of a completely different order of magnitude in a typical Term Structure (the appendage to a Descriptor) and the entire Thesaurus, but the structure is identical, and that is all we are defining at this point.

Conversational Access

Access to the Thesaurus in printed form is by page turning and by eye, using the alphabetized structure inherent in its definition. The human hand and eye represent a potent search mechanism as long as the material is not voluminous and nothing further is to be done with the results.

In on-line conversational access, however, we must be more explicit and precise in calling for sections of the Thesaurus, at most a few lines at a time, by explicit commands rather than implicit page turning and scanning. Therefore we outline here a specific system for conversational access.

The basic format of the conversational access is "Request and Display." The user will make a request for some section of the Thesaurus, and the system will display the results of that request. The results will be the section requested or else an error message, either dealing with the format of the request itself or stating that the section requested could not be located. The basic entry point into the Thesaurus is through Descriptors, possibly further specified by Qualifying Terms and possibly at Subheading levels in the Thesaurus. If the Descriptor is not a preferred term, its request will bring an automatic display of a See Reference list. If a Descriptor has been located that is a preferred term, it will bring a display containing Qualifying Terms, a Scope Note, and a Hierarchical Notation to the extent that these items are present. We call this a "base Descriptor." Now, given such a Descriptor, the user may request access to any of three lists possibly associated with it: the See also References, the Refer from References, and the Subheadings. Having requested one of these three lists, the user may then request References or Subheadings simply by asking for the "Next" item on the list or by asking for the Descriptor itself. The display response to the "Next" request is the next Reference or Subheading, if available. A Reference may be either a definite Descriptor or an indefinite reference to a generic category of Descriptors. If no more items remain on the list (the user presumably having scanned some previously), the message "End of List" is displayed. Attention can be changed from one of the three lists to any of the others by a simple request instead of "Next" or by a Descriptor request.

The user who wants to follow out a Referenced or Subheading Descriptor (for example, to examine its "See also References") can make a "Transfer" request, which replaces the original base Descriptor by its Referenced or Subheading Descriptor, and access continues from the latter as indicated previously. After one or more requests for such a "Transfer," a "Return" request can be made, which replaces the current base Descriptor by the Descriptor which produced it by "Transfer." Thus after a series of "Transfer" requests, an equal number of "Return" requests will proceed (in reverse order) through the same set of Descriptors, back to the original one.

The foregoing Requests and Displays are summarized (and numbered) in syntax form in Table 6-3. An examination of the table will show how each of the commands leads to a specific display. The displays shown with the request refer to new information. Ordinarily, it would be expected that certain information would be carried over (such as the Descriptor currently being used as a base, which reference list is under

TABLE 6-3. *Conversational Access*

	Request	*Display*
1.	Entry <TERM> [<QTL>]	{<TE>, <SR>, no Entry}
2.	See also	{See also, no See also, no Entry}
3.	Refer from	{Refer from, no Refer from, no Entry}
4.	Subheading	{Subheading, no Subheading, no Entry}
5.	Next	{<TE>, <TEXT>, end of list}
6.	Transfer	{<TE>, no Reference/Subheading}
7.	Return	{<TE>, original Entry}

examination, and so on), as long as the condition held during the conversation.

Note that the only syntactic variable which can be used in a request is a <TERM> (a Descriptor), followed optionally by a <QTL> (Qualifying Term List). The syntactic variables displayed are limited to <TE> (Term Extension), <SR> (See References), and <TEXT> (for generic references); but, of course, just these displays permit the user to browse through any part and detail of the Thesaurus desired. The remaining requests and displays are syntactic constants. In practice, this small vocabulary of request items, all but one of which are constants, represents a simple, readily understood means for accessing any information desired in the Thesaurus.

Thesaurus Creation and Maintenance

We define Thesaurus creation and maintenance in terms of the syntactic entities of Table 6-1 above the level of the primitive Natural Language Text. That is, we consider only the addition and deletion of entire Thesaurus items and not portions of text. The addition and deletion of characters in text making up a file item is considered text editing rather than Thesaurus maintenance in this context. It is recognized that text editing is a desirable future facility in the overall process of Thesaurus maintenance, and the present emphasis reflects merely a time phasing of ultimate interests.

The process of Thesaurus creation is simply the construction of a <TSL> that is to be defined as the Thesaurus. (The problem of how such a Thesaurus is to be physically loaded into storage, with directories, and so on, is a programming question not dealt with here.) For example, *The New York Times Thesaurus of Descriptors,* by definition and barring typographical or logical deviations from its designers' intentions, is a <TSL>.

The process of Thesaurus maintenance is likewise very simple in syntactic terms. A Thesaurus addition or deletion can be defined by giving a *location* and a syntactic entity that is to be added or deleted. The location can be given in the Conversational Access requests, namely,

Entry <TERM> [<QTL>]
See also
Refer from
Subheading
Transfer

to prescribe the destination of the syntactic entity to be added or the entity to be deleted. In the case of unique items, such as a Scope Note or a Hierarchical Notation, addition is taken to mean replacement if such an item is already present. In case of listed items, such as See or See also References, or Subheadings, addition is done automatically in alphabetized form. In the case of deletion, deleting a Descriptor automatically deletes all file items accessed by that Descriptor as well.

Illustrations

We use the model page (page 35 of *The New York Times Thesaurus of Descriptors*) to illustrate the foregoing ideas concretely, including the structural description, conversational access, and Thesaurus creation and maintenance.

First, regard the contents of the model page as a miniature Thesaurus. It has the structure of the entire *New York Times Thesaurus of Descriptors,* only with far less text. It is, in fact, a <TSL> (Term Structure List) of exactly 10 alphabetized <TS> (Term Structure) items, which begin with Descriptors:

ADEN Protectorate
ADOPTIONS
ADVERTISING
AMERICA
AMERIKA
BIRTH Control and Planned Parenthood

BLACK Muslims
"BLACK Power"
BLACKLISTING

(Note that Equations 10 and 16 of Table 6-2 express this structural fact.)

Next, any one of these <TS> consists of a <TE> (Term Extension) followed optionally by References and Subheadings (Equation 15). Some <TS> have no References or Subheadings at all, and some <TE> consist only of a <TERM> item (a Descriptor), but these are admissible possibilities in the equations. Nevertheless, in order to keep matters straight we recognize each syntactic entity represented in the miniature (or full) Thesaurus, even though one section of natural language text may stand for several entities at once. For example, the first <TS>,

ADEN Protectorate
See South Arabia, Federation of

represents the diagrammed entities in Figure 6-1. Similarly, the seventh <TS> has the structure in Figure 6-2.

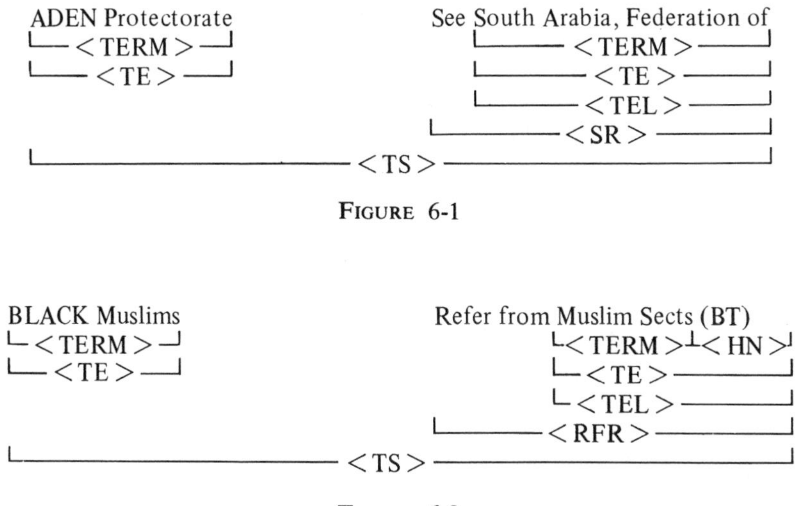

FIGURE 6-1

FIGURE 6-2

In fact, the model page (by design) exhibits nearly every Thesaurus structural possibility; it can be instructive to locate the syntactic equation defining any given structural relationship on the model page.

TABLE 6-4. *A Sample Conversation*

Request	*Display*
Entry ADEN Protectorate	ADEN Protectorate See South Arabia, Federation of
Entry ADEN	No Entry
Entry BLACK Muslims	BLACK Muslims
See also	No See also
Refer from	Refer from
Next	Muslim Sects (BT)
Next	End of List
Subheadings	No Subheadings
Entry ADVERTISING	ADVERTISING
Transfer	No Reference/Subheading
Subheadings	Subheadings
Next	Mass Communications (for inclusion) (BT)
Transfer	Mass Communications (for inclusion) (BT)
Refer from	Refer from
Next	ADVERTISING
Transfer	ADVERTISING
Return	Mass Communications (for inclusion) (BT)
Return	ADVERTISING
Return	Original Term
Subheadings	Subheadings
Next	foreign countries
Transfer	No Reference/Subheading
Next	United States
etc.	

Now consider the miniature Thesaurus given by the model page to be "on-line" for conversational access. Although the eye can take in the entire page, imagine that it cannot and that only one item is available for inspection at a time. We will invoke the "Request and Display" mode of conversational access to browse, in illustration, through this miniature Thesaurus. We show a conversation in Table 6-4.

In the conversation the actual language itself is terse and skeletal —because we are interested only in structural aspects of the Thesaurus and in how Request and Display operations can permit a user to browse and examine the Thesaurus item by item. In practice, the Display side would be more abundant, maintaining "backtrack status" information, and so on, as display space permits.

Thesaurus creation is illustrated by the model page itself: natural language text with structural characteristics satisfying the equations of Table 6-2. For Thesaurus maintenance we consider an addition and a deletion (noting that a modification can be considered a deletion followed by an addition). Suppose we wish to add Television (NT) to the Refer from References of ADVERTISING. We form the Locator

Entry ADVERTISING, Refer from

and the item

<TE> = <TERM> <HN> = Television (NT)

for addition. Then Television (NT) would be automatically added (in alphabetized order) to the Refer from References of ADVERTISING. Similarly, to delete the Hierarchical Notation (BT) in the "BLACK Power" See Reference, we locate by

Entry "BLACK Power"

and delete item

<HN> = (BT)

therein.

ARTICLE

7

Measurements of Program Complexity

(1969)

Introduction

It is increasingly clear in large-scale programming systems that we face problems of almost pure complexity. Five hundred years ago we did not know that air had weight, but we know it now. Some years from now we will learn that complexity has a cost, even though we do not know how to measure that complexity at the present time.

Because of our ignorance, managing a large-scale programming project is a perilous activity. Our technical tools for managing are inadequate. It is difficult to measure performance in programming. It is difficult to diagnose trouble in time to prevent it. It is difficult to evaluate the status of intermediate work such as undebugged programs or design specifications and their potential value to the completed project.

Thus we come to understand that "complexity will exact its price," whether we like it or not. Managing a large programming project involves learning to pay the price of complexity in such a way that we control the destiny of that project development. That price will involve costs in core and storage facilities, costs in running time, and costs in man-hours. It is only too easy in the heat of small programming battles to forget that the price must be paid—to whip up a "small bowl of spaghetti" to get faster throughput, or to save core, or to put off documentation until later in order to get something running.

The best assurance for learning to pay the price of complexity in the right way is to learn how to identify and measure it. The following ideas represent an approach to one aspect of measuring the complexity of programmers' work. The emphasis is on automatic procedures, which can be formulated for widespread common experience in the management of programming projects, rather than on heuristic procedures.

Programming Measurements

One of the most difficult areas in programming from the beginning has been that of programming measurements. We all appreciate the value of providing quantitative measurements in programming, but what to quantify is still very much a question.

The number of instructions is one typical indicator of programming effort. But in some problems the objective is to produce as few instructions as possible (for example, in an operating system scheduler), so that the value of the job is inversely proportional to the number of instructions rather than proportional to it. In general, under assumptions of things being equal, such as programmer capability, program complexity, and machine availability, the number of instructions may not be a bad estimate of program size. However, this typically makes assumptions about the very things we set out to measure.

Viewed at a somewhat deeper level, the place to begin the measurement is the total task being accomplished for a user. This total task will have some size and complexity, which we are hard put to measure at the moment. In addition, there will be some mix of hardware and software capability addressed to the task. For example, the same task will be easier to program in a big, fast computer than in a small, slow one, where both space and time must be optimized; so even though the task is the same to the user, the software/hardware mix may be different.

There are ideas in the mathematical theory of information that may help in quantifying programming measurements. In information theory the concept of information content for a message is quantified, and this concept can be taken over intact from English, say, to a programming language.

Another measure of information content can be deduced from the execution sequences that programs generate. In this case, a program with a great deal of branching will produce execution sequences having higher information content than a program with little branching. This second measure of information content gives a quantitative value for the complexity of operations a program generates in the computer.

Program Content

We will use the phrase "program content" as shorthand for the information content of a program, regarded as an expression in a programming language. Actually, there are several alternative ways we might measure and interpret such program content, and empirical research is clearly in order. Several specific alternatives are given next.

Character-Based Program Content

Perhaps the simplest approach is to regard a source program as a string of characters just as they appear on a keypunch. One would probably want to squash out extra blanks in such programs, but otherwise treat it as a straight character string. There are two ways in which program content could be determined. First, one can regard the universe of character strings that are generated by programmers in a given source language, such as PL/I or Assembly. In this case, one could accumulate statistics over a wide variety of existing source programs that were deemed to be representative in some sense and, from this, compute such quantities as information content per character. Another method is to regard each new source program as a universe in itself and build statistics from that single source program, which then can be used to compute information content per character. Intermediate methods would be to regard classes of scientific programming, system programming, information storage retrieval programming, and so on.

Symbol-Based Program Content

Another level of sophistication would be to identify certain basic symbols in source programs such as identifiers, reserved or key words, and special characters, as characters in a new alphabet and, again, to compute information content per character in this newly derived alphabet. All the possibilities in character content remain in choices of the universe. In addition, the treatment of identifiers and reserved or key words also admits alternatives. At one level, all identifiers may be treated as a single generic character, or they may be treated as individual and distinct characters, symbol by symbol. Intermediate levels would treat classes of identifiers as generic characters, such as data identifiers, entry identifiers, and file identifiers.

Syntactic-Based Program Content

Both the preceding cases are, in fact, special cases of a selection of syntactic elements in a programming language. In the description of a language, one usually begins with characters such as those from the keypunch, builds these into identifiers, reserved words, and so on, and then these further into expressions, conditions, statements, and the like, on to DO groups, procedures, and finally, programs. In the foregoing cases, we have partitioned the physical character string into a new string of syntactic elements at one level or another. However, the program itself has a hierarchical structure, as implied by the linear structure, such as identifiers contained in statements, statements in DO groups, and DO groups in procedures, and one can conceive of computing the information content required to define the hierarchical structure that a program realizes. There is such a wide set of alternatives here that further selection will be desirable, depending in large part on the source language itself and its properties.

Things We Might Learn

Our main target in considering theoretic measures of the information in programs is to identify intrinsic difficulties and measures of performance in programming. These measures will be imperfect, at best, but they could well provide a good deal of insight and calibration that we do not have now, from simple instruction or statement counts.

The different kinds of program content described above may have different advantages, depending on what we are looking for. For example, an apparent disadvantage of the character-based program content is that it may depend upon the length of names used by programmers, that is, two programs that are identical, except that short names in one are substituted for long names in the other, may turn up with different program contents. It is not really known that this will happen with a sizable difference, and, in fact, the definition of information content will implicitly take advantage of long names reappearing to lower the information content per character. Nevertheless, it probably will result in more information content for the total source program. However, this may not necessarily be a fault, for example, in measuring how difficult such a program might be to code or keypunch, where some of the work involved is related to the sheer number of characters. It may also be worth giving a programmer credit for doing more work by using longer names because this helps in the readability of the program and, in fact, may represent more work on the part of the programmer in remembering longer names correctly. So even such a choice of character- versus symbol-based program content turns out not to be quite so simple without further investigation and consideration.

Any use of such measurements will have to be calibrated against some kind of experience built up in an experimental or development period, in which programs with certain already identified characteristics have been analyzed and the program contents correlated with these characteristics. A possible use is to discover the extent to which the full facilities of a programming language are being utilized in a programming system. Again, it is a guess at the moment that programming from a small subset of a language will result in lower program content per character or symbol than otherwise. For example, fewer reserved or key words that identify various types of statements may appear and lower the program content in that way. Whether this actually occurs or not should be a matter of empirical investigation.

Looking farther ahead, we can see that the program content may give new indications of how difficult a program may be to debug or how difficult to document or understand by someone else. It is clear that both debugging and documentation are complex subjects and will not be resolved in any definitive way simply by program content; but it does seem possible that program content may reduce, by a worthwhile amount, the residual of uncertainty that needs to be understood by other means.

Execution Content

We will use the phrase "execution content" as shorthand for the information content of an execution sequence generated by a program. Again, there are many alternative ways to measure and interpret this execution content, and, even more than before, empirical research is in order.

Whereas program content can be applied at any point in the life of a program (as intermediate work not yet debugged or program fragments, for example), execution content can only be determined with a program that has been completed and debugged to the point of executing.

Again, empirical evidence is in order, but it seems that program content and execution content can be quite independent of one another. This may not be true, but if there are relations that develop, knowing that would be valuable in itself.

As in the case of program content, the range of alternatives actually stems from a complete description of the program execution in question. This complete description is typically representable in terms of a sequential state process, where the program takes some machine—hypothetical or real—from state to state in the presence of input data. These states are the alphabet on which information can be computed. In programming languages where individual statements are identified, one of the simplest possibilities is to regard the statements as characters in an alphabet and the execution sequence as the actual statements in the order they are executed. The sequences so generated will typically be much longer than we are used to looking at in an information theoretic context and, indeed, in the case of program content. But the logical basis for computing information content is the same.

Another approach may consider syntactic elements at a higher level than statements, such as procedures, groups, and so on, or simply branch points in the source program.

At more detailed levels, execution content might well involve machine operations, in contrast to source language operations, when, for example, branches would be incurred in subroutines and macros called by the compiler, which is hidden to the programmer. These kinds of investigations would not be aimed so much at programmer measurement as programmer education, and at the effect of source language programs in the machine environment.

What to Do Next

The next thing to do is to develop empirical evidence of how information content depends on actual programs. The main effort required is to generate a small set of analysis programs, which will themselves analyze other programs for either program content or execution content automatically. There are plenty of programs around to analyze, and particular programs can be identified to calibrate the general findings on other programs.

There are three kinds of subprograms required in the analysis of program content or execution content: source program analyzers, execution trace analyzers, and information statistics analyzers.

The source program analyzers should take in PL/I, Assembly, Fortran, or other source programs, and according to various alternatives desired, output-derived character strings for further analysis.

The execution trace analyzers could probably operate on the basis of preprocessing source programs and inserting interrupts or calls at the beginning of each statement, block, or whatever is to be traced, at which time the objects being traced can be identified and put into an output stream. The result should be a string of standard characters, just as from the program analyzers, although possibly these strings may be very much larger and consist of alphabets with many more characters than one would typically find in the program content case.

The information statistics analyzers should take as input a string of characters in standard form, and as output various information theoretic quantities such as information content per character or information content for the string. It should be emphasized that these information statistics can be generated as formal quantities regardless of the statistical assumptions behind the input character string. In particular, there are certain differences between a natural language, such as English, and formal languages such as are used in source programs. One difference is the span of correlation in formal languages, compared with natural languages; for example, a legal PL/I program which contains a DO statement is certain to contain an END statement sometime later, possibly very much later. These kinds of necessary correlations, independent of separations, are not characteristic of natural languages. What their effect is on the computation of information statistics remains to be studied. Among other things, these differences require a slightly different interpretation of what the statistical basis is. It is not usual in a natural language to compute the information content of a message on the basis of the statistics of that message alone. This is, in part, because we are asking different questions in analyzing natural languages, such as how difficult is it to transmit a random English message over a telegraph circuit, for example. However, in the present case we are looking for distinctions among messages themselves that may appear because of subtle patterns, which information statistics may reveal for us. In this case it may be very sensible to consider the information content of a message or program on the basis of the statistics it generates. In the more classical context we might be asking a question such as "If this message were statistically representative of the language in which it is stated, then what is its information content?"

ARTICLE

8

Chief Programmer Teams: Techniques and Procedures

(1970)

An Opportunity

There is an opportunity to improve both the manageability and the productivity of programming to a substantial degree. This opportunity lies in moving programming practices from *private art* toward *public science* and in organizing these programming practices into job structures that reflect appropriate skills and responsibilities in a team effort.

A Chief Programmer Team

A *Chief Programmer Team* is a response to this opportunity. A Chief Programmer Team is a small but highly structured group that is headed by a programmer who assumes responsibility in complete detail for the development of a programming project. The primary idea in a Chief Programmer Team is to go from an unstructured "soccer team" approach in programming to a structured "surgical team" approach. The Chief Programmer Team is made up of members having very specific skills and roles to play. A typical team nucleus consists of a *Chief Programmer,* a *Backup Programmer,* and a *Programming Librarian*. The Programming Librarian is a secretary or other clerical specialist with additional training in dealing with programming materials. In addition to the nucleus, more programmers, analysts, technical writers, technicians, or other specialists may be incorporated as well.

The Chief Programmer Team permits the application of new management standards and new technical standards to programming projects. The management standards derive from the specialization of skills and duties of personnel who are trained independently for various roles in programming systems development. The technical standards are made possible by utilizing higher-level technical skills for the actual programming process, technical skills that are freed up through work structuring and delegation in the Chief Programmer Team.

A Programming Production Library

A *Programming Production Library* (PPL) serves as a focal point and a critical ingredient in the Chief Programmer Team. The PPL records a developing programming project in continuous, visible form. The team members' interface between programming and clerical activities is through this visible project. The Programming Librarian is responsible for maintaining the PPL. The Chief Programmer is responsible for its contents. This structure of responsibility permits a new level of management standardization in project record keeping. The PPL is an "assembly line" concept, in which people work on a common, visible product, rather than carrying pieces of work back to their "benches."

The PPL also represents a major programmer tool for productivity, through isolating and delegating clerical activities out of programming. As such, it permits a programmer to exercise a wider span of detailed control over the programming. This in turn permits fewer programmers to do the same job, which in turn reduces communication requirements, and the time gained thereby enables a still wider span of detailed control in the programming. With advanced programming techniques and technical standards, discussed further below, this span of detailed control can be expanded by an order of magnitude beyond today's practice; the PPL plays a crucial role in this potential expansion.

Technical Standards in Programming

New technical standards play a key role in Chief Programmer Team operations. Recent theoretical developments provide a foundation for greater discipline than before, which insures more uniform and repeatable program development processes. A Chief Programmer is a highly disciplined programmer—the complete opposite of the "mad scientist" producing a creature no one else understands. The PPL imposes an additional discipline on the whole Chief Programmer Team.

It requires good programmers to work within these new technical standards, just as it takes a good engineer to design a complex device using only a few standardized units. In programming these days there is often a confusion between creativity and variability—they are not the same. A high act of creativity in programming is to find deep simplicities in a complex process and to write programs that are easily read and understood by others. This is a major test of a good programmer.

The Chief Programmer

The reintroduction of senior people into the detailed programming process also recognizes a new set of circumstances in programming systems such as OS/360, which was not nearly so critical in previous operating systems. It is that the job control language, data management and utility facilities, and high-level source languages are so rich and complex that there is both an opportunity and a need for using senior personnel at the detailed coding level.

The need is to make the best possible use of a very extensive and complicated set of facilities. OS/360 is neither easy to understand nor easy to invoke. Its functions are impressive, but they are called into play by language forms that require a good deal of study, experience, and sustained mental effort to utilize effectively.

The opportunity is for a good deal of work reduction and simplification for the rest of the system, in both original programming and later maintenance. For example, the intelligent use of a high-level data management capability may eliminate the need to develop a private file processing system. Finding such an intelligent use is not an easy task but can bring both substantial reductions in the code required and easier maintenance of the system.

The Backup Programmer

The concentration of responsibility in a Chief Programmer Team may seem to create undue managerial exposure on projects. However, there are procedures that can reduce this exposure, not only to an acceptable level, but to a level considerably below those we have now in the "soccer team" approach.

One reduction comes from the use of a Backup Programmer, a peer of the Chief Programmer in matters of system design, so that a second person is totally familiar with the developing project and its rationale. Another major function of the Backup Programmer can be to provide independent test conditions for the system.

In addition, the Backup Programmer can serve as a research assistant for the Chief Programmer in questions of programming strategy and tactics. It has already been noted that the use of OS/360 is formidable, but its imaginative and intelligent use can mean very large differences in the amount and kind of detailed code that may be needed. In this way a Backup Programmer can provide a Chief Programmer with more freedom to concentrate on the central problems of the system under development, using results of peripheral investigations that have been assigned to the Backup Programmer.

The Programming Librarian

The job of a Programming Librarian is standard across every Chief Programmer Team and is independent of the subject matter of the project. It is to maintain the records of a project under development, in both an internal, machine-readable form and an external, human-readable form.

The external records of a Chief Programmer Team project are maintained in a set of filed listings, which define the current status and previous history of the project. The current status is maintained in looseleaf notebooks, each headed by a directory and followed by an alphabetized list of member modules. When members and directories are updated and replaced in the status notebooks, the replaced copies are archived in chronological journals. All results of debugging runs are also maintained in journals.

Programmers build and alter the project status by writing programs or data on coding sheets or by marking up status members in the PPL. It is the responsibility of the Librarian to introduce this data into the project records. This responsibility is carried out through a set of interlocking office procedures and machine procedures. Part of the office procedures deal with data entry into the PPL. The remainder deal with the filing of output from the machine procedures; it is this filing process that maintains the visible project.

Programmers also call on the Librarian for all assembling, compiling, linkage editing, and debugging runs required in the project. The results of these runs are filed automatically by the Librarian as part of the visible project.

The Team Idea

Note that we support a Chief Programmer not simply with tools, but with a team of specialists, each having special tools. The Backup Programmer supports the Chief Programmer at the technical design and programming strategy level. The Programming Librarian supports the Chief Programmer at the clerical and data handling level. Other programmers and analysts play roles precisely defined by the Chief Programmers to meet project requirements, designing and coding modules that are originally specified and finally accepted by the Chief Programmer in the system.

A surgeon and a nurse communicate at a terse "sponge and scalpel" level, with little room for misunderstanding and little time wasted. The doctor never says, "Ms. Jones, I am carrying out a cardiovascular operation, etc., and have used this scalpel which may now have some germs on it, etc., so would you please sterilize it, etc., and return it to the rack, etc." Rather, the sponge and scalpel interactions are independent of the type of surgery, and the nurse's role can be prestructured and taught in nursing school, not in the operating room.

The relation of Programmer and Librarian can be made precise and efficient by similar developments and standards. Simply marking up a correction or addition in a listing of the PPL by a Programmer leads to an automatic response by the Librarian to incorporate the new information in the PPL.

The visibility of the PPL and the automatic clerical operations that maintain it permit the programmers to concentrate on programming matters and to communicate more precisely and effectively thereby through the PPL.

The work simplification that is possible through using facilities such as OS/360 effectively in a Chief Programmer Team seems to be considerable. It permits detailed technical control of a programming project by a Chief Programmer who has been provided with sufficient resources in other team members to cope with the complexities of OS/360, system functional requirements, and the clerical problems of creating and maintaining systems definitions.

The Chief Programmer as a Professional

The Chief Programmer Team approach through job assignment and work delegation frees up a Chief Programmer to be a professional in every sense. The first obligation of a professional is to serve the client's needs and to serve them well. This obligation to a client involves financial as well as technical considerations. In programming, it involves making the "right plans" to carry out a project for a client's approval, and to then make the "plans right" in carrying the project out, within a time and dollar budget.

The Chief Programmer is a programmer with high technical competence, not only in details and technique, but also in broad systems analysis and design. The Chief Programmer's tools are programming languages and systems, and he or she must know them in breadth and depth. It is also essential to know the clients' needs and to effectively solve any disparity between those needs and the programming tools available.

In particular, note the Chief Programmer Team relationships, which are prestructured, allowing the Chief Programmer and other team members to look outward to client needs and technical possibilities, rather than inward. This freedom to concentrate on a client's requirements, with facilities for production automatically defined, is a major objective in defining a Chief Programmer Team.

ARTICLE

9

On the Statistical Validation of Computer Programs

(1970)

Abstract

Techniques of statistical inference are introduced into the question of program correctness by the intentional, but randomized, introduction of programming errors into a program before a testing process on it. The introduction of such errors permits a confidence computation through an Assert, Insert, Test (AIT) process.

Key Words and Phrases

testing
correctness of programs
statistical validation of programs
program reliability
systems assurance

The Correctness of Programs

The correctness of computer programs is of increasing concern and importance. Correctness is usually treated as a logical problem, as outlined by Floyd [4], Naur [7], Dijkstra [1], and others. Thus far, correctness proofs have been carried through only for relatively small programs. One of the largest examples is due to London [6]. However, King [5] has mechanized a correctness process, based on a general theorem prover, using the ideas of Floyd. Even so, correctness ideas have been used informally to guide major programming efforts in design and coding, as reported by Dijkstra [2] in the T.H.E. System. The author also attests to a considerable influence on programming practices, due to correctness ideas.

However, questions of correctness and reliability of large programming systems still are crucial as practical matters, whether or not current correctness techniques can address them. Large systems are being tested, and errors found in checked out systems, every day. Thus far, the errors found are treated as unique events and are not much used to shed light on what other errors may remain. It is a cliche in large systems programming that no large system can be free of errors. That may or may not be so in the future, but even now it is not a very useful cliche.

Statistical Inference About Correctness

We introduce techniques of statistical inference about the correctness of computer programs and maximum likelihood estimates of the number of unfound errors at any stage in a testing process. The statistical concepts are carried out here, in part, to motivate a corresponding development that is required in programming concepts.

Given a large computer program to validate, its correctness is a matter of fact and not a matter of probability. But we can convert this question of fact into a question of statistical inference, or estimation, through the intentional, but randomized, introduction of programming errors into a program. These errors then calibrate a testing process and permit statistical inference about the effectiveness of the testing process itself.

The statistical ideal is to introduce errors into a computer program that have the same chance of being found as the errors already there, if any such exist. This is a nontrivial program-theoretic problem. The errors present in a program at any point in time depend on the history of fault-finding activities that have been applied to it up until then. For example, if a program has been compiled successfully, then certain errors of syntax will not be present, or else the compiler would have located them. We assume here that this problem of introducing errors is resolved, in order to motivate work to develop reasonable solutions to it. Because once that problem is solved, then the statistical reasoning that follows is relatively straightforward but quite powerful in comparison with present information we have about the validation of computer programs.

In fact, the question of the number of programming errors in a program needs to be formulated carefully because there are many ways to fix a program that has errors in it—including writing a whole new program that in no way resembles the original program. Informally, we think of correcting an error in terms of changing or adding a statement (for example, an elementary unit of execution or declaration in a program). The correction may require adding a compound statement as well. This in turn suggests the idea of introducing errors by a random process whose basic actions are to change or delete statements. It is not difficult to devise automatic (random) processes for various programming languages to introduce errors but maintain correct syntax, for recompilation and testing. Presumably, these error frequencies can be set to reflect actual experience of programming errors found in a given language at a given stage of testing. These ideas are preliminary, and, as noted, the statistical concepts are intended to motivate a deeper investigation into these program-theoretic problems.

A Statistical Model of Computer Program Errors

In order to separate programming theory and statistical theory we define an abstract model of the process we have in mind. Our model contains a "system," sets of "indigenous errors" and "calibration errors," and a "testing process." The testing process may be executions of the system or some partial correctness proof process.

We begin with a system containing an unknown number of indigenous errors, which are the object of investigation. We are permitted to insert into the system a number of calibration errors and then to perform the testing process to find errors—calibration or indigenous. At any point in the testing process we assume that there is an equal chance for the recovery of any of the errors, indigenous or calibration, that yet remain in the system. During the testing process a certain number of indigenous errors may be found. We use these circumstances to make statistical assertions about what indigenous errors may yet remain in the system.

Feller [3], on page 43, analyzes a similar situation in terms of estimating the number of fish in a lake. The process described there is catching fish, marking them, and making a new catch of fish to determine how many of those caught were marked. He shows there that the hypergeometric distribution describes the probabilities of the various possibilities. In our application, of course, "lake" is synonymous with "system," "unmarked fish" is synonymous with "indigenous errors," "marked fish" with "calibration errors," and "catching fish" with "testing process."

A Maximum Likelihood Estimator for Indigenous Errors

At any point in the testing process, assume the following parameters.

y = calibration errors inserted initially.

u = indigenous errors found to date.

v = calibration errors found to date.

Feller also shows that the maximum likelihood estimator for the original number of indigenous errors—say, x—is the integer part of the expression yu/v. Needless to say, this maximum likelihood estimator will itself be subject to statistical error, but it gives an objective indication of errors remaining in a program as a testing process proceeds.

An Assert, Insert, and Test Process for Statistical Inference

We formulate a sample Assert, Insert, and Test (AIT) process which consists of the following actions.

1. It is *asserted* that a given system has no more than a selected number of indigenous errors, say, $k \geq 0$.
2. A selected positive number of calibration errors are *inserted* into the system, say, $j > 0$.
3. The system is *tested* until the j calibrated errors have been found, and the number of indigenous errors found during that process is recorded as well, say, i. Note that under our hypothesis, i is a random variable.
4. A confidence, C, is computed as

$$C = \begin{cases} 0 & \text{if} \quad i > k \\ \dfrac{j}{j+k+1} & \text{if} \quad i \leq k. \end{cases}$$

The rationale for C is given as follows. If $i > k$, it is obvious that the assertion is false, and the confidence in it is zero. If $i \leq k$, the assertion may or may not be true. For each possible hypothesis for which the assertion is false, we compute the probability in such an AIT process that $i > k$, that is, that we would correctly reject the assertion. With a hypothesis of h indigenous errors the probability of finding i of them *before* the jth calibration error is found is (cf. Feller)

$$(1) \qquad p(h, i, j) = \frac{\binom{h}{i}\binom{j}{j-1}}{\binom{h+j}{i+j-1}} \left(\frac{1}{h-i+1}\right) \qquad h \geq i,\ i \geq 0,\ j > 0$$

that is, we find any i indigenous errors and any $j-1$ calibration errors, in any order, and then find the remaining calibration error among the $h-i+1$ errors remaining.

The probability that we correctly reject a false assertion is given by

$$(2) \qquad c(h, j, k) = \sum_{i=k+1}^{h} p(h, i, j) \qquad h > k, \quad j > 0, \quad k \geq 0.$$

Now, for the assertion to be false, h must be an integer greater than k; we consider all possibilities and the minimum value possible, namely,

$$(3) \qquad C(j, k) = \min_{h>k,}\ c(h, j, k) \qquad j > 0,\ k \geq 0.$$

It can be proved, then, that the value of C is (see the Appendix below)

$$(4) \qquad C(j, k) = c(k+1, j, k) = \frac{j}{j+k+1} \qquad j > 0,\ k \geq 0,$$

as used above.

It is easy to see how to generalize this simple AIT process. The test could be concluded when a certain function of the indigenous errors were found, rather than all of them, with new confidence levels thereby. More complex stopping rules for the test could be used, based on both calibrated and indigenous errors found, for example.

The AIT Process: Interpretation and Examples

The AIT process produces a confidence statement about a programming and testing process, not about a specific system under test. This is a fundamental distinction often misunderstood in statistical inference. As already noted, the number of indigenous errors in the system is a fixed number—no less fixed because of our ignorance about it. Our confidence is in the

TABLE 9-1. *Confidence in the Correctness of a System (Assuming No Indigenous Errors Found in Testing)*

Calibration Errors	1	4	9	19	99
Confidence	.50	.80	.90	.95	.99

AIT process as it is applied over and over to many such systems; we will correctly reject a false assertion a certain fraction of the time. C is a conservative value for this fraction.

A special case of interest in AIT is that in which $k = 0$—the assertion is that the system is correct (no errors). Then C simplifies to $j/(j + 1)$. Thus various levels of confidence in the correctness of a system can be obtained by inserting various numbers of calibration errors and finding only those errors in the testing process. Some samples are given in Table 9-1.

Table 9-2 give a few values of C for small values of the parameters of Assertion, k, and Insertion, j. It is easy to see a general property of the table of confidence values: the larger the asserted bound, or the smaller the number of inserted errors, the easier it is to pass the test, but the less confidence the AIT process then produces. This property indicates a general pragmatic strategy for AIT, which balances an estimate of the state of a system with an objective in establishing a level of confidence. If the objective in confidence is unrealistically high, AIT will usually provide no confidence at all, and a new AIT will be required to establish any confidence. If the assertion is unrealistically loose (in high numbers of errors), the confidence is thereby degraded. (It is important to realize that asserting five errors and finding none gives a much lower confidence than asserting no errors and finding none—when five errors are asserted, finding none and finding five are equivalent to that assertion).

TABLE 9-2. *Confidence (When Indigenous Errors Found Do Not Exceed Asserted Error Bound)*

Asserted Bound	*Inserted Calibration Errors* 1	2	3	4	5	6
0	.50	.67	.75	.80	.83	.86
1	.33	.50	.60	.67	.71	.75
2	.25	.40	.50	.57	.62	.67
3	.20	.33	.29	.50	.56	.60
4	.17	.29	.38	.46	.50	.54
5	.14	.25	.33	.40	.45	.50

The AIT Chart

During the testing process the errors will be found chronologically, and as soon as one calibration error has been found, a maximum likelihood estimator is available for the number of indigenous errors. This estimate will fluctuate in a somewhat predictable way, usually going up with every indigenous error found and down with every calibrated error found. A chart of such estimates can provide a visual status report of the testing process as it progresses through time—say, over several weeks. For example, suppose an AIT with parameters

$$k = 6$$

$$j = 9$$

produces a test with errors found in the following sequence, I = indigenous, C = calibrated error;

$$C\ C\ I\ C\ I\ I\ C\ C\ C\ I\ C\ C\ I\ C$$

The maximum likelihood estimators at each stage of the testing are as shown in Table 9-3.

TABLE 9-3.

Error	*Type*	$[yu/y]$
1	*C*	0
2	*C*	0
3	*I*	4
4	*C*	3
5	*I*	6
6	*I*	9
7	*C*	6
8	*C*	5
9	*C*	4
10	*I*	6
11	*C*	5
12	*C*	4
13	*I*	5
14	*C*	5

This information can be summarized on a single chart for management purposes. At the beginning of the test the chart has the form in Figure 9-1.

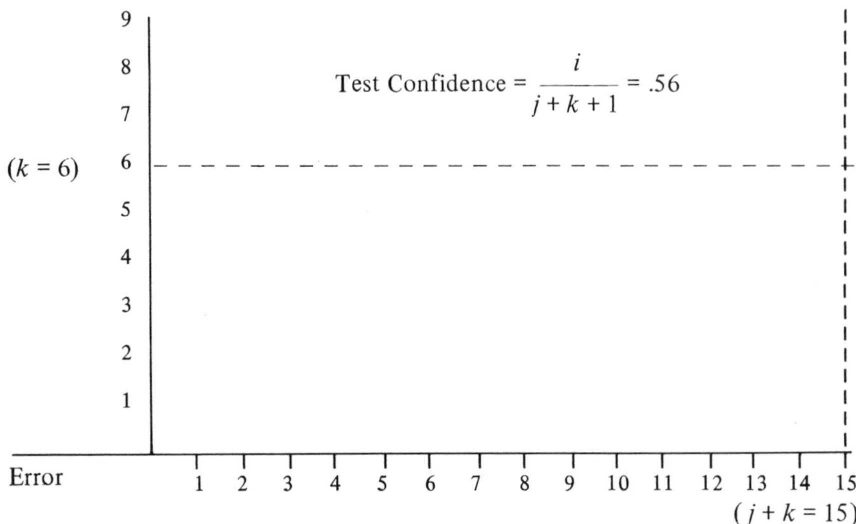

FIGURE 9-1. *AIT Chart at Test Inception*

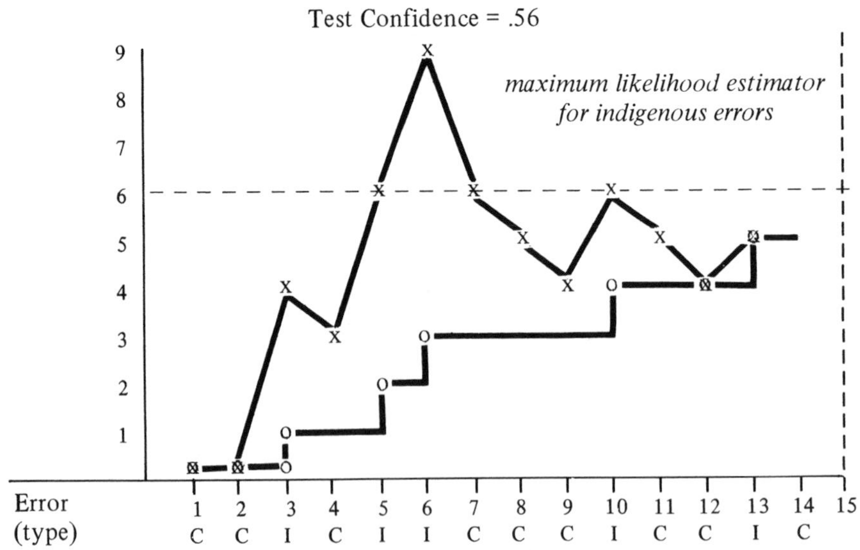

FIGURE 9-2. *AIT Chart at Test Conclusion*

The test confidence is computed from j, k: namely, $j/(j + k + 1) = 9/16 = .56$; the barrier on the right is $j + k$, since if more than $j + k$ errors are found, there are more than k indigenous errors and the AIT fails; the horizontal line is a target to stay below, and certainly to end up below for a successful test.

Using the foregoing assumption about errors found, we show the completed test in Figure 9-2.

At any point in the test, the chart up to that time is known, and a cumulative picture of the test progress is available. This test succeeded (the maximum likelihood curve ended up inside the barriers), although it "looked bad" at error 6.

Acknowledgment

Appreciation is due to M. M. Kessler for discussions and the reference to Feller's treatment of the combinatorial aspects of the problem.

References

1. Dijkstra, E. W. "A Constructive Approach to the Problem of Program Correctness." *BIT* 8 (1968): 174–186.
2. Dijkstra, E. W. "The Structure of the 'T.H.E.' Multiprogramming System." *Comm. ACM* 11 (1968): 341–346.
3. Feller, W. *An Introduction to Probability Theory and its Applications.* 2nd ed. New York: John Wiley, 1957.
4. Floyd, R. W. "Assigning Meanings to Programs." In *Proceedings of the Symposium in Applied Mathematics,* vol. 19, edited by J. T. Schwartz, pp. 19–32. Providence, R. I.: American Mathematical Society, 1967.
5. King, J. C. "A Program Verifier." Ph.D. thesis, Carnegie-Mellon University, Pittsburgh, 1969.
6. London, R. L. "Certification of Algorithm 245 Treesort 3: Proof of Algorithms—A New Kind of Certification." *Comm. ACM* 13 (1970): 371–373.
7. Naur, P. "Proof of Algorithms by General Snapshots." *BIT* 6 (1966): 310–316.

Appendix

Returning to (2), we will show that $c(h, j, k)$ is monotonically nondecreasing for $h > k$, $j > \emptyset$, $k \geq \emptyset$. Then $c(h, j, k)$ must achieve a minimum over h at the value $h = k + 1$, as is asserted in (4). In order to show the monotonic property of $c(h, j, k)$ we prove that

$$\text{(5)} \qquad \Delta c(h, j, k) = \left(\frac{j}{h+j}\right)(1 - c(h-1, j, k)) \qquad h > k,\ j > 0,\ k \geq 0,$$

where we have defined

$$\Delta c(h, j, k) = c(h, j, k) - c(h-1, j, k).$$

Since $c(h-1, j, k)$, for $h > k$, $j > 0$, $k \geq 0$, is a probability, the right-hand side of (5) is nonnegative; $\Delta c(h, j, k)$ in (5) is therefore nonnegative; and $c(h, j, k)$ is thereby nondecreasing as required.

In order to prove (5) we first simplify the expression for $p(h, i, j)$ in (1) to find

$$\text{(6)} \qquad p(h, i, j) = \frac{j(i+j-1)\,(i+j-2)\cdots(i+1)}{(h+j)(h+j-1)(h+j-2)\cdots(h+1)}.$$

Then we calculate

$$\begin{aligned} \Delta c(h, j, k) &= c(h, j, k) - c(h-1, j, k) \\ \text{(7)} \qquad &= \sum_{i=k+1}^{h} p(h, i, j) - \sum_{i=k+1}^{h-1} p(h-1, i, j) \\ &= p(h, h, j) + \sum_{i=k+1}^{h-1} (p(h, i, j) - p(h-1, i, j)). \end{aligned}$$

Now we note that the first term on the right-hand side, using (6), becomes

$$\begin{aligned} \text{(8)} \qquad p(h, h, j) &= \frac{j(h+j-1)\quad(h+j-2)\cdots(h+1)}{(h+j)\,(h+j-1)\,(h+j-2)\cdots(h+1)} \\ &= \frac{j}{h+j}. \end{aligned}$$

Next we note that each term of the summation of the right-hand side can be reorganized, using (6), as

$$
\begin{aligned}
p(h, i, j) - p(h-1, i, j) &= \frac{j(i+j-1)\ (i+j-2)\cdots(i+1)}{(h+j)\ (h+j-1)\ (h+j-2)\cdots(h+1)}\left(\frac{h}{h}\right) \\
(9) \qquad &\quad - \frac{j(i+j-1)\ (i+j-2)\cdots(i+1)}{(h+j-1)\ (h+j-2)\ (h+j-3)\cdots(h)} \\
&= \left(\frac{h}{h+j} - 1\right) p(h-1, i, j) \\
&= \left(\frac{j}{h+j}\right) p(h-1, i, j).
\end{aligned}
$$

Then, summing, we find

$$
\begin{aligned}
\sum_{i=k+1}^{h-1} p(h, i, j) - p(h-1,\ i, j) &= \sum_{i=k+1}^{h-1} \left(1 - \frac{j}{h+j}\right) p(h-1, i, j) \\
(10) \qquad &= -\left(\frac{j}{h+j}\right) c(h-1, j, k).
\end{aligned}
$$

Finally, recombining the two terms of (7), we get

$$
\Delta c(h, j, k) = \left(\frac{j}{h+j}\right) (1 - c(h-1, j, k)),
$$

as asserted in (5).

ARTICLE 10

OS/360 Programming

(1970)

Introduction

Effective OS/360 programming requires a comprehensive understanding of OS/360 concepts and facilities. The collective programming facilities of OS/360 can be regarded as a multilanguage processor; and, in particular in OS/360 programming, the objective should be to:

1. program as far as is reasonable in JCL (Job Control Language); then, as a next resort,
2. program as far as is reasonable in LEL (Linkage Editing Language); then, as a last resort,
3. program in one or more of Assembly, PL/I, BSL, Fortran, Cobol, and so on.

In this strategy we seek to solve problems of program design and coding at the highest possible level in the language hierarchy, in such a way as to solve those problems with as little code as possible written for that purpose. For example, it is preferable to solve a problem in data management in JCL with data description (DD) cards and utilities, rather than writing programs in PL/I or Cobol to accomplish the same ends.

The facilities of OS/360 are complex, arbitrary, and hard to use. In the past, senior-level programmers have, for good reason, been reluctant to be involved directly with all the details and seeming accidentals of JCL, particularly the data descriptions required therein. As a result, such senior personnel have frequently solved programming problems from an IBSYS (the IBM 7094 operating system) viewpoint, and so on, at blackboards and on memos (for example, a checkpoint, restart problem), and then send more junior personnel off to implement these functional solutions in the programming languages at hand, such as PL/I or Assembly. This mode of operation often reinvents facilities that are already present in OS/360. The reinvented code has to be maintained, documented, and otherwise integrated into the overall system with a general overhead and expenditure befitting its size. In fact, however, if the senior-level personnel are aware of the facilities of OS/360, particularly of JCL (for example, in handling a checkpoint, restart problem), what was a blackboard and memo solution leading to considerable programming effort by junior personnel may very well become a few-line JCL addition to the system, in which the senior personnel have total and direct control over what is taking place and the benefit of all future OS/360 improvements and maintenance.

OS/360 as a Natural System

OS/360, as a multilanguage processor, seems better regarded as a "natural system" than a rational one at this point in time. To be sure, in its planning stages there was a definite sense of rationality in it. But by this time it has grown into a rather homely collection of facilities that are called in oftentimes mysterious formats. Nevertheless, for all its homeliness, OS/360 is far and away the most powerful programming environment yet provided to programmers for production programming. As a result, if we regard OS/360 as a natural system, like a cow, we are in a much healthier mental condition than if we try to regard it as a rational system. In the latter case, most senior-level programmers simply get mad and do not get much accomplished. We simply use a cow, not questioning whether it should have four legs or six legs, whether its body temperature should be 93 or 99 degrees, and so on, and there is a great deal of benefit to be gained thereby. That is our attitude here toward OS/360.

Describing OS/360 as the natural system it really amounts to is no easy task. The manuals provide many insights, generalizations, and observations about OS/360, but they represent just that—not really complete information. The only really authoritative information about OS/360 is the code itself, and the main purpose of documentation is to make that kind of examination unnecessary. Nevertheless, there are places, when one is looking to get the most possible out of this or that feature, that you cannot trust the manuals, you cannot trust the PLMs, you need to go to the code itself. That will not happen often, but it will happen.

We can do better and better at describing OS/360 just as we do in describing cows in descriptive zoology. We attempt such a description, particularly with respect to JCL and LEL, in order to put those languages on a better footing for senior personnel to use directly in the definition and control of programming systems development. This involves, first of all, treating both the JCL and LEL as bona fide programming languages. It is pretty clear that JCL is a programming language. It embodies ideas of conditional execution, symbolic parameters, algorithm passing, and so on, that are hallmarks of programming languages. LEL is harder to see as a language. Linkage editing is a generalization of assembling, in which the "instructions" are load modules and object modules, rather than hand-coded instructions of a line or so. It is a simple fact that linkage editing, except for the size of these "instructions," has exactly the same function as the assembler, requires symbol tables, requires a second pass to resolve references, and so on. Thus we regard LEL as a real language.

Compared with simpler operating systems, it seems that the role of OS/360 utilities is more often overlooked or reinvented, partly because these utilities, as conceived in OS/360, are more complex and less directly usable than in previous systems and partly because of the complexities of JCL itself. For example, it is relatively difficult to do a simple utility operation, such as list a deck of cards, in OS/360, but with little more difficulty one can do some very substantial data handling jobs, such as unloading a partitioned data set from disk onto a tape.

JCL as a Programming Language

JCL occupies a particular place in OS/360. It is the system programming language usually referred to as the control language, which is interpreted automatically by OS/360. Every other language in OS/360 has a specific language processor, which treats programs as data and converts them into new data that is eventually treated as programs by references in JCL. But a PL/I program, for example, has no more connection with OS/360 than a file to be sorted or any other input to a processing program.

The historical development of job control languages began with the idea of a "few control cards" to permit better utilization of hardware. In the beginning these control cards did very simple things and represented a very simple interpretation of commands. But in OS/360 these control cards invoke extensive data management task control and other activities, and the language for invoking these more sophisticated activities has grown up somewhat haphazardly. Even though JCL has grown up without the benefit of a central motivating design concept, it is still a programming language and permits the development of a programming style for better understanding and maintenance of JCL programs. In particular, JCL admits a syntax that is reasonably straightforward if one suppresses default possibilities that have been historically used in JCL for the convenience of individual programmers. For example, JCL statements consist of an operator and a series of optional operands. These operands can be lumped together on a single card, so that a line of JCL looks much like gibberish, or the operands can be separated, line by line, and exhibit more structure and simplicity to the reader.

The syntax of JCL, which itself has grown up quite haphazardly, provides for a bewildering variety of forms—for example, missing parameters, multiple commas, and so on, but this variety can be reduced to a considerable extent without reducing the function by taking certain forms as preferred and displaying them in the syntax in a full and always appearing fashion. In illustration, the disposition parameter, DISP, can be set simply to NEW to indicate that a data set is to be created in a particular job step. However, if a disposition at the end of the job step is required, the parameters must be set equal to (NEW, OLD), that is, not only does one require a second suboperand, OLD, but also enclosing parentheses and a separating comma. If, in addition, one wishes to handle an ABEND disposition for that data set in the job step, one needs to define a third suboperand, for example, (NEW, KEEP, PASS). Because of default conditions, one may also encounter an operand such as (NEW, , PASS), etc. A way to simplify all these considerations is simply to define the disposition operands to always contain three suboperands—one for entry, one for exit, and one for abnormal exit—always enclosed by parentheses and separated by commas. Then the syntax becomes easier to describe; and, in fact, if these operands are always written out, there is no danger of programmer mistakes or misunderstandings due to hidden defaults. Such a syntax is given in Table 10-1.

TABLE 10-1 *JCL Syntax*

```
<JCL procedure> ::= [<procedure statement>]
                     <procedure body>
<procedure statement> ::= //[<name>] <b> PROC <c>
                          [// <b> <name> = <parameter> <,>
                           ...                            ]
<procedure body> ::= <procedure step>
                     [<procedure step>
                      ...            ]
<procedure step> ::= <execute statement>
                     [<data statement>
                      ...             ]
<execute statement> ::= //[<name>] <b> EXEC <c>
                        // <b> PGM = <program> <,>
```

TABLE 10-1 *JCL Syntax (Continued)*

```
                          [// <b> COND = (<bypass conditions>) < , >]
                          [// <b> PARM = (<parameter>) < , >]
                          [// <b> RD = ( <restart>) < , >]
                          [// <b> REGION = (<integer> K,
                                          <integer> K) < , >]
                          [// <b> ROLL = (<yesno>, <yesno>) < , >]
                          [// <b> TIME = (<integer>, <integer>) < , >]
                          [// <b> ACCT = (<parameter>)]
<data statement> ::= <file statement>
                        [<concatenated data>
                         . . .               ]
<file statement> ::= // <name> <b> DD <c>
                       <data set>
<data set> ::= // <b> <data identity> < , >
                 [// <b> LABEL = (<label data>) < , >]
                 [// <b> DCB = (<attribute data>) < , >]
                 [// <b> <status data> < , >]
                 [// <b> UCS = (<character set>) < , >]
                 [// <b> UNIT = (<unit data>) < , >]
                 [// <b> VOLUME = (<volume data>) < , >]
                 [// <b> <space allocation> < , >]
                 [// <b> <channel usage>]
<program> ::= [*. <name> .] <name>
<bypass conditions> ::= <first condition> [ , <condition> ··· ]
<first condition> ::= EVEN | ONLY | <condition>
<condition> ::= <integer>, <comparison>, <name>
<comparison> ::= GT | GE | EQ | NE | LE | LT
<restart> ::= R | NC | NR | RNC
<yesno> ::= YES | NO
<data identity> ::= DUMMY| DSNAME=<data name> | <deferred name>
<data name> ::= [<data prefix>] <name> [(<argument>)]
<data prefix> ::= && | *. <name>
<argument> ::= <name> | <integer> | INDEX | PRIME | OVFLOW
<deferred name> ::= DDNAME = <name>
<label data> ::= [<integer>] [ , [<label type>]] [ , [PASSWORD]]
                   [ , <inout>] [ , <expret>]
<label type> ::= SL | SUL | NSL | NL | BLP
<inout> ::= IN | OUT
<expret> ::= EXPDT = <integer> | RETPD = <integer>
<attribute data> ::= <attributes> | <attribute reference> [ , <attributes>]
<attributes> ::= <<see Attribute Table>>
<attribute reference> ::= [*.<name>. ] <name>
<status data> ::= DISP = <disposition> | SYSOUT = <routing>
<disposition> ::= <entry status> , <exit status> , <abend status>
<entry status> ::= NEW | OLD | MOD | SHR
```

TABLE 10-1 *JCL Syntax (Continued)*

```
<exit status> ::= DELETE | KEEP | PASS | CATLG | UNCATLG
<abend status> ::= DELETE | KEEP | CATLG | UNCATLG
<character set> ::= <char code> [ , [FOLD] [ , VERIFY]]
<char code> ::= AN | HN | PCAN | PCHN | PN | QNC | QN | RN |
                SW | TN | XN | YN
<unit data> ::= <group> [ , <multiunit> [ , DEFER]]
<group> ::= <three byte address> | <unit number> |
            <<unit group name>>
<three byte address> ::= <byte> <byte> <byte>
<unit number> ::= <integer> [ - <digit>]
<multiunit> ::= P | <integer>
<volume data> ::= [PRIVATE], [RETAIN], <integer>, <integer>,
                                                   <seref>
<seref> ::= SER = (<integer>, • • •) | REF = [*. [<name>.]] <name>
<space allocation> ::= SPACE = (<space data>) | SPLIT = <split data> |
                       SUBALLOC = (<suballoc data>)
<space data> ::= <space layout>, [RLSE] [<contiguity>], [ROUND]
<space layout> ::= <space units>, (<integer> [ , <integer> [ , <integer>]])
<space units> ::= TRK | CYL | <integer>
<split data> ::= <integer> | % | (<integer>), CYL, (<integer>
                 [ , <integer>]) | (%, <integer>), (<integer>
                 [ , <integer>])
<suballoc data> ::= <space layout>, [<name>.] <name>
<channel usage> ::= SEP (<name>, • • •) | AFF = <name>
<name> ::= <letter> [<alphameric> • • • ]
<parameter> ::= <<character string>>
<c> ::= <<non blank in column 72>>
<,> ::= <<comma, except omitted in last line of actual code for this entity>>
```

JCL Programming

Beyond the vocabulary of JCL and its functions we seek to develop a rationality and style for programs written in it. We do this by organizing each type of statement into an ordered sequence of parameter choices. This ordered sequence gives a programmer a checklist to ensure that all critical parameters are included in a statement.

In typical format we set out parameters, one per line, for easier inspection and interpretation. Catalogued procedures contain essentially EXEC and DD statements, and for each of those JCL statements we define the following sequence of parameter choices.

EXEC Parameters

1. Identity of Program
   PGM
2. Conditions for Execution
   COND
3. Parameters of Execution
   PARM
4. Restart Conditions
   RD
5. Time Constraints
   TIME
6. Region Allocations
   REGION
7. Roll-out Conditions
   ROLL
8. Accounting Requirements
   ACCT

DD Parameters

1. Identity of Data Set
   DUMMY/DSNAME/DDNAME
2. Data Set Attributes
   DCB
3. Disposition of the Data Set
   DISP
4. Special Print Characters
   UCS
5. Unit Information
   UNIT
6. Volume Information
   VOLUME
7. Label Requirements
   LABEL
8. Space Requirements
   SPACE | SPLIT | SUBALLOC
9. Channel Utilization
   SEP | AFF

ARTICLE

11

Top Down Programming in Large Systems

(1970)

Abstract

Structured programming can be used to develop a large system in an evolving tree structure of nested program modules, with no control branching between modules except for module calls defined in the tree structure. By limiting the size and complexity of modules, unit debugging can be done by systematic reading, and the modules can be executed directly in the evolving system in a top down testing process.

Introduction

Large systems programming today is dominated by the integration and debugging problem because it is commonly assumed that logic errors are inevitable in programming systems (in contrast to syntax errors, which are detected by translators). There is no doubt that programmers are fallible and always will be. But it now appears possible to organize and discipline the program design and coding process in order to (1) prevent most logic errors in the first place and (2) detect those errors remaining more surely and easily than before.

We will use the term "structured programming" to denote a complex of ideas of organization and discipline in the programming process.

© 1971. Reprinted, with permission, from *Debugging Techniques in Large Systems,* R. Rustin (Editor), Prentice-Hall, 1971, pp. 41–55.

There are two major principles involved. First, beginning with a functional specification, we will show that it is possible to generate a sequence of intermediate systems of code and functional subspecifications so that at every step, each system can be verified to be correct, that is, logically equivalent to its predecessor system. The initial system is the functional specification for the program, each intermediate system includes the code of its predecessor, and the final system is the code of the program. The transitivity of these step-by-step equivalences then insures the correctness of the final code with respect to the initial functional specifications. The code of the program is generated from the "top down" in this sequence of intermediate systems. Second, it can also be shown that the control logic of each successive system of code and functional subspecifications can be completely organized in terms of a few basic control structures, each with a single entry and a single exit. Three basic control structures sufficient for control logic are (1) simple sequencing, (2) IF-THEN-ELSE, and (3) DO-WHILE structures, already known in several languages, for example, PL/I [9]. For efficiency, a CASE structure may also be desirable, for example, as defined in PL360 [15].

The iterated expansions of functional specifications and of intermediate functional subspecifications into code and possibly into more detailed functional subspecifications reflect a rigorous step-by-step process of program design. Each functional subspecification defined in an intermediate system represents only a mapping of initial data into final data for some segment of coding yet to be specified. The expansion process describes the means selected for this mapping, using possibly more detailed mappings to be similarly described later.

In traditional terms this programming design process is carried out top down on paper, using flowcharts or any other conceptual objects available to describe the design structure selected for each portion of the system. Once the design is completed, the resulting modules defined are coded, unit tested, integrated into subsystems, then into a system, and finally debugged as a system, in a bottom up coding and testing process.

In the structured programming process this design structure is carried out directly in code, which can be at least syntax checked, and possibly executed, with *program stubs* standing in for functional subspecifications. Instead of paper flowcharts, the structured design is defined in IF-THEN-ELSE and DO-WHILE code, which connect newly defined subspecifications. In fact, program stubs can be used to simulate the estimated core and throughput requirements of the code yet to be developed for given functional subspecifications, during executions of intermediate systems.

The functional expansion process can be carried out literally in a page of code at a time, in which new functional subspecifications are denoted by names of dummy members of a programming library, which will eventually hold the code for the next level of expansion. Such a page, called a *segment,* is itself identified by a name and corresponding functional subspecification at the next higher level segment in the programming system. The segments of a program form a tree structure.

A functional subspecification, as a mapping from initial data to final data, has no implicit control logic, and this is reflected in its corresponding segment. A segment has only one entry, at the top; and one exit, at the bottom. If other segments are named within it, such segments are in turn entered at the top and exited out the bottom, back into the naming segment. As such, a named segment behaves precisely as a simple data transformation statement (possibly quite complex, according to its functional subspecification), without any possible side effects in program control.

The problem of proving the correctness of any expansion of a functional subspecification is thereby reduced to proving the correctness of a program of at most one page, in which there possibly exist various named subspecifications. The verification of the given segment requires a proof that the segment subspecification is met by the code and named subspecifications. These named subspecifications will be subsequently verified, possibly in terms of even more detailed subspecifications, until segments with nothing but code are reached and verified.

The foregoing process provides a rigorous format for an activity that all programmers do, more or less, and good programmers do well, in designing programs. But it further converts the design into code directly and provides a vehicle for maintaining the integrity of the developing system step by step. The coding is produced "top down," rather than "bottom up" as called for by traditional standards. Integrating and control code is produced before functional code, and no unit checking of modules occurs.

Some Background

E. W. Dijkstra has provided several illuminating arguments for the ideas of structured programming [2, 3, 4] and has exhibited a substantial application of it in the development of the T.H.E. system [5]. The critical theorem that the control logic of any program can be represented in the three basic control structures of simple sequencing, IF-THEN-ELSE, and DO-WHILE structures is due to C. Böhm and G. Jacopini [1]. The result of Böhm and Jacopini permits a new level of discipline in the programming process, which, as Dijkstra [4] also points out, can help reduce to practical terms the problem of proving program correctness in today's real programming systems.

There are several important developments in proving program correctness in the recent literature, which at the very least indicate procedures that programmers can follow in documenting and giving heuristic argumentation for the correctness of the programs they develop. Building on ideas of Floyd [6] and Naur [14], London and associates have produced formal proofs of substantial programs, themselves written for other purposes without proof methods in mind [8, 12]; King [11] and, more recently, Good [7] have elaborated on these ideas with automatic and semiautomatic procedures for proof.

In fact, the correctness problem integrates the specification and documentation questions into programming in a natural, inevitable, and precise way. The documentation of a program should provide evidence that the program meets its functional specifications. One cannot prove a program to be correct without a definition of what it is supposed to do—its functional specification. And sufficient evidence that a program meets its functional specification can serve as its documentation.

It may appear at the outset that proving a system to be correct (that is, not to depart from its original functional specifications), step by step in implementation, would be agonizingly slow and totally impractical. In fact, such an impression is no doubt behind the usual approach of coding "bottom up" from paper designs. However, when the integration and debugging activities are taken into account as well, then the step-by-step construction and verification process may turn out not to be so slow after all.

Our point of view is also very close to concepts of "functional programming," under the interpretation that functional specifications are indeed mathematical functions without side effects in control and that connectives IF-THEN-ELSE, DO-WHILE, and so on are convenient forms for defining composite functions in terms of other functions.

The Idea of Structured Programs

We are interested in writing programs that are highly readable, whose major structural characteristics are given in hierarchical form and are tied in closely to functional specifications and documentation. In fact, we are interested in writing programs that can be read sequentially in small segments, each under a page in length, such that each segment can be literally read from top to bottom with complete assurance that all control paths are visible in the segment under consideration.

There are two main requirements through which we can achieve this goal. The first requirement is GO TO–free code, that is, the formulation of programs in terms of a few standard and basic control structures, such as IF-THEN-ELSE statements, DO loops, CASE statements, and DECISION tables, with no arbitrary jumps between these standard structures. A critical characteristic of each such control structure is that it contains exactly one entry and one exit. The second requirement is library and macro substitution facilities, so that the segments themselves can be stored under symbolic names in a library, and the programming language permits the substitution of any given segment at any point in the program by a macrolike call.

PL/I in OS/360 [10] has both the control logic structures and the library and macro facilities necessary. Assembly language in OS/360 has the library and macro facilities available, and a few standard macros can furnish the control logic structures required.

Böhm and Jacopini [1] give a theoretical basis for programming without arbitrary jumps (that is, without GO TO or RETURN statements), using only a set of standard programming figures such as those mentioned above. We take such a possibility for granted and note that any program, whether it be one page or a hundred pages, can be written using only IF-THEN-ELSE and DO-WHILE statements for control logic.

The control logic of a program in a free form language such as PL/I can be displayed typographically, by line formation and indentation conventions. A "syntax-directed program listing" (a formal description for such a set of conventions) is given by Mills [13]. Conventions often are used to indent the body of a DO-END block, such as

```
DO I = J TO K;
    statement 1
    statement 2
    . . .
    statement n
END;
```

and clauses of IF-THEN-ELSE statements such as

```
IF X > 1 THEN
   statement 1
ELSE
   statement 2
```

In the latter case, if the statements are themselves DO-END blocks, the DO, END are indented one level and the statements inside them are indented further, such as

```
IF X > 1 THEN
   DO;
          statement 1
          statement 2
            . . .
          statement k
   END;
ELSE
   DO;
          statement k + 1
            . . .
          statement n
   END;
```

In general, DO-END and IF-THEN-ELSE can be nested in each other indefinitely in this way.

Segment-Structured Programs

Since it may not be obvious at the outset how a structured program can be developed, we begin with a more conventional approach. Suppose any large program has been written in PL/I—say, several thousand lines of code—by any means of design and coding available. The theorem of Böhm and Jacopini [1] is proved constructively, so that it is possible, mechanically, to transform the program we have in mind into a GO TO–free program. Ordinarily, using programming insight, this can be done with little loss of efficiency. Now we are in a position to imagine a hundred-page PL/I program already written in GO TO–free code. Although it is highly structured, such a program is still not very readable. The extent of a major DO loop may be 50 or 60 pages, or an IF-THEN-ELSE statement take up ten or 15 pages. There is simply more than the eye can comfortably take in or the mind retain for the purpose of programming.

However, with our imaginary program in this structured form we can begin a process that we can repeat over and over until we get the whole program defined. This process is to formulate a one-page skeleton program that represents that hundred-page program. We do this by selecting some of the most important lines of code in the original program and then filling in what lies between those lines by names. Each new name will refer to a new segment to be stored in a library and called by a macro facility. In this way we produce a program segment with something under 50 lines, so that it will fit on one page. This program segment will be a mixture of control statements and macro calls, with possibly a few initializing, file, or assignment statements as well.

The programmer must use a sense of proportion and importance in identifying what is the forest and what are the trees out of this hundred-page program. It corresponds to writing the "high-level flowchart" for the whole program, except that a completely rigorous program segment is written here. A key aspect of any segment referred to by name is that its control should enter at the top and exit at the bottom, and have no other means of entry or exit from other parts of the program. Thus when reading a segment name, at any point, the reader can be assured that control will pass through that segment and not otherwise affect the control logic on the page being read.

In order to satisfy the segment entry/exit requirement we need only to be sure to include all matching control logic statements on a page. For example, the END to any DO and the ELSE to any IF-THEN should be put in the same segment.

For the sake of illustration this first segment may consist of some 20 control logic statements, such as DO-WHILEs, IF-THEN-ELSEs, perhaps another ten key initializing statements, and some ten macro calls. These ten macro calls may involve something like ten pages of programming each, although there may be considerable variety among their sizes.

Now we can repeat this process for each of these ten segments. Again we want to pick out some 40 to 50 control statements, segment names, and so on, that best describe the overall character of that program segment, and to relegate further details to the next level of segments. We continue to repeat the process until we have accounted for all the code in the original program. Our end result is a program, of any original size whatsoever, that has been organized into a set of named member segments, each of which can be read from top to bottom without any side effects in control logic, other than what is on that particular page. A programmer can access any level of information about the program, from highly summarized data at the upper-level segments to complete details in the lower levels.

In our illustration this hundred-page program may expand into some 150 separate segments because (1) the segment names take up a certain amount of space and (2) the segments, if kept to a one-page maximum, may average only some two-thirds full on each page. Each page should represent some natural unit of the program, and it may be natural to fill up only half a page in some instances.

Creating Structured Programs

In the preceding section we assumed that a large-size program somehow existed, already written with structured control logic, and discussed how we could conceptually reorganize the program into a set of more readable segments. In this section we observe how we can create such structured programs a segment at a time in a natural way. It is evident that program segments as we have defined them are natural units of documentation and specification, and we will describe a process that develops code, subspecifications, and documentation concurrently. First we note that a functional specification corresponds to the mathematical idea of a function. It is a mapping of inputs into outputs, without regard to how that mapping may be accomplished. Each segment defined in the preceding development represents a transformation of data, namely, a mapping of certain initial values into final values. In fact, intermediate values may be created in data as well. Corresponding to this mapping of initial into final data is a subspecification that ordinarily will be deduced directly from the specification for the naming segment. It represents part of the work to be done in the segment. The entire page of code and new segment names must produce precisely the mapping required by the functional specification of that naming segment.

When all segments named have been assigned functional specifications, then the logical action of that naming segment can be deduced from the code and those named specifications. Methods of proving the correctness of programs can be applied to this single page. The specifications may be too complex to carry out a completely rigorous proof of correctness, but at the very least there is on one page a logical description of a function that can be heuristically compared with the functional specification for that segment. The argumentation that the function does indeed duplicate the functional specification for that segment is the documentation for that segment.

Our main point is to observe that the process of coding can take place in practically the same order as the process of extracting code from our imaginary large program in the previous section. That is, armed with a program design, one can write the first segment, which serves as a skeleton for the whole program, using segment names where appropriate to refer to code that will be written later. In fact, by simply taking the precaution of inserting dummy members into a library with those segment names, one can compile or assemble, and even possibly execute, this skeleton program while the remaining coding is continued. Very often, it makes sense to put a temporary write statement, "got to here OK," as a single executable statement in such a dummy member. More elaborately, a dummy member can be used to allocate core and to simulate processing time required during executions of the intermediate system containing it.

Now the segments at the next level can be written in the same way, referring as appropriate to segments to be written later (also setting up dummy segments as they are named in the library). As each dummy segment becomes filled in with its code in the library, the recompilation of the segment that includes it will automatically produce updated, expanded versions of the developing program. Problems of syntax and control logic will usually be isolated within the new segments so that debugging and checkout go correspondingly well with such problems so isolated.

It is clear that the programmer's creativity and sense of proportion can play a large part in the efficiency of this programming process. The code that goes into earlier sections should be dictated, to some extent, not only by general matters of importance, but also by the question of getting executable segments reasonably early in the coding process. For example, if the control logic of a skeleton module depends on certain control variables, their declarations and manipulations may need to be created at fairly high levels in the hierarchy. In this way the control logic of the skeleton can be executed and debugged, even in the still skeleton program.

Note that several programmers may be engaged in the foregoing activity concurrently. Once the initial skeleton program is written, each programmer could take on a separate segment and work independently within the structure of an overall program design. The hierarchical structure of the programs contribute to a clean interface between programmers. At any point in the programming, the segments already in existence give a precise and concise framework for fitting in the rest of the work to be done.

Function Description and Expansion

We have noted above that the structured programming process represents a step-by-step expansion of a mathematical function into simpler mathematical functions, using such control structures as IF-THEN-ELSE and DO-WHILE. Ordinarily, we think of this expansion in terms of a page of code at a time. However, we can break that expansion down to much more elementary steps, namely, into a single control structure at a time. In this case we ask the question "What elementary program statement can be used to expand the function?" The expansion chosen will imply one or more subsequent functional specifications, which arise out of the original specification. Each of these new functional specifications can be treated exactly as the original functional specification, and the same questions can be posed about them.

As a result, the top down programming process is an expansion of functional specifications to simpler and simpler functions until, finally, statements of the programming language itself are reached. Part of such a process is shown below, expanding the functional specification "Add member to library." Such a functional specification will require more description, but the breakout into subfunctions by means of programming statements can be accomplished as indicated here.

In the example the single letters identifying function names will be multiple-character library names, and the small quoted phrases may be very substantial descriptions of logical conditions or processes.

Specification (Level 0):

f = "Add member to library"

f expands to: g THEN h

Subspecifications (Level 1):

g = "Update library index"

h = "Add member text to library text"

g expands to: IF p THEN i ELSE j

Subspecifications (Level 2):

p = "Member name is in index"

i = "Update text pointer"

j = "Add name and text pointer to index"

Restatement of two levels of expansion:

f = IF "Member name is in index" THEN
"Update text pointer" ELSE
"Add name and text pointer to index"
"Add member text to library text"

References

1. Böhm, Corrado, and Jacopini, Giuseppe. "Flow Diagrams, Turing Machines and Languages with Only Two Formation Rules." *Comm. ACM* 9 (1966): 366–371.
2. Dijkstra, E. W. "A Constructive Approach to the Problem of Program Correctness." *BIT* 8, No. 3 (1968): 174–186.
3. Dijkstra, E. W. *Notes on Structured Programming,* Technische Hogeschool Eindhoven, 1969.
4. Dijkstra, E. W. "Structured Programming." In *Software Engineering Techniques,"* edited by J. N. Burton, and B. Randell, pp. 88–93. NATO Science Committee, 1969.
5. Dijkstra, E. W. "The Structure of the "T.H.E." Multiprogramming System." *Comm. ACM* 11 (1968): 341–346.
6. Floyd, R. W. "Assigning Meanings to Programs." In *Proceedings of the Symposium in Applied Mathematics,* Vol. 19, edited by J. T. Schwartz, pp. 19–32. Providence, R. I: American Mathematical Society, 1967.
7. Good, D. I. "Toward a Man-Machine System for Proving Program Correctness." Ph.D. thesis, University of Wisconsin, 1970.
8. Good, D. I., and London, R. L. "Computer Interval Arithmetic: Definition and Proof of Correct Implementation." *J. ACM* 17, No. 4 (1970): 603–612.
9. *IBM System/360 Operating System: PL/I(F) Language Reference Manual,* Form C28-8201. IBM Corporation.
10. *IBM System/360 Operating System: Concepts and Facilities,* Form GC28-6535. IBM Corporation.
11. King, J. C. "A Program Verifier." Ph.D. thesis, Carnegie Mellon University, Pittsburgh, 1969.
12. London, R. L. "Certification of Algorithm 245 Treesort 3: Proof of Algorithms—A New Kind of Certification." *Comm. ACM* 13 (1970): 371–373.
13. Mills, H. D. "Syntax-Directed Documentation for PL360." *Comm. ACM* 13 (1970): 216–222.
14. Naur, P. "Proof of Algorithms by General Snapshots." *BIT* 6 (1966): 310–316.
15. Wirth, N. "PL360, a Programming Language for the 360 Computers." *J. ACM* 15 (1968): 37–74.

ARTICLE
12

Programming Techniques: From Private Art to Public Practice

(1970)

A Science of Programming

The computer has introduced a need for highly complex, precisely formulated systems on a scale never before attempted. Systems may be large and highly complex, but if human beings or even analog components are intrinsic in them, then various error tolerances are possible, which such components can adjust and compensate for. But a digital system, hardware and software, not only makes the idea of perfect precision possible—it requires perfect precision for satisfactory operation. This complete intolerance to the slightest error gives programming a new character, unknown previously, in its requirements for precision on a large scale.

The combination of this new requirement for precision and the commercial demand for computer programming on a broad scale has created many false values and distorted relationships in the past decade. They arise from intense pressure to achieve complex and precise results in a practical way without adequate theoretical foundations. As a result, a great deal of programming today uses people and machines highly inefficiently, as the only means presently known to accomplish a practical end.

It is one thing to understand the mechanisms of a computer such as OS/360 and to write down a set of detailed operations that will produce a payroll, for example. It is another thing to produce a payroll programming system that has intrinsic technical value in its own right—technical value that permits others to understand it readily or to add onto it, or permits it to use hardware efficiently.

In the first case, one has merely the problem of writing down all the conditions and cases that might occur and dealing with them individually with the computer instruction repertoire. In the second case, one has a problem in general systems design and implementation. This problem is poorly defined, and high professional creativity and skill are required to handle it effectively.

There have been, from the beginning of programming activities, certain general principles from general systems theory that good programmers have identified and practiced in one way or another. These include developing systems designs from a gross level to more and more detail until the detail of a computer is reached, dividing a system into modules in such a way that minimal interaction takes place through module interfaces, creating standard subroutine libraries, and using programming languages for the coding process.

These general principles will eventually find themselves codified and integrated into a general science of programming. It is premature to say that there is a science of programming at the present time, but it is becoming possible to move programming from being a private art (although supported by various principles in ad hoc ways) toward being a public science (in which work processes are repeatable and understandable by people other than the original programmers). A Chief Programmer approach will lead in this area by reintroducing high-level technical capabilities into programming, which will permit the propagation of principles and their use in practical affairs, with resultant feedback into the emerging science of programming.

Two Key Technical Principles

Programming in a Chief Programmer Team is based primarily on a renewal and a reapplication of classical ideas in system development such as system modularity and clean interface construction. However, there are also two key principles, relatively new in their application to programming, that play a major role in the definition of Chief Programmer Team techniques.

The first key technical principle is that the control logic of any programming system can be designed and coded in a highly structured way. In fact, arbitrarily large and complex programming systems can be represented by iterating and nesting a small number of basic and standard control logic structures.

This principle has an analog in hardware design, where it is known that arbitrary logic circuits can be formed out of elementary AND, OR, and NOT gates. This is a standard in engineering so widespread that it is almost forgotten as such. But it is based on a theorem in Boolean algebra that arbitrarily complex logic functions can be expressed in terms of AND, OR, and NOT operations. As such, it represents a standard based on a solid theoretical foundation that does not require ad hoc management support, case by case, in actual practice. Rather, it is the burden of a professional engineer to design logic circuits out of these basic components. Otherwise, considerable doubt exists about this person's competence as an engineer.

One practical application of this principle is writing PL/I programs without explicit GO TO statements in them. Instead, the branching control logic can be effected entirely in terms of DO loops and IF-THEN-ELSE and ON conditions. The resulting code is read strictly from top to bottom, typographically, and is much more easily understood thereby. It takes more skill and analysis to write such code, but the debugging and maintenance are greatly simplified. Even more important, such structured programming can increase a single programmer's span of detailed control by a large amount.

The second key technical principle is that programs can be coded in a sequence that requires no simultaneous interface hypotheses. That is, programs can be coded in such a way that every interface is defined initially in the coding process itself and referred to thereafter in its coded form.

This principle has an analog in the theory of computable functions. The key point in characterizing a computable function is that its valuation can be accomplished in a sequence of elementary computations, none of which involves solving a simultaneous system of equations. Any program that is to be executed in a computer can be coded in an execution sequence, and the very fact that the computer evaluates only computable functions means that no interfaces can be defined hypothetically and simultaneously in computation.

In practical application this principle leads to "top down" programming where code is generated in an execution sequence, for example, job control code first, then linkage editor code, then source code. The opposite (and typical implementation procedure) is "bottom up" programming, where source modules are written and unit tested to begin with and later integrated into subsystems and, finally, systems. This integration process in fact tests the proposed solutions of simultaneous interface problems generated by lower-level programming; and the problems of system integration and debugging arise from the imperfections of these proposed solutions. Top down programming circumvents the integration problem by the coding sequence itself.

Standards, Creativity, and Variability

Many reactions to standards in programming show a basic confusion between creativity and variability. Programming these days is a highly variable activity. Two programmers may solve the same problem with very different programs; that is, the results are highly variable. Two engineers asked to design a "half adder" with economical use of gates will be much less variable in their solutions but, in fact, no less creative than two programmers in a typical programming project. Carried to an extreme, two mathematicians asked to solve a differential equation may use different methods of thinking about problems but will come up with identical solutions and still be extremely creative in the process.

The present programming process is mostly writing down all the things that have to be done in a given situation. There are many different sequences that can accomplish the same thing in most situations, and this is reflected in extreme variability. A major problem in programming at the present time is simply not to forget anything—that is, to handle all possible cases and to invent any intermediate data needed to accomplish the final results. Thus as long as programming is primarily the job of writing everything down in some order, it is in fact highly variable. But that in itself is not creative.

It is possible to be creative in programming, and that deals with far more ill-defined questions, such as minimizing the amount of intermediate data required, or the amount of program storage, or the amount of execution time, and so on. Finding the deep simplicities in a complicated collection of things to be done is the creativity in programming. However, it is not standards that inhibit such creativity in the programming process; it is simply the lack of creativity in the programmers themselves.

Controlling Complexity through Technical Standards

A major purpose in creating new technical standards in programming is to control complexity. Complexity in programming seems sometimes to be a "free commodity." It does not show up in core or throughput time, and it always seems to be something that can be dealt with indefinitely at the local level.

In this connection it is an illuminating digression to recall that 500 years ago, no one knew that air had weight. Just imagine, for example, the frustrations of a water pump manufacturer, building pumps to draw water out of wells. By tightening up seals, one can raise water higher and higher—five feet, ten feet, then 15 feet, and so on, until one gets to 34 feet. As soon as it is known that air *has* weight and it is, in fact, the weight of a column of 34 feet of water, then the frustration clears up right away. Knowing the weight of air allows a better pump design, for example, in multiple-stage pumps, if water has to be raised more than 34 feet.

We have a similar situation in programming today. Complexity has a "weight" of some kind, but we do not know what it is. We know more and more from practical experience that complexity will exact its price in a qualitative way, but we cannot yet measure that complexity in operational terms that, for example, would cause us to reject a program module because it had "too many units of complexity in it." (These units of measure will, in all probability, be in "bits of information." But just how to effect the measurements still requires development and refinement.)

Nevertheless, we have qualitative notions of complexity, and standards can be used to control complexity in a qualitative way, whether we can measure it effectively yet or not. One kind of standard we can use to control complexity is structural, as in the first principle noted above. Then we can require that programs be written in certain structural forms rather than be simply arbitrary complex control graphs generated at a programmer's fancy. The technical basis for the standard is to show that arbitrarily complex flowcharts can be reformulated in equivalent terms as highly structured flowcharts that satisfy certain standards. This is like theorems in Boolean algebra that state a priori that half adders can be written in terms of AND, OR, and NOT gates.

We define, through standards, work processes that are more repeatable. People may think differently about the same problem but, just like the mathematicians above, may come up with the same differential equation. When the problems and standards are stated sufficiently well, people will come up with the same answers. In programming at the moment, we define neither the problems nor the tools with sufficient standards, but as we improve our standards, the work processes in programming will become more and more repeatable in terms of final results.

Structured Programming

There are new results in graph theory that show that the control logic of any programming system can be designed and coded in a highly structured way. Any programming system, no matter how large or complex, can be represented as a finite set of flowcharts (hardware interrupt mechanisms may be used to transfer control from one flowchart to another in such a programming system). The new theoretical results deal with converting arbitrarily large and complex flowcharts into standard forms so that they can be represented by iterating and nesting a small number of basic and standard control logic structures.

A sufficient set of basic control logic structures consists of three members:

1. A sequence of two operations (Figure 12-1).
2. A conditional branch to one of two operations and rejoined (an IF-THEN-ELSE statement) (Figure 12-2).
3. Repeating an operation while some condition is true (a DO-WHILE statement) (Figure 12-3).

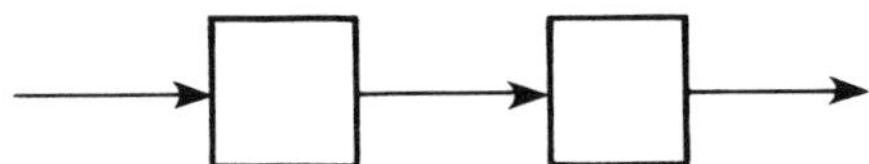

FIGURE 12-1. SEQUENCE

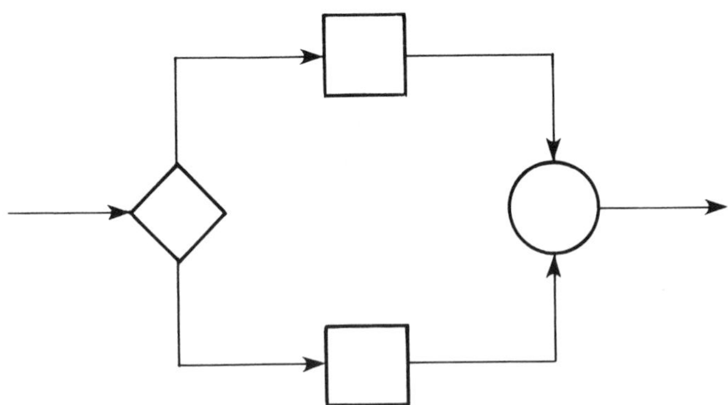

FIGURE 12-2. IF-THEN-ELSE

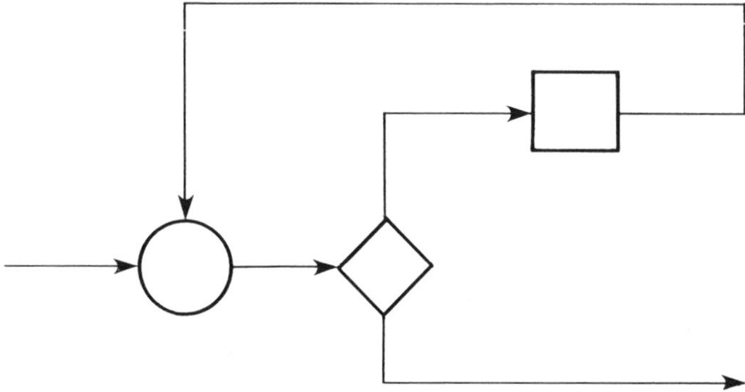

FIGURE 12-3. DO-WHILE

The basic theorem (due to Böhm and Jacopini, "Flow Diagrams, Turing Machines, and Languages with Only Two Formation Rules," *Comm. ACM* 9, May 1966) is that any flowchart can be represented in an equivalent form as an iterated and nested structure in these three basic and standard figures.

Note that each structure has one input and one output and can be substituted for any box in a structure, so that complex flowcharts can result. The key point (not obvious here) is that an arbitrary flowchart has an equivalent representative in the class so built up. In fact, Figure 12-1, a simple sequence, is so natural that it rivals the number zero (in algebra) in the difficulty of its discovery as a bona fide structural figure.

Needless to say, there is no compelling reason in programming to use such a minimal set of basic figures, and it appears practical to augment the DO statement with several variations, such as ordinary "Fortran DO loops" in order to provide more flexibility for programmers and greater adaptability to given machine characteristics.

When converted into PL/I terms, the foregoing theorem demonstrates that PL/I programs can be written in terms of IF-THEN-ELSE and DO-WHILE statements. Note that the idea of a general GO TO is never introduced in these basic structures and is thus never required in a representation. Because of questions of efficiency, one may in fact wish to use GO TO's occasionally in some PL/I programs, but not through any logical necessity. The use of GO TO's can be made on an exception basis, so that special justification and documentation would be called for in any such use.

A major characteristic of programs written in these structures is that they can be literally read from top to bottom typographically; there is never any "jumping around" as is so typical in trying to read code that contains general GO TO's. This property of readability is a major advantage in debugging, maintaining, or otherwise referencing code at later times. Another advantage of possibly even greater benefit is the additional program design work that is required to produce such structured code. The programmer must think through the processing problem, not only writing down everything that needs to be done, but writing it down in such a way that there are no afterthoughts with subsequent jump-outs and jump-backs nor indiscriminate use of a section of code from several locations because it "just happens" to do something at the time of the coding. Instead, the programmer must think through the control logic of the module completely at one time, in order to provide the proper structural framework for the control. This means that programs will be written in much more uniform ways because there is less freedom for arbitrary variety than there is with general GO TO's.

Such structured programming can also be carried out in OS/360 assembly language using macroprocessing facilities. The 360 macroprocessing is sufficiently powerful to allow standard block structure macros to be developed so that assembly language programs can be written without instruction labels or branches except those generated in the standard macros. The assembler language also has enough facility (though it is seldom used) to permit the typographical representation of control logic through indentation, that is, so that code which is nested (within a DO loop, for example) is indented to show that nesting typographically.

It is expected that Chief Programmers write in highly structured forms; this represents a high degree of creativity on their part. This serves a major function in permitting communication at a precise level between the Chief Programmer and the Backup Programmer and any other programmers to whom coding is delegated. That is, the Chief Programmer expects to read and understand all the code going into the system no matter who wrote it. If others write code in the same block structured way, this facilitates the code reading by the Chief Programmer to verify its content and correctness for the system under development.

Top Down Programming

There is a new principle in system implementation that has been followed intuitively in module development (but not in system development) for some time. It is to produce code in execution sequence, that is, to code only instructions that could be executed by the machine because all previous instructions required have already been coded. Note that this principle is being applied here to the sequence in which code is created, not the sequence in which it is executed.

In general, system development has evolved as a "bottom up" process, where the lowest level modules are coded, then the next level, on up to subsystems and systems. In the top down approach, the system level code is written first, then the subsystem code, and so on, down to the lowest levels of code.

These two ways of coding have a direct counterpart in the theory of computable functions. Computable functions have the property, at any point of computation, that all the elements required to compute the next value have already been computed. That is, one never incurs a set of simultaneous equations, even though those equations may be well defined and have a unique solution. Note that a solution to a system of simultaneous linear equations is not included in the theory of computable functions; but an algorithm for solving such a system (in finitely many steps) is so included.

It would be possible to develop a far more complex theory of computability in which simultaneous equations were permitted. Such a theory might require that at each point of computation there would exist a set of equations for several variables that had a unique solution. It would be vastly more complex than the ordinary theory of computable functions, and no real development of such an extended theory even exists.

However, it is this latter, highly complex process that has been going on in system development right along. That is, while coding at the low-level modules in the bottom up approach, programmers are assuming hypothetical interfaces. That is, they are attempting to solve "simultaneous interface equations" in their programming process to arrive at a consistent set of low-level modules. The next level of modules check out these consistencies, and in fact a great deal of the debugging and reworking is usually required because of inadvertent inconsistencies that appear. This process of combining more and more modules represents, in a computability theory, the process of solving simultaneous interface equations at higher and higher levels until finally the entire interface system has been "solved," or the program has been debugged.

In contrast, the principle defined above follows the computable function approach. The proof that this is possible comes directly out of the machine execution itself. Hardware cannot execute hypothetical data. Its function is to always produce new data out of old data in a computable way.

In programming terms this means that an external data set must be defined in its format, and so on, before a file can access it. The file must be defined with its records before a program can make use of data from it, and so on. Notice in the process that there are no hypothetical interfaces and no logical points at which confusion or misunderstanding can arise. Human fallibility cannot be eliminated, but we can eliminate the hypothetical interface communication, and this may indeed eliminate the majority of the errors that are now made through human fallibility in programming.

At first glance, the idea of top down programming may sound prohibitive in terms of elapsed coding time. It is typical in a large project to get coding started at the lower levels early because there seems to be so much of it and the feeling is that it will be the bottleneck in the development process. This will probably turn out to be false; it is likely that what actually happens in projects is that at the integration time, programs are checked, modified, and corrected with more than sufficient time spent on them to write them from the beginning to firm interfaces. For many programming systems, writing top down is not expected to take any more elapsed time than writing bottom up, particularly with the high-level languages and macroprocessing facilities that are available today.

There is another facet of system implementation standards and the top down approach. It deals with an idea called "main-line programming." Usually, most programs have paths that can be called main-line paths because that is the expected control path for typical program execution and the additional "exception" code that handles unusual or error conditions. It is common in programming development to write main-line code and get that running first and then to write exception data later on at a more leisurely pace. This can be done in the top down approach simply by recognizing that debug data can be written in top down manner as well. That is, debug data should be written to exercise the main-line path to begin with, and be augmented later, as exception paths are developed in code, to exercise that code. Again the principle is exactly the same, only now regarding debug data and programming code as a unit in a top down approach. (It should be pointed out here that debug data is distinguished from test data, which is defined at the point of functional specification of the system and not referred to here. The debug data referred to here is used in development to identify programmer fallibility and serve as a continuous check on the system development to date for the programmer. Of course, at acceptance the system should be subjected to data called for by functional specifications, but that is considered as a separate matter, outside the programming development itself.)

In OS/360, for example, job control, linkage editor, "supervisory" and "data management" source code is written in that order, and only then the source modules that typically give a system its functional capability. Thus system development proceeds through the controlled addition of new modules to an always checked out system. That is, supervisory programs run early in the development phase, first calling on dummy modules into which later functional modules can be substituted. The system is then developed by expanding the set of modules it can call and run. In this process the Chief Programmer can maintain complete and direct control over the system, usually having written the nucleus and personally specifying and checking out the modules produced by other programmers or specialists in the very system environment for which they are intended.

The top down approach permits the effective use of OS/360 languages in a project. No matter what is written in memos or discussed in meetings, the machine will end up reading what is punched on cards in OS/360 languages. Concepts that cannot be stated in OS/360 languages cannot be utilized in the machine. Instead, module interface specifications can be done entirely in OS/360 languages, with less opportunity for misunderstanding and error. As was noted, in the top down programming approach there is no programming to hypothetical or temporary interfaces; every interface is defined at one logically defined point in the project and used as a fully specified reference from there on.

ARTICLE

13

Mathematical Foundations for Structured Programming

(1972)

Introduction

The first name in structured programming is Edsger W. Dijkstra (Holland), who has originated a set of ideas and a series of examples for clear thinking in the construction of programs. These ideas are powerful tools in mentally connecting the static text of a program with the dynamic process it invokes in execution. This new correspondence between program and process permits a new level of precision in programming. Indeed, it is contended here that the precision now possible in programming will change its industrial characteristics from a frustrating, trial-and-error activity to a systematic, quality-controlled activity.

However, in order to introduce and enforce such precision programming as an industrial activity the ideas of structured programming must be formulated as technical standards, not simply as good ideas to be used when convenient, but as basic principles that are always valid. A good example of a technical standard occurs in logic circuit design. There, it is known from basic theorems in Boolean algebra that any logic circuit, no matter how complex its requirement, can be constructed by using only AND, OR, and NOT gates.

Our interest is similar: to provide a mathematical assurance, for

---

Reprinted with permission from International Business Machines Corporation.

management purposes, that a technical standard is sound and practical. This mathematical assurance is due, in large part, to Corrado Böhm and Giuseppe Jacopini (Italy), who showed how to prove that relatively simple (structured) program control logics were capable of expressing any program requirements.

Initial practical experience with structured programming indicates that there is more than a technical side to the matter. There is a psychological effect as well, when programmers learn of their new power to write programs correctly. This new power motivates in turn a new level of concentration, which helps avoid errors of carelessness. This new psychology of precision has a mathematical counterpart in the theory of program correctness, which we formulate in a new way.

The mathematical approach we take in formulating structured programming and the correctness problem emphasizes these combinatorial aspects, in order to demonstrate for programmers that correct programming involves only combinatorial selection and not problems requiring perfect precision on a continuous scale. Because of this we are confident that programmers will soon work at a level of productivity and precision that will appear incredible compared to early experience with the programming problem.

Complexity and Precision in Programming

The digital computer has introduced a need for highly complex, precisely formulated, logical systems on a scale never before attempted. Systems may be large and highly complex, but if human beings, or even analog devices, are components in them, then various error tolerances are possible, which such components can adjust to and compensate for. However, a digital computer, in hardware and software, not only makes the idea of perfect precision possible—it requires perfect precision for satisfactory operation. This complete intolerance to the slightest logical error gives programming a new character, little known previously, in its requirements for precision on a large scale.

The combination of this new requirement for precision and the commercial demand for computer programming on a broad scale has created many false values and distorted relationships in the past decade. They arise from intense pressure to achieve complex and precise results in a practical way without adequate technical foundations. As a result, a great deal of programming uses people and computers highly inefficiently, as the only means presently known to accomplish a practical end.

It is universally accepted today that programming is an error-prone activity. Any major programming system is presumed to have errors in it; only the very naive would believe otherwise. The process of debugging programs and systems is a mysterious art. Indeed, more programmer time goes into debugging than into program designing and coding in most large systems. But there is practically no systematic literature on this large undertaking.

Yet even though errors in program logic have always been a source of frustration, even for the most careful and meticulous, this may not be necessarily so in the future. Programming is very young as a human activity—some 20 years old. It has practically no technical foundations yet. Imagine engineering when it was 20 years old. Whether that was in 1620 or 1770, it was not in very good technical shape at that stage either! As technical foundations are developed for programming, its character will undergo radical changes.

We contend here that such a radical change is possible now, that in structured programming the techniques and tools are at hand to permit an entirely new level of precision in programming.

This new level of precision will be characterized by programs of large size (from tens of thousands to millions of instructions) that have a mean time between detected errors of a year or so. But to accomplish that level of precision, a new attitude toward programming expectations will be required in programmers as well.

The Psychology of Precision

A child can learn to play the game of tic-tac-toe perfectly—but a person can never learn to saw a board exactly in half. Playing tic-tac-toe is a combinatorial problem, selecting at every alternative one of a finite number of possibilities. Sawing a board exactly in half is a physical problem for which no discrete level of accuracy is sufficient.

The child who has learned to play tic-tac-toe need never make a mistake, except through a loss of concentration. In any game the child believes important (say, played for a candy bar), he or she is capable of perfect play.

Computer programming is a combinatorial activity, like tic-tac-toe, not like sawing a board in half. It does not require perfect resolution in measurement and control; it only requires correct choices out of finite sets of possibilities at every step. The difference between tic-tac-toe and computer programming is complexity. The purpose of structured programming is to control complexity through theory and discipline. And with complexity under better control it now appears that people can write substantial computer programs correctly. In fact, just as a child moves from groping and frustration to confidence and competence in tic-tac-toe, so people can now find solid ground for program development.

Children, in learning to play tic-tac-toe, soon develop a little theory, dealing with "center squares," "corner squares," "side squares," and the self-discipline to block possible defeats before building threats of their own. In programming, theory and discipline are critical as well at an adult's level of intellectual activity. Structured programming is such a theory, providing a systematic way of coping with complexity in program design and development. It makes possible a discipline for program design and construction on a level of precision not previously possible.

But for children, knowing how to play tic-tac-toe perfectly is not enough. They must know that they know. This knowing that they know is a vital ingredient in self-discipline—knowing that they are capable of analyzing the board and do not need to guess and hope.

It is the same with programmers. If programmers know that what is in their minds is correct, then getting it onto paper precisely is more important, as is checking details of data definitions, and whatever, in the coding process. On the other hand, if programmers think that what is in their minds is probably all right, but are subconsciously counting on debugging and integration runs to iron out logic and interface errors, then the entire process of getting it onto paper and into the computer suffers in small ways to later torment them.

It takes some learning on the part of experienced programmers to discover that structured programs can be written with unprecedented logical and interface precision. As with the child, it is not enough to be able to program with precision. Programmers must know their capabilities for precision programming in order to supply the concentration to match their capabilities.

The Problem of Complexity

Five hundred years ago, it was not known that the air we breathe and move through so freely had weight. Air is hard to put on a scale, or even to identify as any specific quantity for weighing at all. But now we know that air has weight—at sea level, the weight of a column of water 34 feet high.

It is easy to imagine, in hindsight, the frustrations of a well pump manufacturer, whose "research department" is operating on the theory that "nature abhors a vacuum." Water can be raised up a well pipe 15, 20, then 25 feet, by using a plunger and tightening its seals better and better. All this merely seems to confirm the "current theory" about the operation of such pumps. But at 35 feet, total frustration ensues. No matter how tight the seals, the water cannot be raised.

In computer programming today we do not yet know that "complexity has weight." Since it is not easily measured or described, like storage requirements or throughput, we often ignore the complexity of a planned program or subprogram. But when this complexity exceeds certain unknown limits, frustration ensues. Computer programs capsize under their own logical weight or become so crippled that maintenance is precarious and modification is impossible. Problems of storage and throughput can always be fixed, one way or another. But problems of complexity can seldom be adequately recognized, let alone fixed.

The syndrome of creating unsolvable problems of complexity because of anticipated problems of storage and throughput is well known. It is the work of amateurs. It arises in a misguided arrogance that "what happened to them won't happen to me!" But it keeps happening, over and over.

The Idea of Structured Programming

Closely related to many original ideas of E. Dijkstra [10] and using key results of C. Böhm and G. Jacopini [5], P. Naur [31], and R. Floyd [13], structured programming is based on new mathematical foundations for programming (in contrast to the use of programming to implement mathematical processes or to study foundations of mathematics). It identifies the programming process with a step-by-step expansion of mathematical functions into structures of logical connectives and subfunctions, carried out until the derived subfunctions can be directly realized in the programming language being used. The documentation of a program is identified with proof of the correctness of these expansions. Aspects of this approach are illustrated as well in work of Ashcroft and Manna [3], Hoare [17], and Wirth [39]. A major application to a programming system of considerable size is described by Baker [4].

Four mathematical results are central to this approach. One result, a "Structure Theorem" due in original form to Böhm and Jacopini, guarantees that any flowchartable program logic can be represented by expansions of as few as three types of structures, for example, (1) f THEN g, (2) IF p THEN f ELSE g, (3) WHILE p DO f, where f and g are flowcharts with one input and one output, p is a test, and THEN, IF, ELSE, WHILE, and DO are logical connectives. This is in sharp contrast to the usual programming practice of flowcharting arbitrary control logic with unrestricted control branching operations.

In block-structured programming languages, such as Algol or PL/I, such structured programs can be GO TO–free and can be read sequentially without mentally jumping from point to point. In a deeper sense the GO TO–free property is superficial. Structured programs should be characterized not simply by the absence of GO TO's, but by the presence of structure. Structured programs can be further organized into trees of program "segments," such that each segment is at most some prescribed size, for example, one page (some 50 lines) in length, and with entry only at the top and exit at the bottom of the segment. Segments refer to other segments at the next level in such trees, each by a single name, to represent a generalized data processing operation at that point, with no side effects in control. In this way the size and complexity of any programming system can be handled by a tree structure of segments, where each segment—whether high level or low level in the system hierarchy—is of precisely limited size and complexity.

The Structure Theorem has a constructive proof, which itself provides insight into program design and construction techniques. Although a flowchart may be of any size, the Structure Theorem guarantees that its control logic can be represented on a finite basis, with a corresponding reduction in the complexity characteristic of arbitrary flowcharts. The Structure Theorem also provides a canonical form for documenting and validating programs, to help define operational procedures in programming.

The second mathematical result is a "Top Down Corollary," which guarantees that structured programs can be written or read "top down," that is, in such a way that the correctness of each segment of a program depends only on segments already written or read and on the functional specifications of any additional segments referred to by name. The application of this corollary requires a radical change in the way most programmers think today, although advocates of "functional programming" have proposed such ideas independently (as Zurcher and Randell [40], Landin [22], Strachey [37], Burge [6], and Scott [35]). It is a nearly universal practice at the present time to write large programs "bottom up"—coding and unit testing program modules, then subsystems, and finally systems integration and testing. In top down programming, the integration code is written first, at the system, then subsystem levels, and the functional modules are written last. As discussed by Mills [29], top down programming can eliminate the necessity for the simultaneous interface assumptions that frequently result in system errors during integration.

The third mathematical result is a "Correctness Theorem," which shows how the problem of the correctness of structured programs can be reduced to function theoretic questions to which standard mathematical practices apply. These questions necessarily go into the context of intentions and operations available for writing programs. Ordinarily, they will require specific mathematical frameworks and procedures for their resolution. Indeed, for complex programs the mathematical question may be more comprehensive and detailed than is practical to resolve at some acceptable level of mathematical rigor. In any case the questions can be formulated on a systematic basis, and technical judgments can then be applied to determine the level of validation that is feasible and desirable for a given program.

In this connection we note that mathematics consists of a set of logical practices, with no inherent claim to absolute rigor or truth (for example, see Wilder [38, p. 196]). Mathematics is of human invention and subject to human fallibilities, in spite of the aura of supernatural verities often found in a schoolboy world. Even so, the reduction of the problem of program meanings to such mathematical practices permits the classification and treatment of ideas in terms of processes that have been subjected to considerable analysis and criticism by humankind.

The fourth mathematical result is an "Expansion Theorem," which defines the freedom available in expanding any functional specification into a structure at the next level. Perhaps the most surprising aspect of this result is how little freedom a programmer has in correctly expanding programs top down. For example, it will be clear in defining the structure "IF p THEN f ELSE g" that the choice of p automatically defines f and g—that the only freedom in such a structure is in its predicate. Even more surprising is the result that in the expansion "WHILE p DO f" no freedom exists at all in the selection of p—the looping predicate will be seen to be totally determined by the functional specification itself.

Our motivation in this final result is to exhibit programming as an analysis, rather than a synthesis, activity, that is, to identify the top down programming process as a sequence of decompositions and partitions of functional specifications and subspecifications, each of which produces simpler subspecifications to handle, until finally the level of programming language instructions or statements is reached. This is in contrast to programming as a synthesis of instructions or statements that "accomplish" the functional specifications. It is in this distinction that programming emerges as a readily perceived combinatorial activity.

The Correctness of Structured Programs

With structured programming, programmers are capable of high-precision programming, but, as in tic-tac-toe, it is important for their concentration to know their own capability for this high precision. The Correctness Theorem provides concepts and procedures for realizing this precision in programming. Correctness proofs are demonstrations of human devising for human consumption. There is no such thing as an absolute proof of logical correctness. There are only degrees of rigor, such as "technical English," "mathematical journal proof," "formal logic," and so on, each of which is an informal description of mechanisms for creating agreement and belief in a process of reasoning.

It is clear that a whole spectrum of rigor will be useful in correctness proofs. A casual program, used in an experimental investigation, may warrant no more than a few lines of explanation. A heavily used program —say, a text editor or a compiler—may warrant a much more formal proof. London has furnished several realistic examples of proof at a mathematics level [23, 24, 25], including the proof of an optimizing LISP compiler. Jones [20] has given an example of a proof in more formal terms. King [21] and Good [14] have developed more automatic machinery. Dijkstra [9] has illustrated less formal ideas that may be even more convincing in some programs. The persuasion of a proof depends not only on its formality, but on its brevity. Unfortunately, formality and brevity do not often cooperate, and the programmer has a difficult balancing problem in selecting the best compromise between formality and brevity.

Our approach is functional (or denotational, as used by Ashcroft [2]), rather than computational; instead of proving assertions about computational steps in a program (as introduced by Naur [32], Floyd [12], and others), we formulate assertions about functions whose values are computed by programs and subprograms. In this approach, the set theoretic definition of a function as a set of ordered pairs is of critical convenience. For example, an IF-THEN-ELSE subprogram corresponds to a partition of a corresponding function into two subsets of ordered pairs, which, as subfunctions, correspond to the THEN clause and ELSE clause of the original subprogram.

As noted, structured programs admit decompositions into subprograms of very simple types, such as THEN, IF-THEN-ELSE, and DO-WHILE subprograms. Our main interest is to show that each type leads to a characteristic logical assertion about the correctness of a subprogram. These assertions are eventually embodied in function theoretic questions, dealing with composition and partition of functions; for example, for some sets f, g, h, (not necessarily distinct), it is to be proved that

$$f = g * h \qquad \text{or} \qquad f = g \cup h.$$

These relations assert equalities between sets of ordered pairs. There are many acceptable ways in current mathematical practice to prove such assertions, such as an induction over some common structural feature of the sets involved. But such ways are outside our current interest in formulating the assertions themselves.

We recognize, with Floyd [12], that the question of program correctness is simply the question of program meaning, that is, knowing what a program does. Any program, including pure gibberish, exhibits some behavior, and it is correct with respect to that behavior, independent of what other capabilities may be envisioned for it. In this context it is crucial to distinguish between correctness and capability. A program under construction top down can be correct at every stage but not capable of its eventual requirements until completed. An error in a program is an unexpected action. A function theoretic description of the behavior of a program can thus be regarded as a pure description or a normative prescription, but the correctness problem comes down to the agreement between a functional description and a program behavior.

Functions

We adopt the common mathematical notion that a *function* is a set of ordered pairs (see Halmos [15]), say,

$$f = \{(x_1, y_1),\ (x_2, y_2), \ldots\}$$

such that if $(x, y) \in f$, $(u, v) \in f$, $x = u$, then $y = v$. The relation $(x, y) \in f$ is often written as

$$y = f(x),$$

and x is called the *argument*, and y is called the *value* of function f. The sets of first and second members of the ordered pairs of a function are called the *domain* and *range* of the function, respectively. In the example above,

$$\text{domain } (f) = \{x_1, x_2, \ldots\}$$

$$\text{range } (f) = \{y_1, y_2, \ldots\}$$

Note that these definitions for domain and range include *only* arguments and values of the function, and no other elements.

Since a function is a set, it makes sense to use the terms "empty function," "subfunction," "function partition," and so on, with the word, suffix or prefix "set" replaced by "function" whenever the conditions further required by a function can be guaranteed to hold. Instances that violate these conditions include the case of the power set (the set of subsets of a function is not itself a function, but is a set of functions), and the union of functions (the uniqueness of a value for a given argument may be lost in forming the union of two functions). However, the union of disjoint functions or intersection of two functions is again a function, as is the difference (set) of two functions.

Functions and Rules

In the description of a function f as a set of ordered pairs it is often convenient to give a *rule* for calculating the second member from the first, as in

$$f = \{(x, y) \mid y = x^2 + 3x + 2\}$$

or

$$(x, x^2 + 3x + 2) \in f$$

or even

$$f(x) = x^2 + 3x + 2,$$

where domain (f) is given in some broader context. A rule used in defining a function in this way is not unique. For example, if

$$x^2 + 3x + 2 = (x + 1)(x + 2),$$

then the new function and rule

$$g = \{(u, v) \mid v = (u + 1)(u + 2)\}$$

or

$$g(u) = (u + 1)\ (u + 2)$$

defines the same set as before, that is, $f = g$ (as sets).

If a function is finite, then its enumeration can serve in a rule. The rule is to find any given argument as a first member of an ordered pair, if possible, and to extract the second member, if found, as the value for that argument. Otherwise, if enumeration is impossible or impracticable, a rule must be expressed as an algorithm, possibly very complex but with unambiguous outcome for every argument.

In programming there is a direct correspondence to the relationship between functions and rules—it is between functional specifications and programs. The problem of program correctness then becomes the problem of showing that a given function is defined by a given rule. Perhaps the simplest form of the program correctness problem is defined by function rules of enumeration, or "table lookup." If a table lookup program has previously been proved to be correct, then any finite functional specification, entered as a table, can be verified to be correct by verifying the table entries therein.

Since functions are merely sets of ordered pairs, we regard the usual idea of a "partial function" to be a relationship between two sets, one of which is the domain of some function under consideration. In our case we use the term *partial rule* to mean a rule of computation not always defined over some given set.

Function Composition and Completion

Beyond operations directly inherited from sets, *function composition* is based on the fact that functions are sets of ordered pairs. A composition of two functions is a new function that represents the successive use of the values of one function as the arguments of the other. That is, we define the new function composition, using an infix notation:

$$f * g = \{(x, y) \mid \exists z\ (z = g(x) \wedge y = f(z))\}.$$

If range (g) and domain (f) are disjoint, then $f * g$ is the empty function; otherwise, $f * g$ is just the set of ordered pairs that is defined through the application of g then f to arguments of g to get values of f.

Conversely, we say that an ordered pair of functions, (f, g), is a *decomposition* of a function, h, if $h = f * g$. Clearly, for any function h, there may be many decompositions.

It is clear that function composition is associative, that is, that

$$(f * g) * h = f * (g * h)$$

for all functions f, g, and h; hence the parentheses can be omitted without ambiguity, as in

$$f * g * h.$$

Then the composition of a function with itself can also be denoted simply by an exponent notation:

$$f^2 = f * f$$

$$f^3 = f * f^2 = f^2 * f = f * f * f$$

$$f^4 = f * f^3 = f * f * f * f.$$

It will occasionally be convenient to permit a zero exponent and interpret f^0 as an identity function (see below).

Given a function, we consider its repeated composition with itself, reusing values as new arguments until, if ever, such values are not members of the domain of the function. The number of compositions then possible depends on the original argument, of course. Thus we define a *function completion,* say, for function f, to be

$$* f * = \{(x, y) \mid \exists k ((x, y) \in f^k) \wedge y \notin \text{domain}(f)\}.$$

Special Functions

We identify for future convenience, several general classes of functions, namely:

1. Identity functions:

$$I = \{f \mid (x, y) \in f \supset y = x\}$$

2. Constant functions:

$$C(a) = \{f \mid (x, y) \in f \supset y = a\}$$

3. Permutation functions:

$$P = \{f \mid \text{domain}(f) = \text{range}(f)\}$$

4. Inverse function pairs:

$$R = \{(f, g) \mid f * g = g * f \in I\}$$

(If $(f, g) \in R$, we say $g = f^{-1}$ or $f = g^{-1}$.)

Programs

We abstract the commonly known idea of a (computer) *program* as a finite set of functions, called *instructions,* each with a finite domain contained in a common set, called the *data space,* and a finite range contained in the Cartesian product of the data space and the program, called the *state space*. Members of the data space and state space are called data values and state values, respectively.

A program *execution* is a sequence of state values, say,

$$s_i = (d_i, f_i), i = 0, 1, \ldots$$

such that

$$s_{i+1} = f_i\ (d_i), i = 0, 1, \ldots$$

which terminates, if ever, when $f_i(d_i)$ fails to exist—that is, when $d_i \notin$ domain (f_i). The state value s_0 is called the *initial value* of the execution. If the execution is finite, say,

$$s = s_0, s_1, \ldots, s_n = t,$$

then t is called the *final value* of the execution.

Since the state space of a program is finite, it is decidable, for every initial value, s, whether that execution terminates and, if so, what the final value, t, is. Therefore a program automatically defines a function of ordered pairs (s, t) defined by terminating executions, called the *program function*. If a program is given by a set P, we denote its program function by $[P]$. In retrospect, a program is a specific (nonunique) rule for calculating the values of its program function.

A *subprogram* is a subset of a program, which inherits its state space. A *subprogram execution* is a contiguous subsequence of a program execution which terminates, if ever, when an instruction not in the subprogram appears in the state value. To each subprogram corresponds a *subprogram function* as well.

Control Graphs

The instructions (functions) of a program determine a directed *control graph* whose nodes are instructions and whose directed lines are the next possible instructions. A node of such a graph may have several *input lines* and several *output lines,* which denote the direction of control flow, as shown in Figure 13-1.

An instruction (node) has a natural decomposition between control and data effects that can be displayed by its partition (of its set of ordered pairs) into subsets, each of whose values contains identical (next) instruction components. The instruction node displayed in Figure 13-1 then has the form in Figure 13-2, where the diamond (control node) represents an identity function for values in the data space and a square (*process node*) represents a constant function for values in the program (next instruction). Since the program (set) is finite, this partition can be

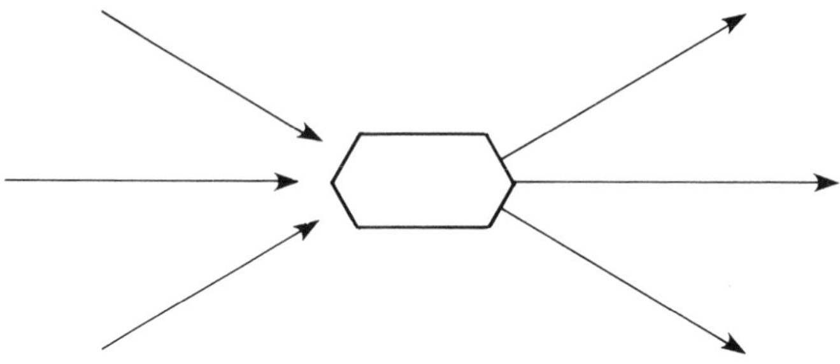

FIGURE 13-1

refined so that control nodes each contain exactly two output lines, called *predicate nodes*.

From these considerations we are led to directed graphs with predicate and process nodes of the form shown in Figure 13-3.

It will be convenient to introduce a symmetry into such directed graphs by augmenting the original program with "no-op" instructions (*collecting nodes*), which collect and transfer control from exactly two input lines each, which we diagram as shown in Figure 13-4. Control graphs are also called program schemas (see Ianov [19]).

Programs in Flowchart Form

We can represent a program in *flowchart* form. A flowchart is defined by a control graph and by operations and tests to be carried out on data in

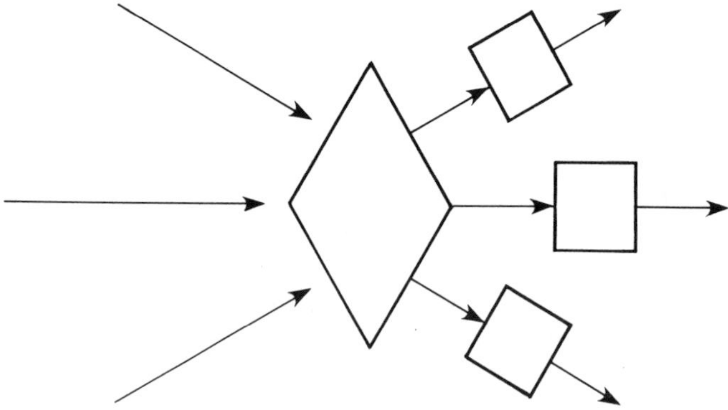

FIGURE 13-2

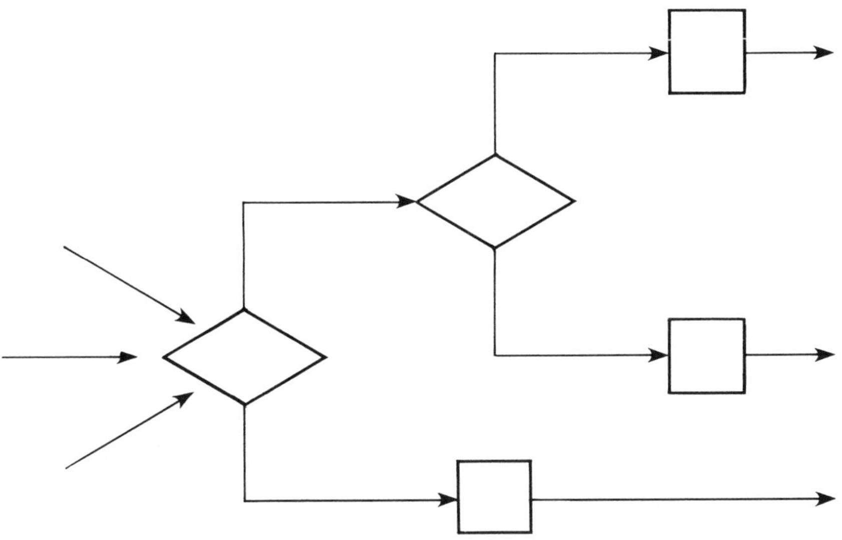

FIGURE 13-3

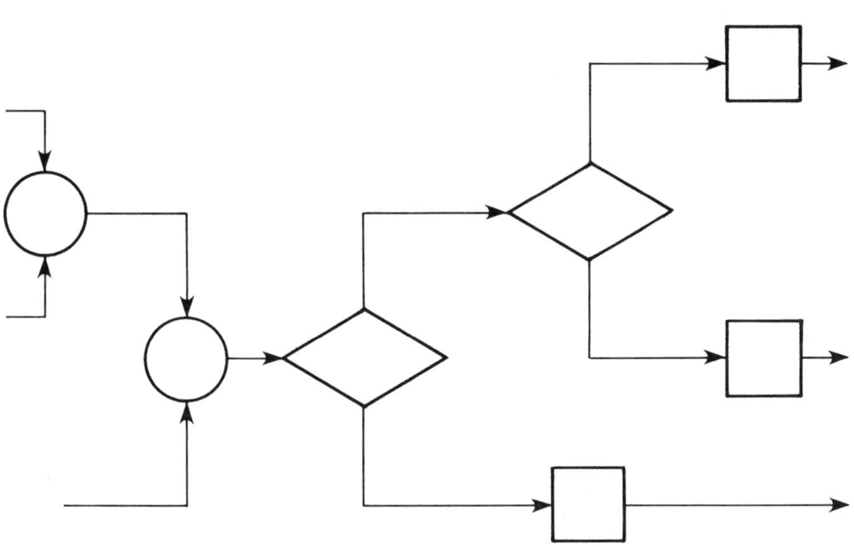

FIGURE 13-4

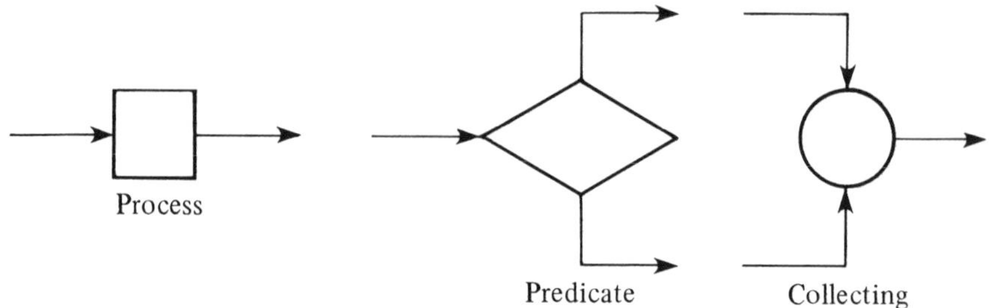

FIGURE 13-5

a sequence determined by that control graph. As noted, we consider control graphs with only three types of nodes (see Figure 13-5). The upper and lower lines out of a predicate node are labeled "True" and "False," respectively, just to be definite, unless otherwise noted.

In a flowchart each process node is associated with a function, or data transformation, and each predicate node is associated with a predicate function, or a binary-valued data test. Each line of a flowchart is associated with a set of possible data states. A set of data states may be the set of all possible machine states, for a program in a machine language, or may be the set of all variables allocated at a point in a program in a programming language. The function associated with a process node maps a set of data states associated with its input line into a set of data states associated with its output line. A function f from X to Y is identified in a flowchart as

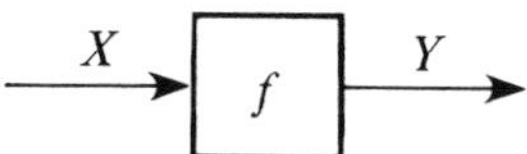

This mapping is a subfunction, say, g, of f, namely:

$$g = \{(x, y) \mid x \in X \land (x, y) \in f \land y \in Y\}.$$

If $x \notin X$, no such input is possible; if $y \notin Y$, no such output is possible; if $x \in X$ but $(x, y) \notin f$ or $y \notin Y$, the operation is not completed.

The predicate function associated with a predicate node maps the set of data states associated with its input line into the set {True, False}

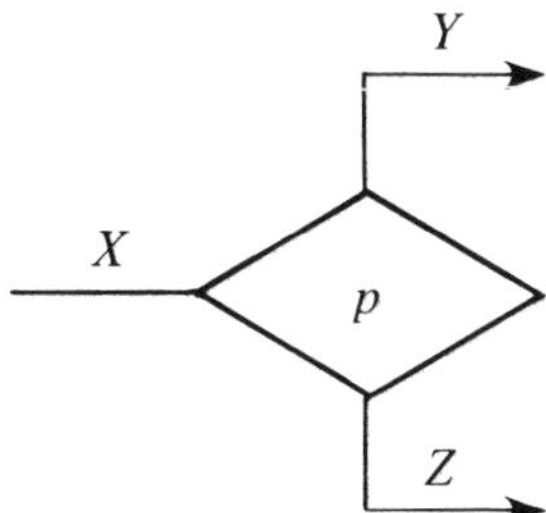

but does not transform data otherwise; that is, the flowchart figure is associated with the identity mappings of data from input to output. But in order to complete the test satisfactorily, the condition

$$x \in X \wedge (((x, \text{True}) \in p \wedge x \in Y) \vee ((x, \text{False}) \in p \wedge x \in Z))$$

must be satisfied.

The collecting node is also associated with an identity mapping, from the flowchart figure.

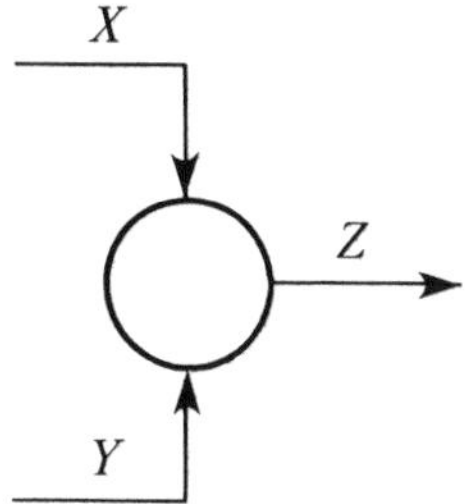

Also, to complete the transfer of control, the condition

$$(x \in X \wedge x \in Z) \vee (y \in Y \wedge y \in Z)$$

must be satisfied. In early practice and in current programming theory the sets associated with control lines are often taken to be identical—a "state vector" set. However, with data scoping and dynamic storage allocation, as found in contemporary practice, the data space is variable, rather than constant, over a program or flowchart.

Program Execution

The execution of a program is easily visualized in a flowchart, using the control graph to identify the sequence of operations and tests on data required. For example, consider the program f in flowchart form as shown in Figure 13-6.

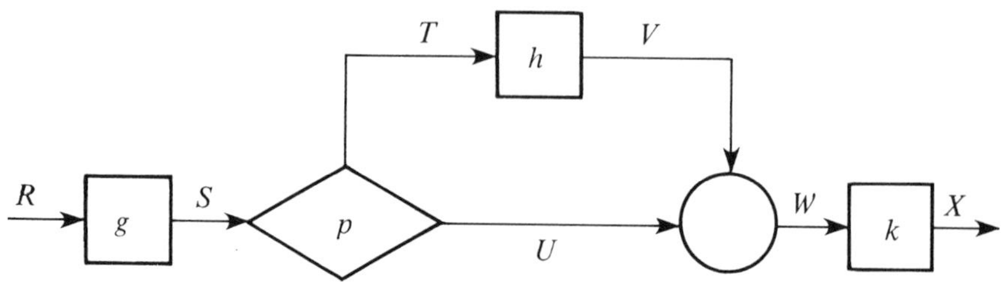

FIGURE 13-6

Where possible, *initial data* $r \in R$ is converted by f into *intermediate data* $s \in S$, then $t \in T$ and $v \in V$, or $u \in U$, then $w \in W$, and ultimately into *final data* $x \in X$, by functions g, h, and k, under the control of predicate p. That is, the program function $[f]$ of program f has values, when they exist, given by

$$x = k(h(g(r))) \quad \text{if} \quad p(g(r)) = \text{True}$$

$$x = k(g(r)) \quad \text{if} \quad p(g(r)) = \text{False}.$$

More precisely, we mean

$$[f] = \{(r, x) \mid r \in R \wedge (\exists\, s, v\ ((r, s) \in g \wedge (s, \text{True}) \in p \wedge (s, v) \in h \wedge (v, x) \in k)) \vee (\exists\, s\ ((r, s) \in g \wedge (s, \text{False}) \in p \wedge (s, x) \in k)) \wedge x \in X\}.$$

Proper Programs

We define a *proper program* to be a program in which:

1. there is precisely one input line and one output line, and
2. for every node, there exists a path from the input line through that node to the output line.

Note that we admit the possibility of programs with no nodes and a single input/output line. We call such a program λ. Clearly, the program function [λ] is an identity function; [λ] ∈ *I*. In illustration, the flowcharts in Figure 13-7 are not proper programs.

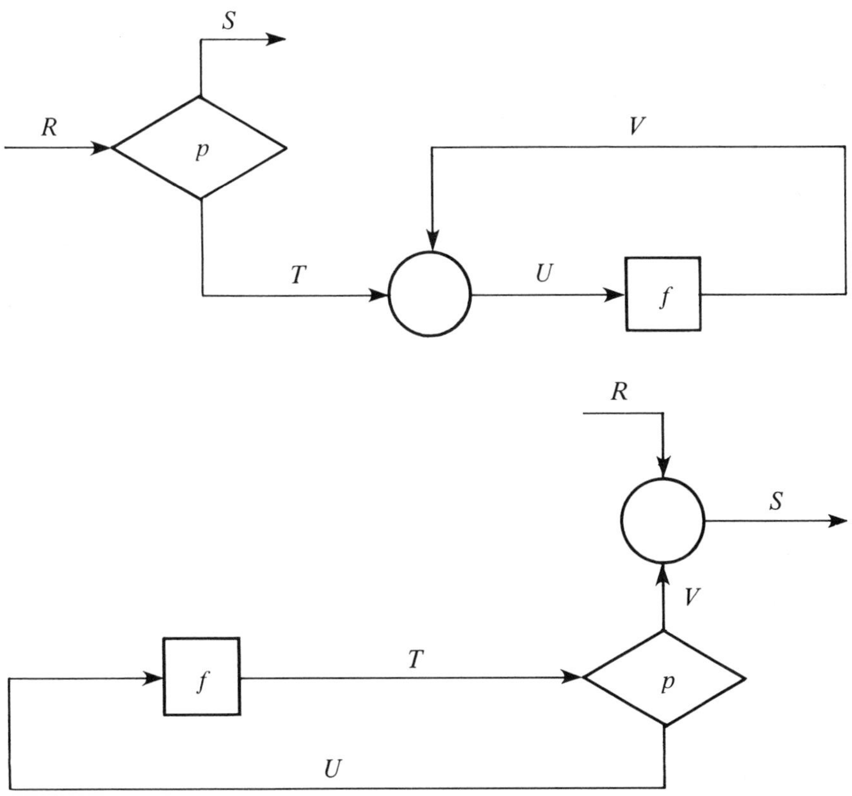

FIGURE 13-7

This definition of proper programs is primarily motivated by the interchangeability of proper programs and process nodes in larger programs.

Henceforth, we take "proper program" and "program" to be synonymous. If necessary, we will use the term "improper program" to refer to a program that is not a proper program.

Program Equivalence

We will say that two proper programs are *equivalent* when they define the same program function, whether or not they have identical control graphs, require the same number of operations, and so on. For example, the two programs

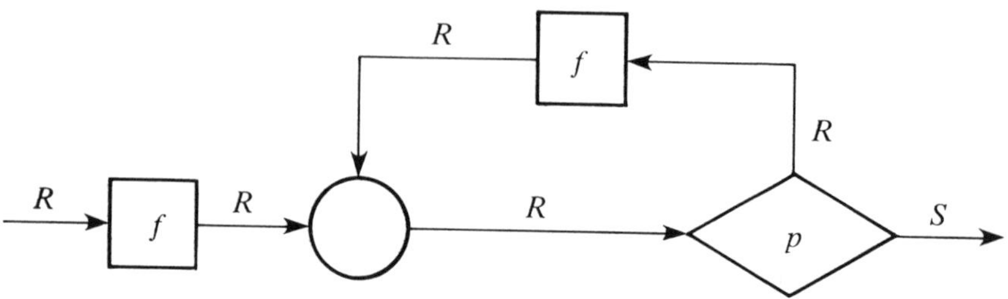

and

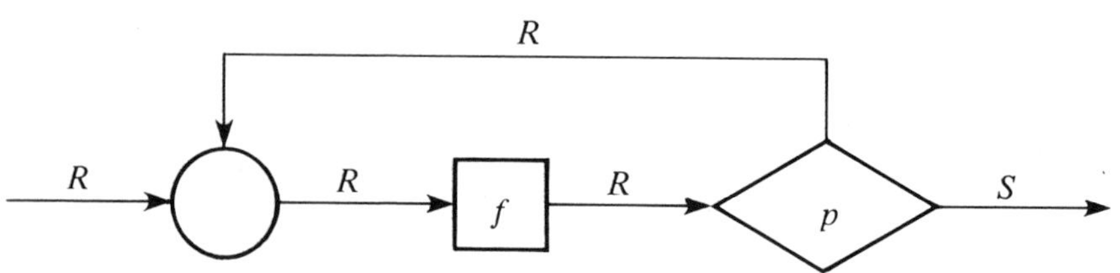

have the same program function, as do the two programs in Figure 13-8. That is, two programs are equivalent if they define the same program function, even though the programs may represent different rules for computing the values of the program function. In particular, given program f and its program function $[f]$, the new program g

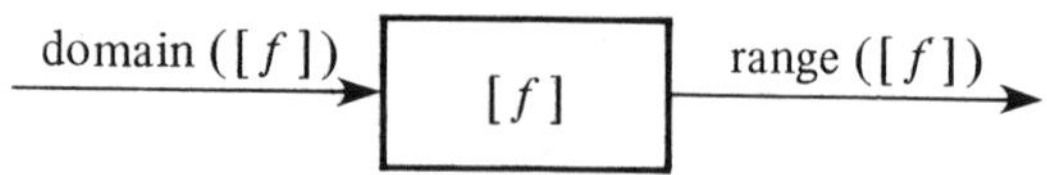

is equivalent to f. In this case, g is a table lookup version of f.

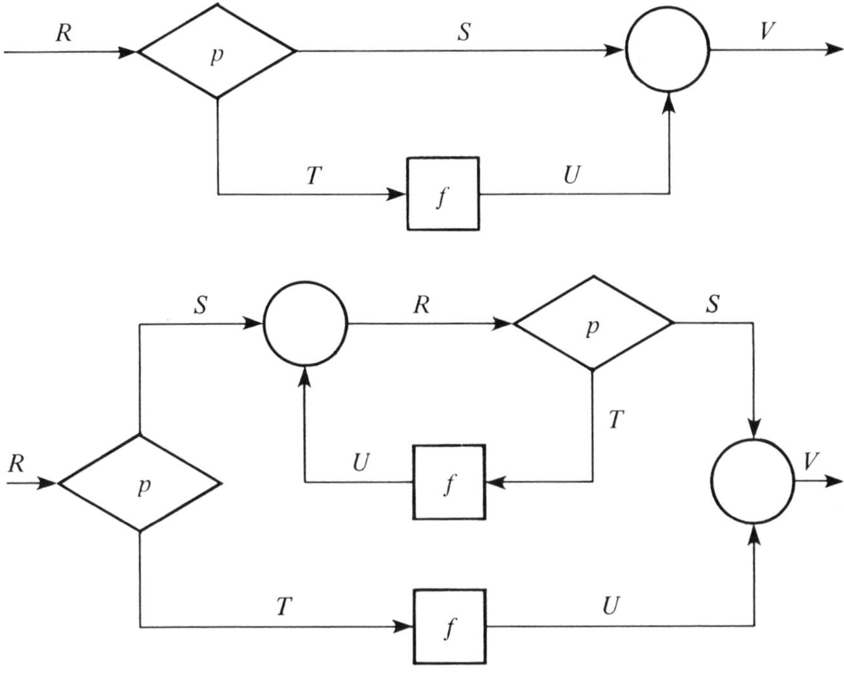

FIGURE 13-8

Program Expansions

If a program contains a process node, as

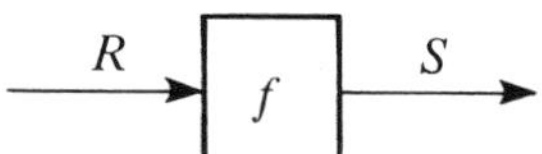

it may happen, that a rule for computing the values of f is defined as another program. We call such a program an *expansion* of the function f, such as is shown in Figure 13-9.

In this case it is asserted that the program function of the latter program is f. That is, any expansion of a function is simply a rule for computing its values, possibly using other functions and predicates to do so.

Programs with loops may or may not terminate. This property of

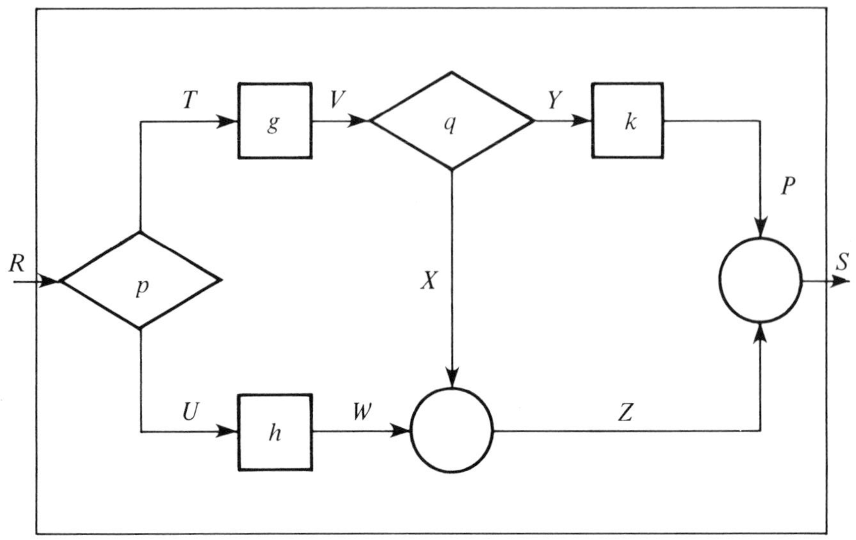

FIGURE 13-9

termination partitions an input set R into R_t and $R - R_t$, where R_t is the subset of inputs for which the evaluations terminate. If $R_t \neq R$, then the program defines a partial rule rather than a rule. Note that in fact a program may terminate by reaching an output line (*normal termination*) or by reaching a node with a data value not in the domain of the corresponding function (*abnormal operation termination*) or by reaching a line with a data value not in the data space (*abnormal storage termination*).

Control Graph Labels

The set of all control graphs of proper programs can be enumerated and labeled. The beginning of such an enumeration is given in Figure 13-10.

In fact, a few such control graphs are given special mnemonic labels in various programming languages. For example, the following labels in Figure 13-11 are common. (IF-THEN is 9, in the enumeration started above, IF-THEN-ELSE might be 37, 42, and so on.)

However, there is nothing special about these graphs except for their simplicity. Any control graph possibly more complicated than these

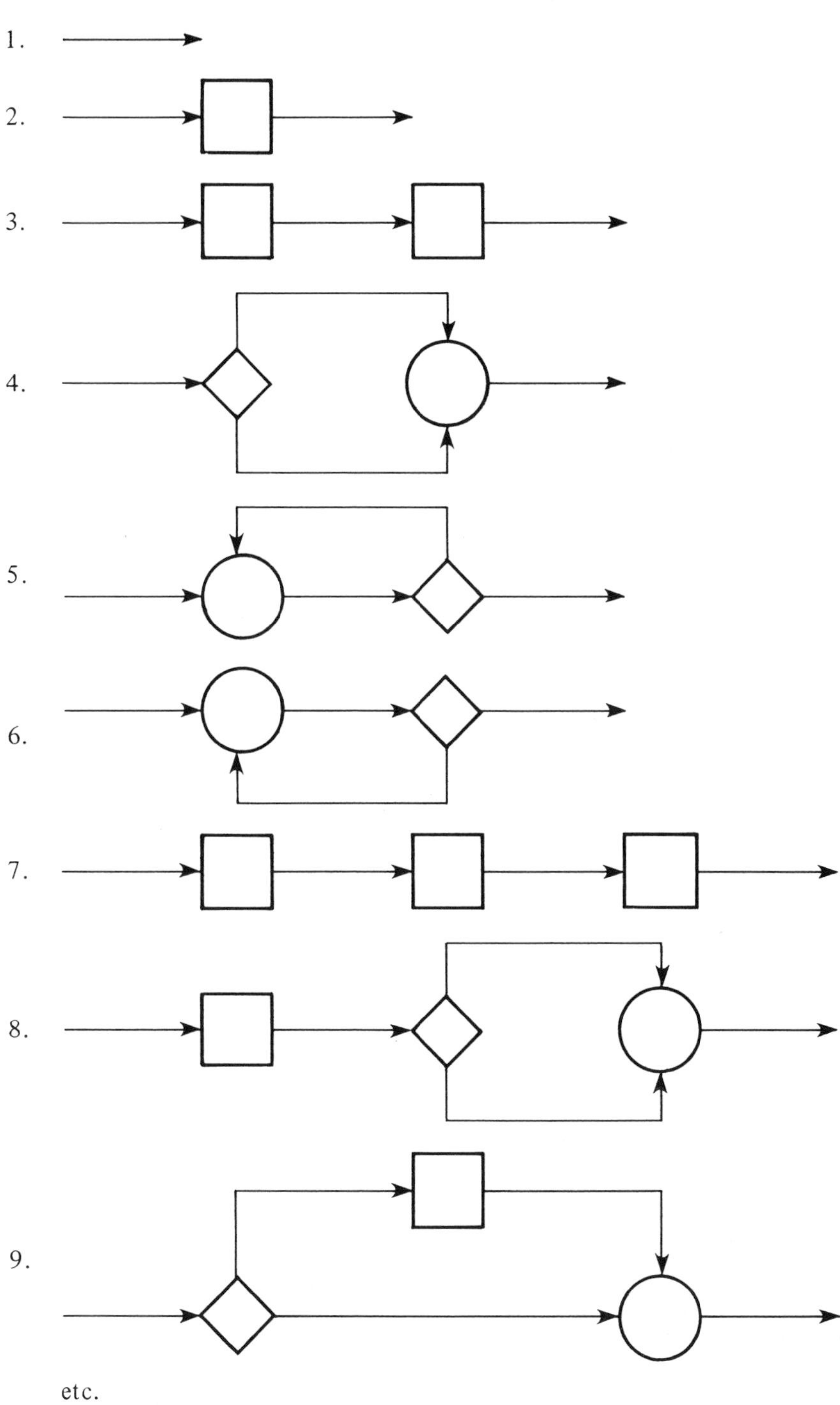

FIGURE 13-10. *Control Graphs*

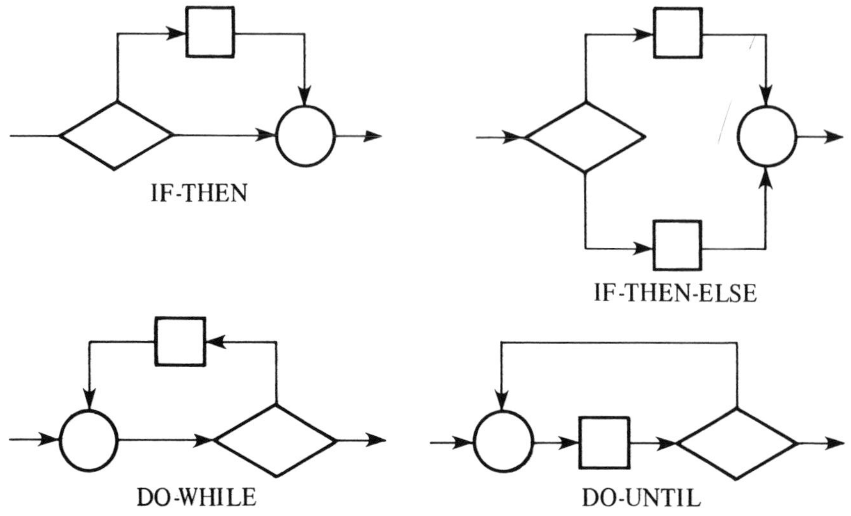

FIGURE 13-11

might be so labeled if it were useful. In particular, we label the sequence of two process nodes

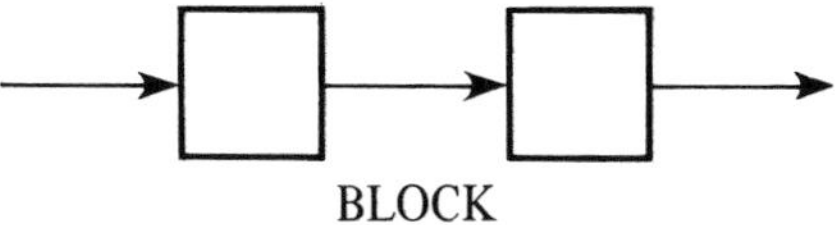

for future reference.

Program Formulas

A program can be given as a *formula,* by associating an ordering with the set of process nodes, predicate nodes, and control lines of its control graph and by listing the label of its control graph, followed by labels for the functions, predicates, and state sets of the program. For notational convenience we will use parentheses and commas to denote the list structure of a program formula; for example,

$$(A, p, q, f, g, h, R, S, T, U)$$

means a program given by a control graph labeled A, with predicates p and q, functions f, g, and h, and state sets R, S, T, and U, associated with the nodes and lines of A. For example,

$$(\text{BLOCK } f, g, R, S, T)$$

defines a program

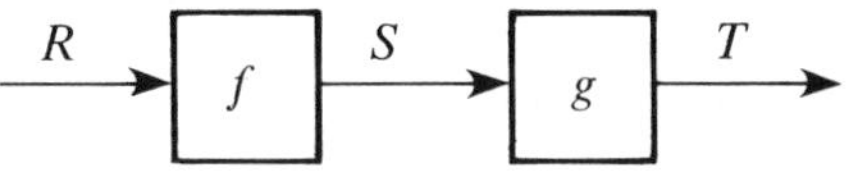

whose action on an input $r \in R$ is to produce output $t \in T$ if it exists, such that

$$t = g(f(r))$$

or, more precisely,

$$[(\text{BLOCK}, f, g, R, S, T)] = \{(r, t) \mid \exists\, s\, (r \in R \wedge s \in S \wedge t \in T \wedge (r, s) \in f \wedge (s, t) \in g)\}.$$

The list

$$(\text{IF-THEN-ELSE}, p, f, g, R, S, T, U, V, W)$$

defines a program

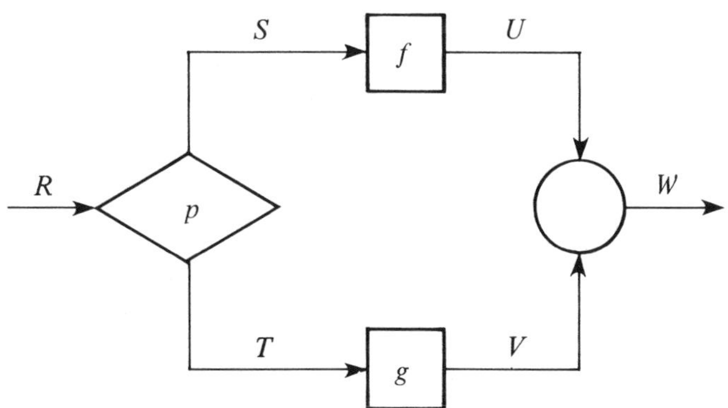

which maps any $r \in R$ into some $w \in W$, if it exists, such that

$$w = \begin{cases} f(r) \text{ if } p(r) = \text{True} \\ g(r) \text{ if } p(r) = \text{False}. \end{cases}$$

More precisely,

$$[(\text{IF-THEN-ELSE}, p, f, g, R, S, T, U, V, W)]$$

$$= \{(r, w) \mid r \in R \wedge w \in W \wedge (((r, \text{True}) \in p \wedge r \in S \wedge (r, w) \in f \wedge w \in U) \vee ((r, \text{False}) \in p \wedge r \in T \wedge (r, w) \in g \wedge w \in V))\}.$$

In much of what follows, the list of data sets is not central to the ideas under development. In this case they will be suppressed. However, such data sets are always implicit to program descriptions and discussions.

Since function composition is associative, that is,

$$(f * g) * h = f * (g * h),$$

then so is BLOCK formation, that is,

$$[(\text{BLOCK}, [(\text{BLOCK}, f, g)], h)] = [(\text{BLOCK}, f, [(\text{BLOCK}, g, h)])],$$

and no ambiguity results by extending the meaning of BLOCK to several nodes, for example

$$(\text{BLOCK3}, f, g, h) = (\text{BLOCK}, (\text{BLOCK}, f, g), h),$$

and so on. In particular, we permit zero or one nodes in a BLOCK as in Figure 13-12. Then, for example, we have the identity

$$f = [(\text{BLOCK1}, f, \text{domain}(f), \text{range}(f))].$$

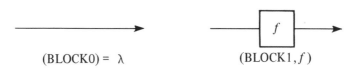

(BLOCK0) = λ

(BLOCK1, f)

FIGURE 13-12

It may happen that a function listed in a program formula is itself a program function given by another formula, such as

$$(\text{IF-THEN}, p, [(BLOCK, g, h)]).$$

We extend the idea of program formula to permit the replacement of a program function by its program formula, such as

$$(\text{IF-THEN}, p, (\text{BLOCK}, g, h)).$$

It is clear that while these are different programs they have identical program functions, just by the definition of program functions.

Program Descriptions

Flowcharts and formulas are simply two alternative ways of describing (possibly partial) rules, with some internal structure, in terms of other rules (or partial rules). Still another method of description is in programming language text such as

```
IF p THEN
   f
ELSE
   g
ENDIF
```

and

```
WHILE p DO
   f
ENDDO
```

and

```
BLOCK
   f
   g
ENDBLOCK
```

and so on. We find all three types of description useful in various circumstances in programming. Typically, flowcharts are useful in general discussions because of their graphics, formulas are useful in stating and proving theoretical properties of such rules, and the text is useful in the actual construction of large complex programs. For example, the same program is given in the formula

$$(\text{IF-THEN-ELSE}, p, (\text{DO-WHILE}, q, f), (\text{BLOCK}, g, h)),$$

in the flowchart

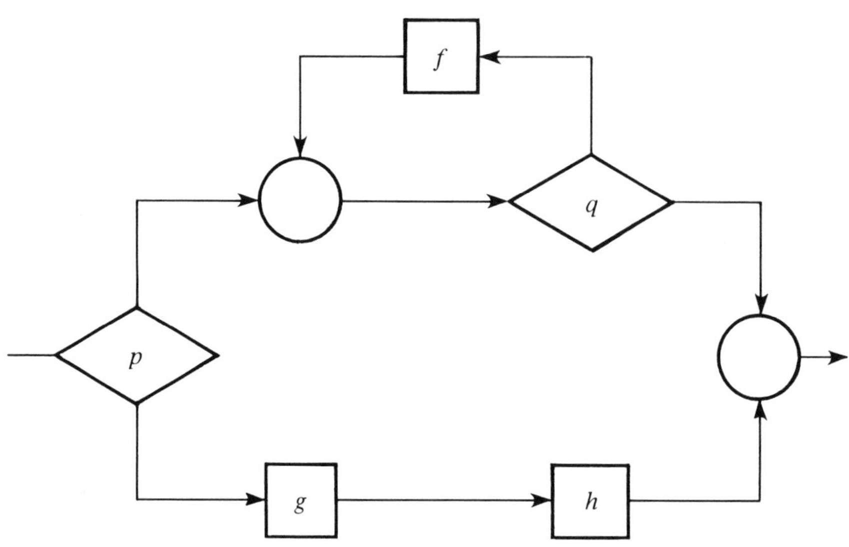

or in program text

```
IF p THEN
      WHILE q DO
          f
      END DO
ELSE
      BLOCK
          g
          h
      END BLOCK
END IF
```

Structured Programs

As flowcharts increase in size, we can often identify patterns that give more coherence and understandability to a whole flowchart. For example, the control graph in Figure 13-13 has three definite nested substructures,

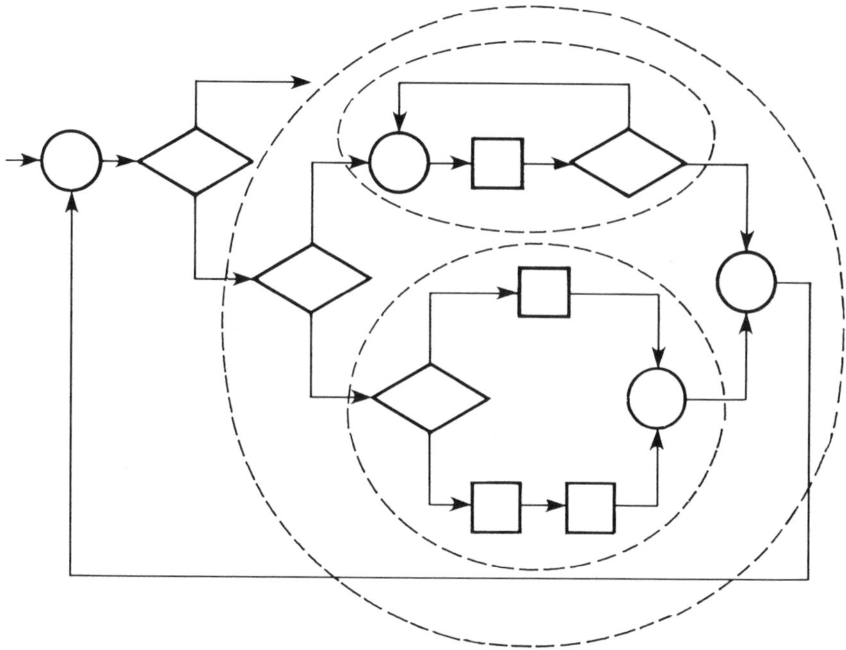

FIGURE 13-13

which are control graphs for proper programs, that make the whole more easily considered. But the control graph in Figure 13-14 admits no such structuring. By simply continuing this last pattern indefinitely it is easy to see that indecomposable control graphs of any size exist.

Having noted that programs of arbitrary size may be indecomposable, we next add the possibility of operations and tests on data outside the original data sets of a program. The additional operations and tests correspond to "flag" setting and testing. But we can couch these operations in the concept of a push down stack to show their economy. In addition to the functions and predicates original to a given program we introduce three new functions and one predicate.

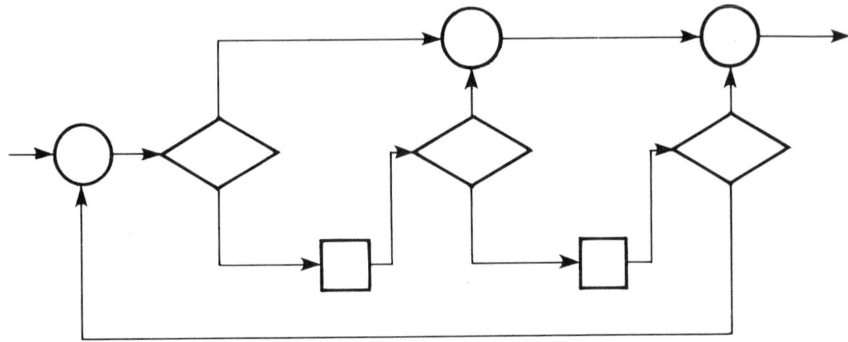

FIGURE 13-14

More specifically, we define process nodes with functions named TRUE, FALSE, and POP, and a predicate node with function named TOP, which add truth values True and False, remove, and test such truth values in an input data set, respectively. That is, for any data set Y, and $y \in Y$ and $z \in$ {True, False},

$$\text{TRUE}(y) = (y, \text{True})$$

$$\text{FALSE}(y) = (y, \text{False})$$

$$\text{POP}(y, z) = y$$

$$\text{TOP}(y, z) = z$$

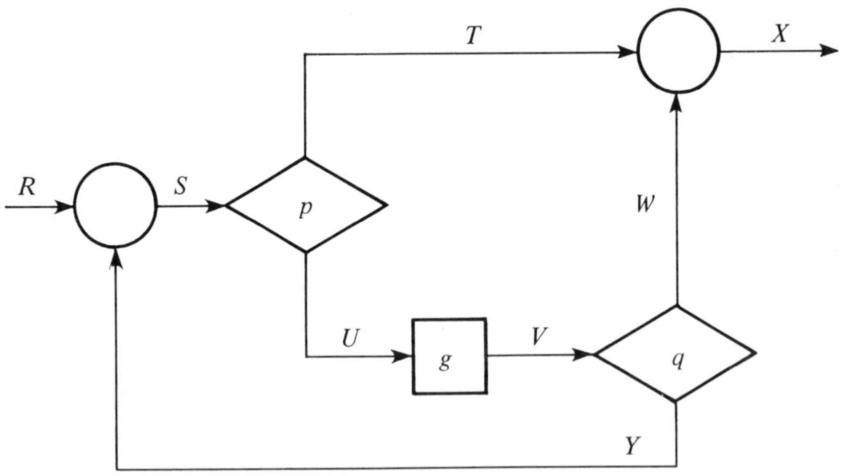

FIGURE 13-15

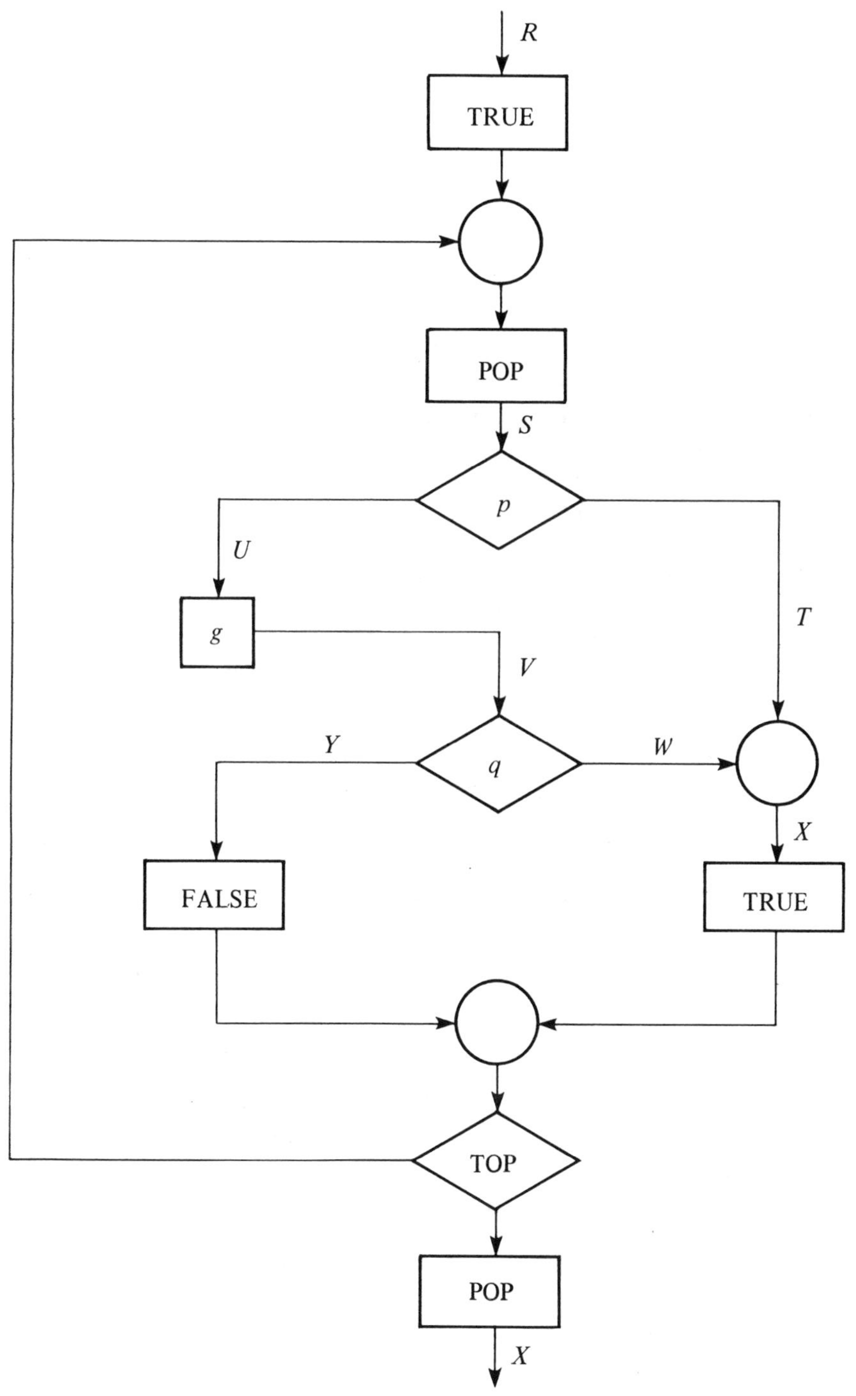

FIGURE 13-16

These new functions and predicate allow us to construct explicit control logic in the form of flags. For example, a program whose control structure is in the indecomposable pattern above is shown in Figure 13-15. This program is equivalent to the new program, where the output line X and return line Y are tagged, and the tag is later tested.

Only the original data sets have been shown in Figure 13-16; the remaining ones can be inferred from the definitions above. Close inspection will reveal that the net effect of TRUE, FALSE, POP, and TOP is to present just the correct original data set to each of the original functions and predicates of the program. It may not be obvious that this equivalent program is of any value in this case. It seems rather more complex—except that there is now a substructure, a proper program, which contains all the original functions and predicates and, furthermore, has no loop in it. This particular application previews a fundamental construction in the proof of the main Structure Theorem below. As a result, this new program can now be decomposed into two sections, of the forms shown in Figure 13-17, where process node f is given by Figure 13-18.

Before proving this Theorem we introduce a simple lemma, which counts the control lines of a proper program in terms of its function and predicate nodes.

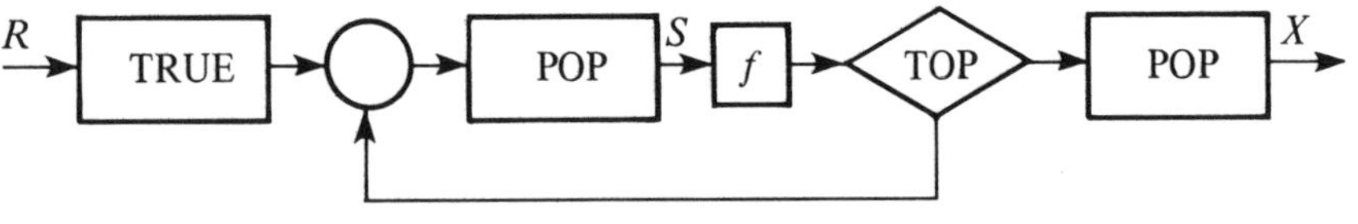

FIGURE 13-17

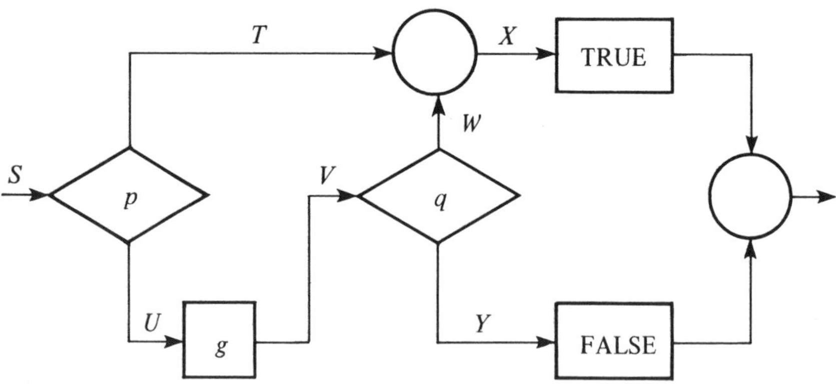

FIGURE 13-18

The Number of Control Lines in a Proper Program

Lemma: If the number of function, predicate, and collecting nodes is ϕ, π, and γ, respectively, and the number of control lines (that is, edges) is e, in a proper program, then

$$\pi = \gamma$$

and

$$e = 1 + \phi + 3\pi .$$

Proof: In order to prove this lemma, count the "heads and tails" of the control lines, adjacent to all the nodes, and at the input and output of the program, to get Table 13-1.

TABLE 13-1

Control Line	*Input*	*Function Node*	*Predicate Node*	*Collecting Node*	*Output*	*Total*
Heads		ϕ	π	2γ	1	$\phi + \pi + 2\gamma + 1$
Tails	1	ϕ	2π	γ		$\phi + 2\pi + \gamma + 1$

Since the total number of heads must equal the total number of tails and each must equal e,

$$\phi + \pi + 2\gamma + 1 = e = \phi + 2\pi + \gamma + 1,$$

and the equations of the lemma follow.

Structure Theorem

Theorem: Any proper program is equivalent to a program whose formula contains at most the graph labels BLOCK, IF-THEN-ELSE, and DO-UNTIL, and additional functions TRUE, FALSE, and POP, and predicate function TOP.

*Proof:** We prove the theorem by induction on the number of lines of a proper program. The induction step is constructive and identifies, for any proper program of more than one node, an equivalent proper program that is a formula in at most graph labels BLOCK, IF-THEN-ELSE,

---

* Thanks go to J. Misra for suggestions and assistance in developing the following proof. Thanks are also due to S. Cole for discussions about the theorem and methods for its proof.

and DO-UNTIL and new proper programs, each with fewer lines than the initial program.

In order to carry out the induction, we first define a structuring process, S, on any proper program, f, whose result we denote by $S(f)$, as follows. For convenience, we abbreviate the graph labels BLOCK, IF-THEN-ELSE, DO-UNTIL to BLK, IF, DO, respectively, in the remainder of the proof.

Since f is a proper program, it has exactly one input and one output. We identify several cases that are possible.

Case 1: No Nodes. If f has no nodes, we define

$$S(f) = \lambda.$$

Case 2: One or More Nodes. If f has at least one node, we examine the unique node reached by the input line. There are three possible cases:

Case 2a: Predicate Node. If the first node is a predicate node, then f is of the form in Figure 13-19. Since f is a proper program, the line z can

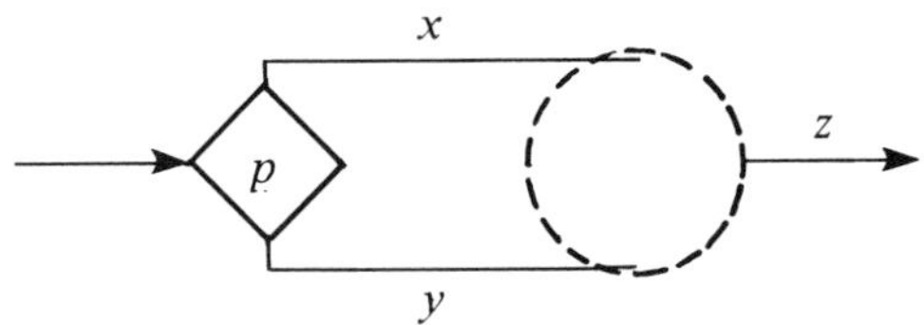

FIGURE 13-19

be reached from both x and y,* and we construct two *constituent* programs that consist of all nodes accessible in f from x and y, respectively, calling them g and h, respectively.

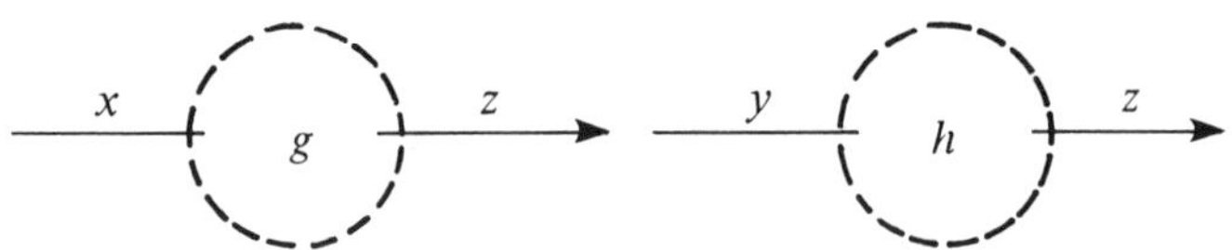

FIGURE 13-20

* Our definition of proper programs is necessary for this assertion. The proof of Böhm and Jacopini [5] breaks down at this point.

The constituents may contain identical nodes from f, so that g and h represent duplications of parts of f. If a collecting node in g or h is reached by only one input line (the other line in f being in the other constituent), we suppress that collecting node, that is,

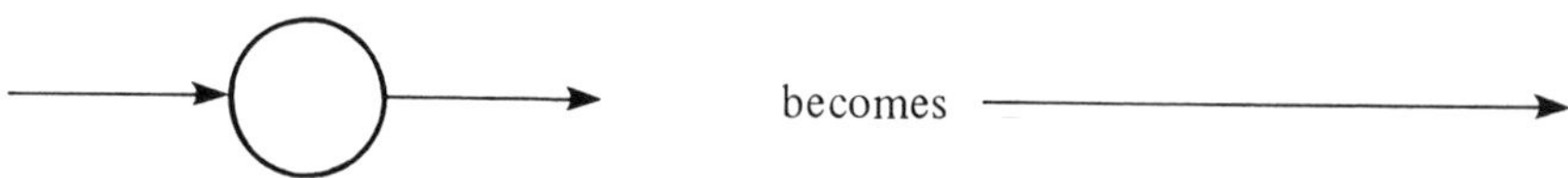

Note that g and h are proper programs; otherwise, f is not a proper program. Note also that g and/or h may be λ, a program with no nodes.

Since each of g and h contains at least one less predicate node than does f, at least one collecting node is suppressed in each constituent. Next we consider the new proper program, (IF, p, g, h), as shown in Figure 13-21, with the original predicate p and the constituents g and h of f (and a new collecting node, not from g or h). In this case we define

$$S(f) = (\text{IF}, p, g, h).$$

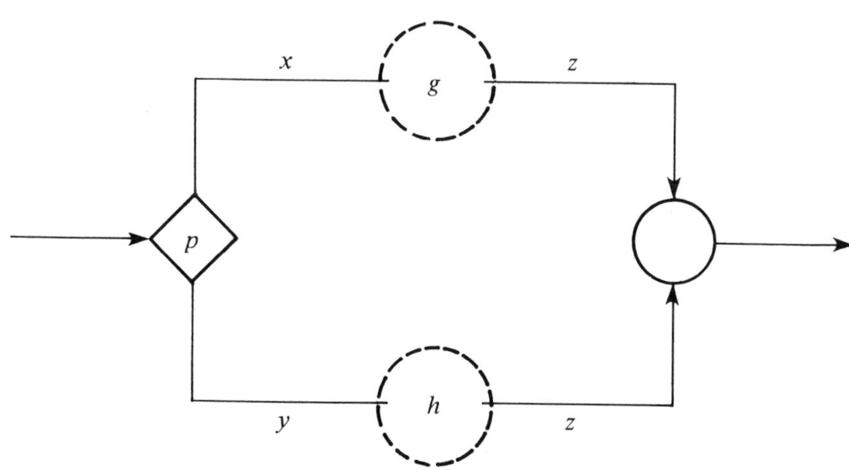

FIGURE 13-21

Also, in this case we observe that

$$e(g) \leq \phi(f) + 3(\pi(f) - 1) + 1 = e(f) - 3$$
$$e(h) \leq \phi(f) + 3(\pi(f) - 1) + 1 = e(f) - 3,$$

since g and h at least do not contain predicate note f. (We use $e(f)$, $\phi(f)$, and $\pi(f)$ to denote the number of lines, function nodes, and predicate nodes, respectively, in f.)

Finally, it is clear by construction that $S(f)$ is equivalent to f.

Case 2b: Function Node. If the first node is a function node, then f is of the form shown in Figure 13-22, and h is a proper program, possible λ. In this case we define

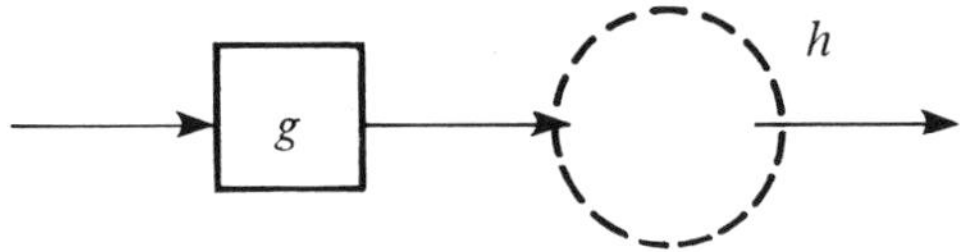

FIGURE 13-22

$$S(f) = (\text{BLK}, g, h).$$

Also, in this case it is easy to count the number of lines in h, given that there are $e(f)$ lines in f. The number is

$$e(h) = (\phi(f) - 1) + 3\pi(f) + 1 = e(f) - 1.$$

Finally, it is clear by construction that $S(f)$ is equivalent to f.

Case 2c: Collecting Node. If the first node is a collecting node, then f must be of the form shown in Figure 13-23, and we examine the next unique node reached from this collecting node. It is clear that such a next node exists, because a predicate node, at least, must be reached in the

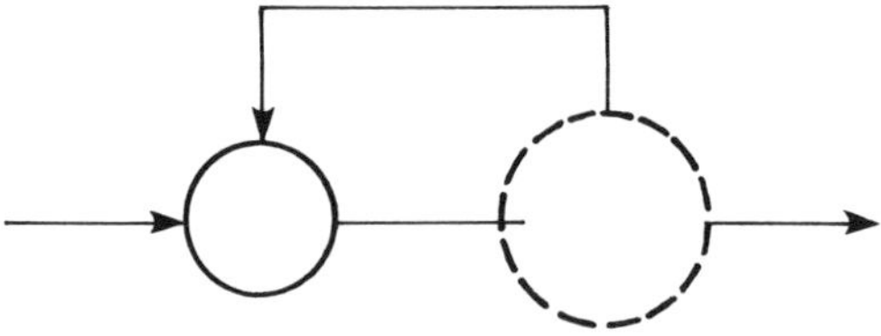

FIGURE 13-23

remaining improper program in order to have two output lines. There are three subcases to be examined.

2.c.(1). Predicate Node. If the next node is a predicate node, then f is of the form shown in Figure 13-24.

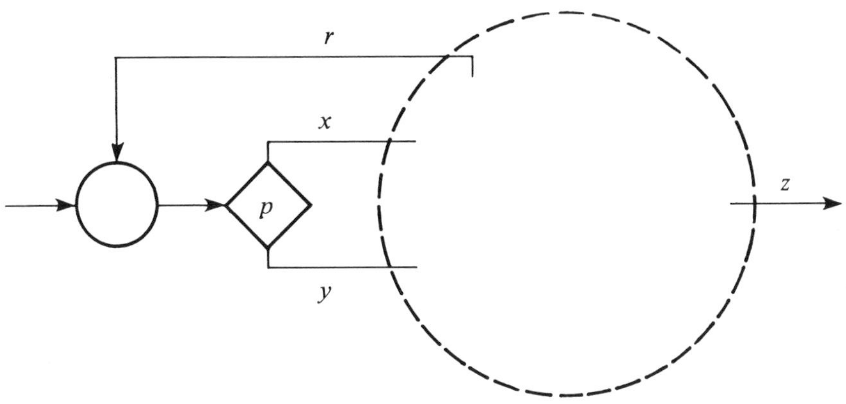

FIGURE 13-24

As before, we construct two programs that consist of all nodes that can be reached from x and y, which terminate in z or r. We suppress collecting nodes with only one input, as before. These programs will not be proper programs if both r and z can be reached from x or y. However, since f is a proper program, we know that each constructed program must reach at least z or r and that each z and r must be reached by at least one constructed program. These constructed programs have the form shown in Figure 13-25, where the solid output line is necessary and the dotted output line may or may not exist. We use TRUE and FALSE function nodes (to set flags) and possibly collecting nodes to construct new proper pro-

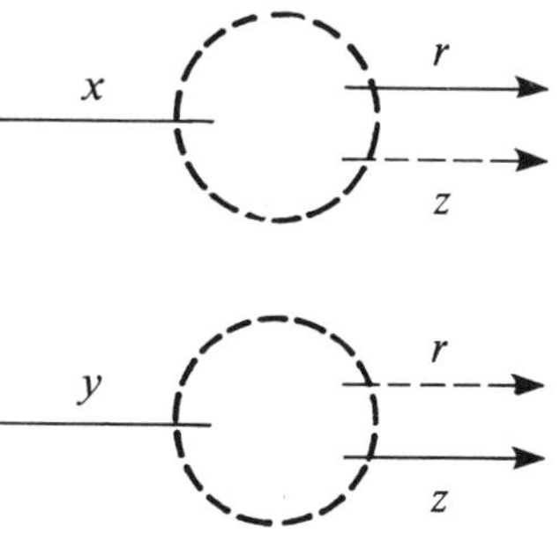

FIGURE 13-25

grams from these shown, of the form in Figure 13-26, the forms in Figure 13-27, or the form in Figure 13-28, depending on whether or not the dotted output lines r and z exist.

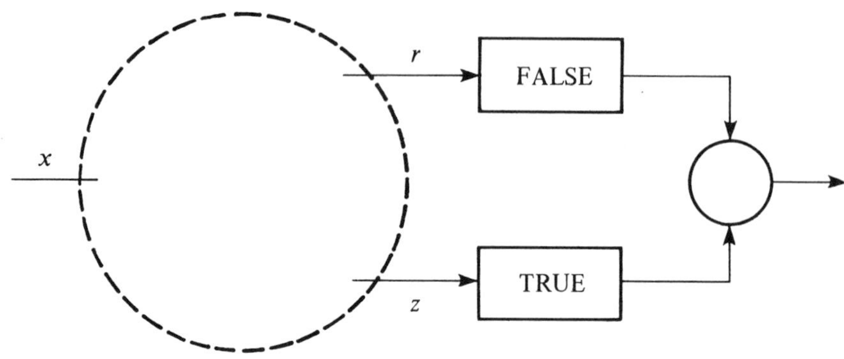

FIGURE 13-26

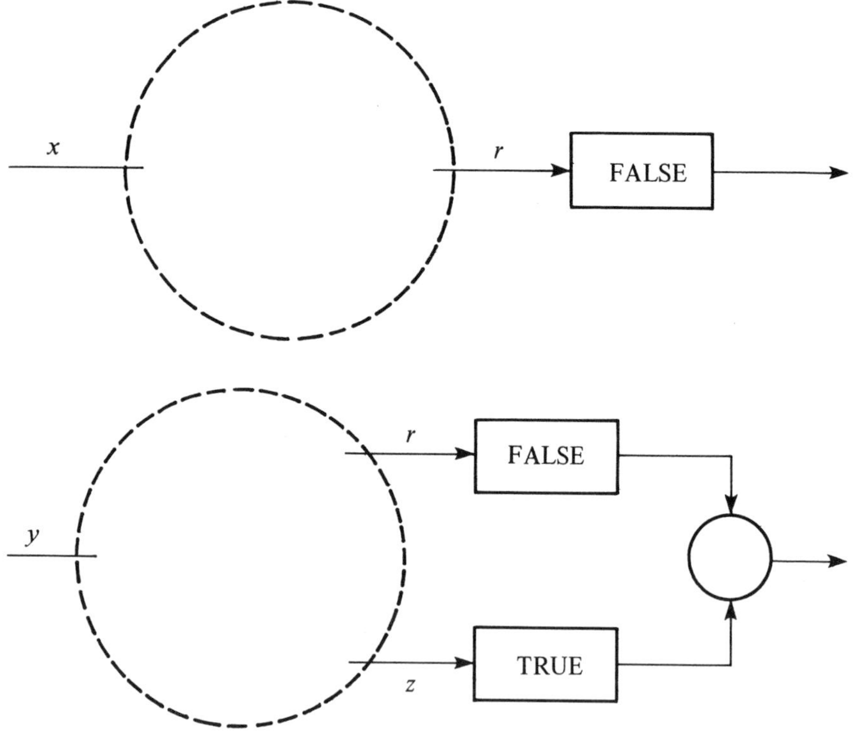

FIGURE 13-27

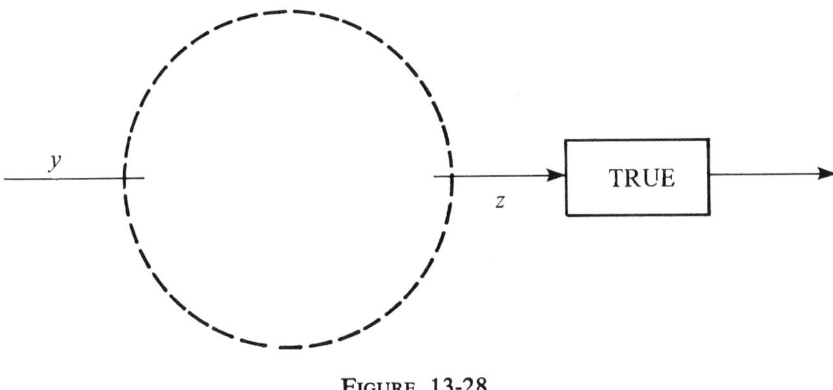

FIGURE 13-28

We label these proper programs g and h (such that g has at least the r output line and h has at least the z output line). Now we consider the new program shown in Figure 13-29, with g and h as constituent programs. In this case we define

$$S(f) = (\text{BLK}, \text{TRUE}, (\text{BLK}, (\text{DO}, \text{TOP}, (\text{BLK}, \text{POP}, (\text{IF}, p, g, h))), \text{POP})).$$

We observe that g and h do not have the predicate node p, and each has at most two more function nodes. Hence,

$$e(g) \leq \phi(f) + 2 + 3(\pi(f) - 1) + 1 = e(f) - 1$$
$$e(h) \leq \phi(f) + 2 + 3(\pi(f) - 1) + 1 = e(f) - 1$$

Finally, it can be verified that $S(f)$ is equivalent to f.

2.c.(2). Function Node. If the next node is a function node, then f is of the form shown in Figure 13-30, and we consider the new program shown in Figure 13-31, with new program labeled h. In this case we define

$$S(f) = (\text{BLK}, g, h).$$

Also, in this case we observe directly that

$$e(h) = e(f)$$

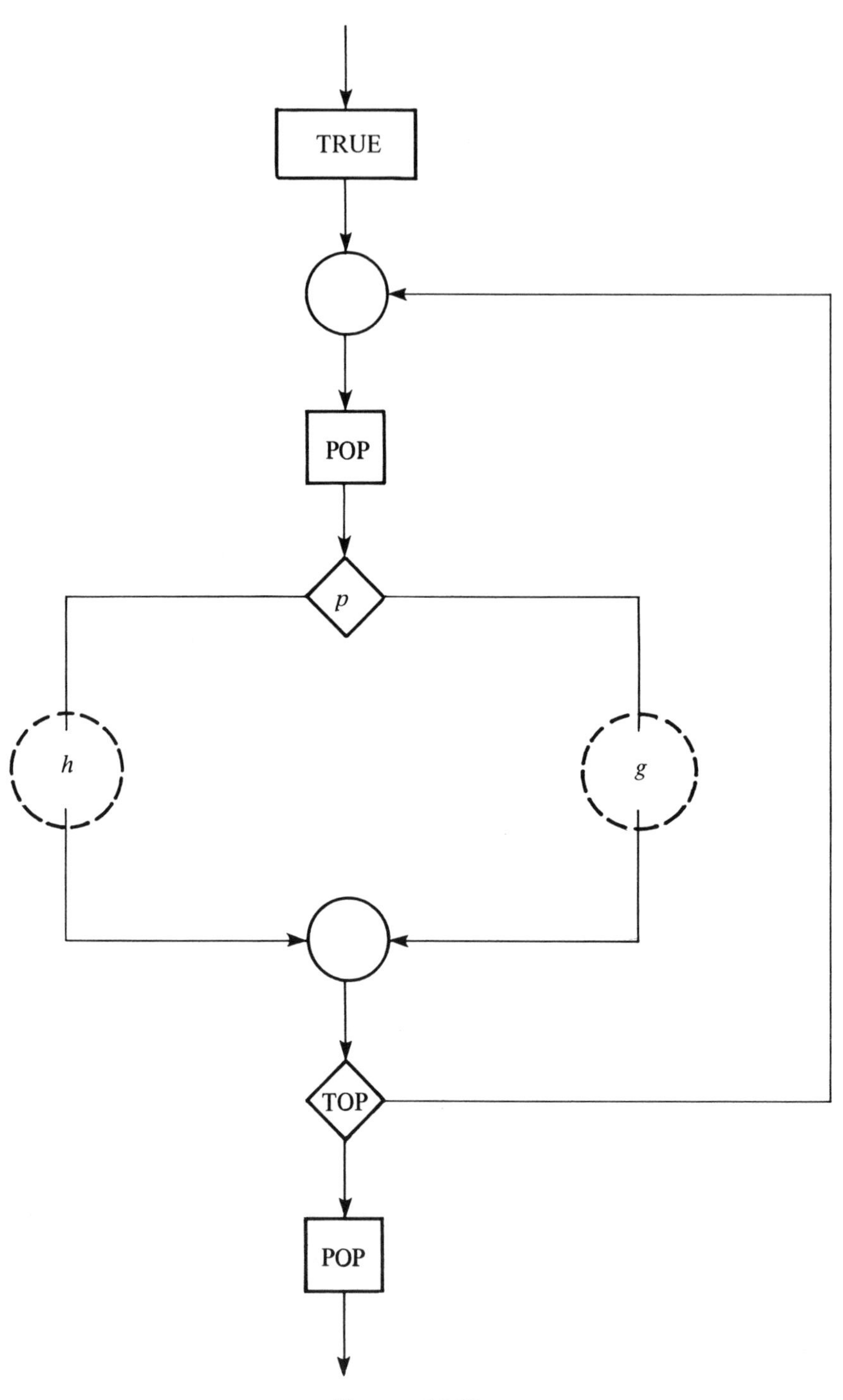

FIGURE 13-29

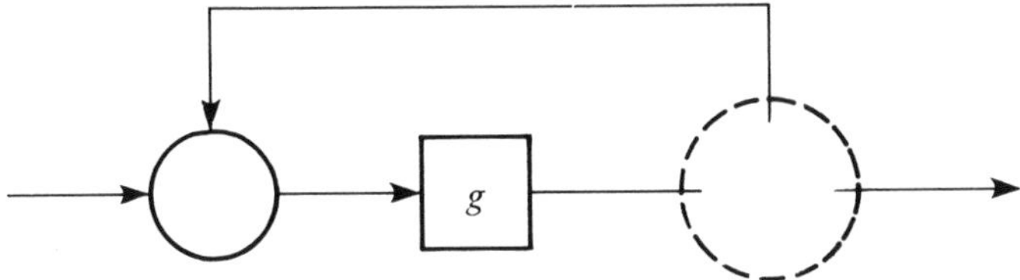

FIGURE 13-30

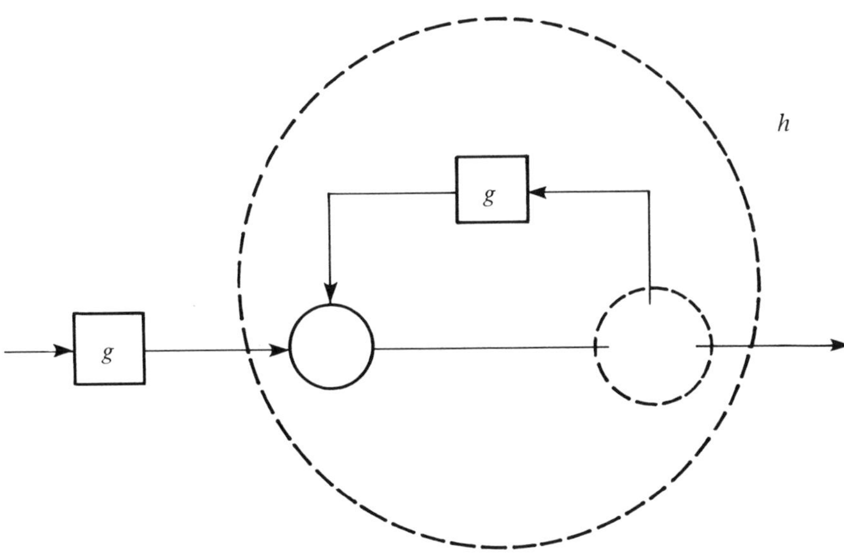

FIGURE 13-31

but that also, the number of lines, say, $i(f)$, required to reach the first predicate of f is reduced by one, that is,

$$i(h) = i(f) - 1$$

Finally, it is clear that $S(f)$ is equivalent to f.

2.c.(3). Collecting Node. If the next node is a collecting node, then f is of the form shown in Figure 13-32, and we consider the new program shown in Figure 13-33, called g. In this case we define

$$S(f) = g$$

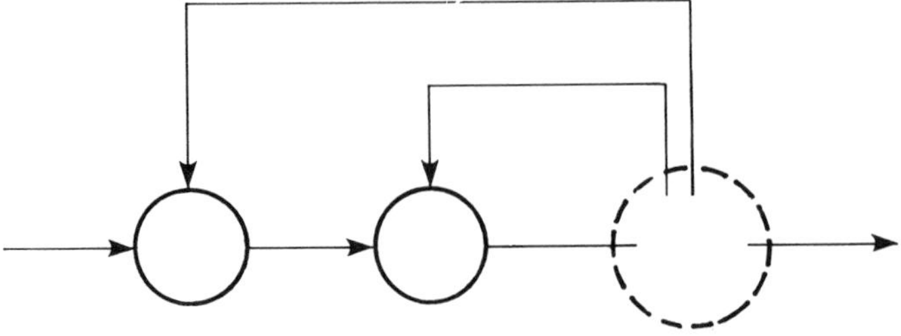

FIGURE 13-32

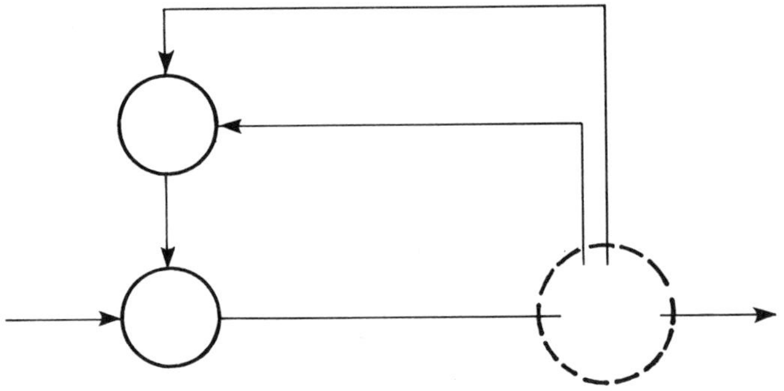

FIGURE 13-33

Also, in this case we observe directly that

$$e(g) = e(f)$$
$$i(g) = i(f) - 1$$

It is clear that $S(f)$ is equivalent to f.

Summary. This completes the analysis of cases for the input region of f and the definition of the structuring process, S. In summary, in each case we have defined a new program, $S(f)$, equivalent to f, such that $S(f)$ is a formula in, at most, graph labels BLOCK, IF-THEN-ELSE, and DO-UNTIL, functions, predicates, and constituent proper programs. In several cases the number of edges of the constituents of f is seen to be less than the number of edges in f. In two cases this number of edges was not decreased, but the number of edges from input to the first predicate node was decreased. It is clear that the number of edges from input to the first predicate node is bounded by the number of edges of a program. When we apply this information to that generated in the case analyses above, we get Table 13-2.

We are now ready to summarize our proof, as follows:

First, it is clear that the Structure Theorem is true for proper programs with one line, for such a program is simply λ.

Next, suppose that the Structure Theorem is true for proper programs of n lines or less for $n > 1$. Let f be a proper program with $n + 1$ lines. We apply S to f. If case 2a, 2b, or 2c(1) applies, we have a new equivalent program, whose constituent programs are proper and have at most n lines; and each such constituent, by our induction hypothesis, satisfies the theorem. Moreover, the new equivalent program has a formula in, at most, graph labels BLOCK, IF-THEN-ELSE, DO-UNTIL, predicates, and their constituents. Therefore the new program satisfies the theorem. If none of cases 2a, 2b, or 2c(1) applies, then $i(f) \leq n$, and case 2c(2) or 2c(3) must apply. In each such case there remains only one constituent, say, g, and

$$e(g) = e(f),\ i(g) = i(f) - 1$$

Therefore after, at most, n such applications, case 2c(1) must apply, and the final equivalent program satisfies the theorem.

This completes the proof of the Structure Theorem.

TABLE 13-2. *Case Analysis: Structuring Process*

Case	*e values*	*i values*
2a	$e(g) \leq e(f)$ - 3 $e(h) \leq e(f)$ - 3	$i(g) \leq e(f)$ - 3 $i(h) = e(f)$ - 3
2b	$e(h) = e(f)$ - 1	$i(h) \leq e(f)$ - 1
2c(1)	$e(g) \leq e(f)$ - 1 $e(h) \leq e(f)$ - 1	$i(g) \leq e(f)$ - 1 $i(h) \leq e(f)$ - 1
2c(2)	$e(h) = e(f)$	$i(h) = i(g)$ - 1
2c(3)	$e(g) = e(f)$	$i(g) = i(f)$ - 1

Top Down Corollary

Any proper program is equivalent to a program of one of the forms

$$(\text{BLOCK}, g, h)$$
$$(\text{IF-THEN-ELSE}, p, g, h)$$
$$(\text{DO-UNTIL}, p, g)$$

where p is a predicate of the original program or TOP, and g, h are proper programs, functions of the original program, TRUE, FALSE, or POP.

S-Structured Programs

The Structure Theorem motivates the definition of a structured program as follows:

Let S be any finite set of labels associated with control graphs of proper programs. Then any program whose formula contains only graph labels from S is said to be an S-structured program.

When the prefix "S" is not critical, or understood, it will be suppressed.

Program Representations

The result of the Structure Theorem is similar to representation theorems in other branches of mathematics, in which it is shown that all elements of a set, or "space," can be represented by combinations of a subset of "basic elements" of the space. For example, three nonplanar vectors span a three-dimensional Euclidean space, the set $\{\sin nx, \cos nx \mid n = 0, 1, \ldots\}$ spans a set of real functions in the interval $[0, 2\pi]$—that is, a "function space." The foregoing examples refer to linear combination for representation.

In the Structure Theorem it is shown that three simple types of programs, defined by BLOCK, IF-THEN-ELSE, and DO-UNTIL control graphs, span the set of all proper programs, using substitution of proper programs for process nodes as the only rule of combination. Such a representation theorem permits the resolution of questions of the adequacy of a programming language simply and effectively. For example, all one needs in order to show that a new set of basis programs will span the set of all proper programs is that one can represent BLOCK, IF-THEN-ELSE, and DO-UNTIL programs in this new set.

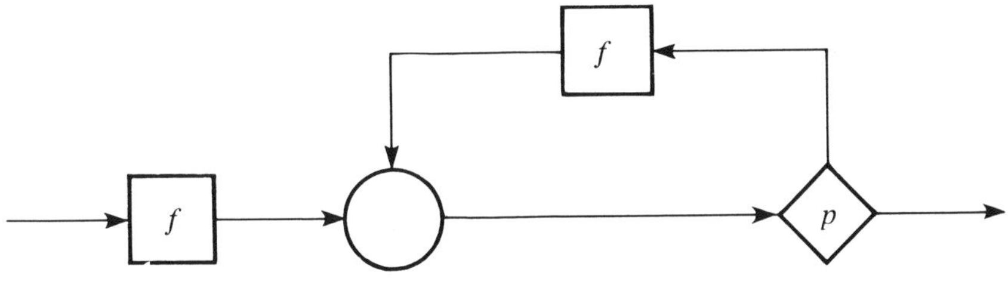

FIGURE 13-34

One simple illustration of a new basis is to represent DO-UNTIL in terms of BLOCK, and DO-WHILE, as shown in Figure 13-34, or

$$(\text{DO-UNTIL}, p, f) = (\text{BLOCK}, f, (\text{DO-WHILE}, p, f)).$$

Hence BLOCK, IF-THEN-ELSE, and DO-WHILE provide a sufficient control structure to represent all proper programs as well as BLOCK, IF-THEN-ELSE, and DO-UNTIL.

Program Trees

The formula of a structured program can be displayed in a program tree in a natural way, with the graph labels, functions, and predicates assigned to nodes of the tree. For example, the formula

$$(\text{IF-THEN-ELSE}, p, g, h)$$

defines the program tree in Figure 13-35; and the formula

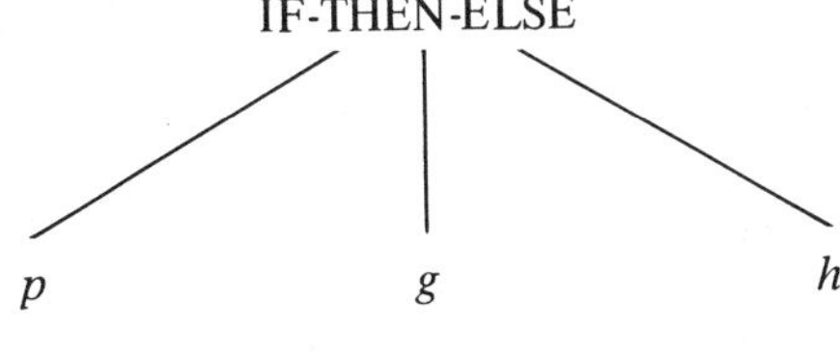

FIGURE 13-35

$$(\text{DO-WHILE}, p, (\text{IF-THEN-ELSE}, q, g, (\text{BLOCK}, h, k)))$$

defines the program tree in Figure 13-36.

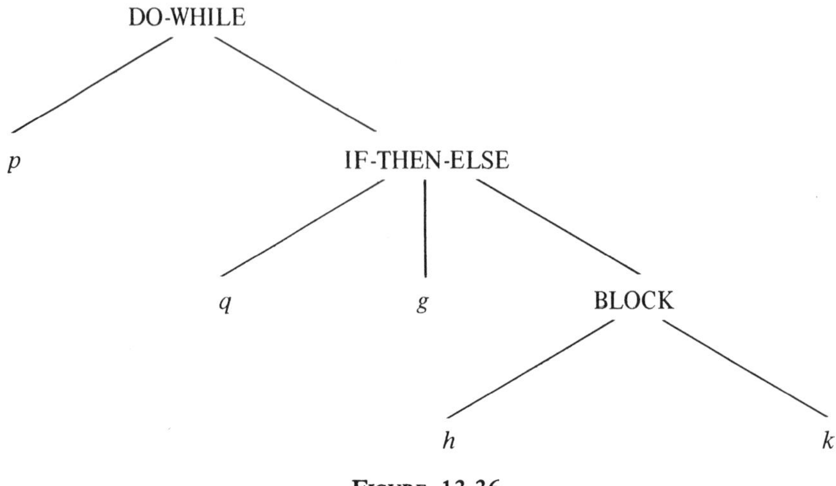

FIGURE 13-36

Conversely, given any program tree of graph labels, functions, and predicates, the original program can be recovered. In particular, any subtree defined by a node plus all its successors in the tree defines a subprogram of the original program.

The program tree provides a convenient way of visualizing program structure in the form of subprograms. By labeling subprograms and referring to their program functions at higher levels in the program, an original program of any size can be organized as a set of subprograms, each of a prescribed maximum size.

It is clear that each subprogram so defined is a proper program. That is, each maps an input data set into an output data set, with no control side effects.

Program Correctness

We have already noted that program correctness is a question of predictability. More precisely, given a program, f, and a function, g, we are interested in whether g is the same as the program function $[f]$. If we know both g and $[f]$, we can resolve the question by comparison. Carrying out such a comparison of two sets is a general mathematics problem whose solution will depend on how the sets are defined. In a few cases they will be enumerated. Then their elements can be ordered and matched, a pair at a time. In most cases such sets will be defined by conditions or rules in some broader (less formal) context than set theory per se. There may be natural numbers involved, in which case inductive definitions and comparisons may be possible. In any case the techniques for comparison are beyond our present interest and must be formulated in whatever terms are available.

In the case of structured programs the program tree permits the decomposition of the correctness problem into a series of nested problems, each of a simple type that can be prescribed in advance.

Correctness Theorem

Theorem: If the formula of a program contains at most graph labels BLOCK, IF-THEN, IF-THEN-ELSE, DO-WHILE, and DO-UNTIL and satisfies a loop qualification, then it can be proved correct by a tour of its program tree, in which, at each node, the relevant one of five cases must be proved (data sets suppressed; see below for data set versions):

1. If $f=$ (BLOCK, g, h), prove

$$[f]=\{(r,t) \mid \exists s((r,s) \in [g] \wedge (s,t) \in [h])\}$$

2. If $f=$ (IF-THEN, p, g), prove

$$[f]=\{(r,s) \mid ((r,\text{True}) \in p \wedge (r,s) \in [g]) \vee ((r,\text{False}) \in p \wedge (r,s) \in p \wedge r=s)\}$$

3. If $f=$ (IF-THEN-ELSE, p, g, h), prove

$$[f]=\{(r,s) \mid ((r,\text{True}) \wedge p \wedge (r,s) \wedge [g]) \vee ((r,\text{False}) \in p \wedge (r,s) \in [h])\}$$

4. If $f=$ (DO-WHILE, p, g), prove

$$[f]=[(\text{IF-THEN}, p, (\text{BLOCK}, [g], [f]))]$$

5. If $f=$ (DO-UNTIL, p, g), prove

$$[f]=[(\text{BLOCK}, [g], (\text{IF-THEN}, p, [f]))]$$

Proof: By hypothesis each node in the program tree is one of the five types listed. Beginning at the root of the tree, the program function $[f]$ of program f is determined by possibly a predicate, and program functions $[g]$, $[h]$ of constituent subprograms g, h, and so on, until functions are reached at the endpoints of the tree. If the program function at each node is known with respect to program functions of its successor nodes, then by finite induction the program function at the root of the tree is known with respect to the functions in the program.

It remains to validate the detailed assertion case by case.

Case f = (BLOCK, g, h)

In flowchart form,

f = —R→ [g] —S→ [h] —T→

Now

$[f]$ = [—R→ [$[g]$] —S→ [$[h]$] —T→]

by the definition of program functions $[g]$, $[h]$. Then program function $[f]$ can be formulated directly as

$$[f] = \{(r, t) \mid r \in R \; \exists \; s((r, s) \in [g] \wedge s \in S \wedge (s, t) \in [h]) \wedge t \in T\}.$$

This agrees with the statement of the theorem with the data sets suppressed.

Case f = (IF-THEN, p, g)

In flowchart form,

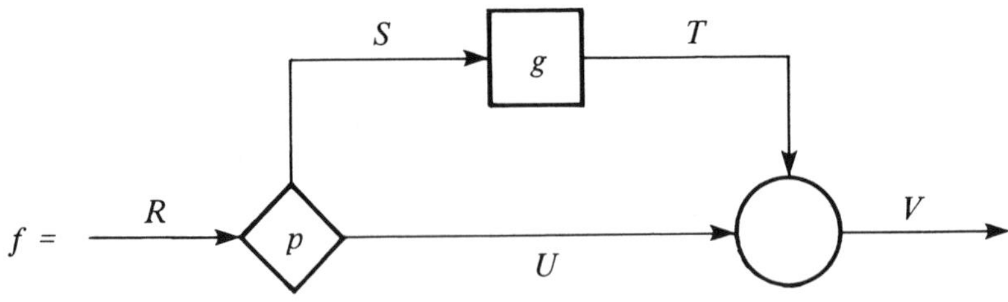

Now

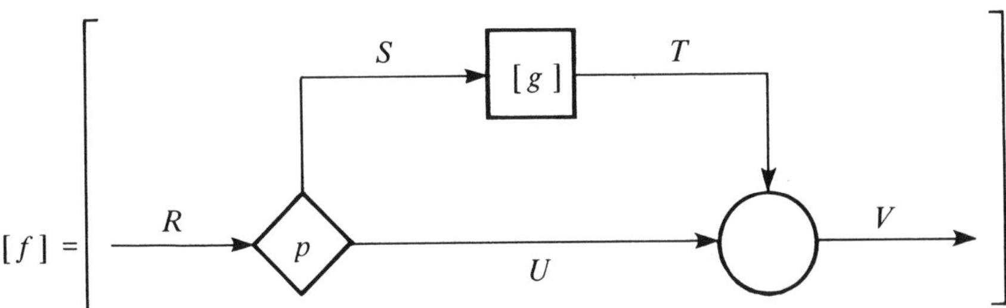

Then

$$[f] = \{(r, v) \mid r \in R \wedge (((r, \text{True}) \in p \wedge r \in S \wedge (r, v) \in [g] \wedge v \in T) \vee ((r, \text{False}) \in p \wedge f = v \wedge v \in U)) \wedge v \in V\}.$$

This agrees with the statement of the theorem with the data sets suppressed.

Case $f =$ (IF-THEN-ELSE, p, g, h)

In flowchart form,

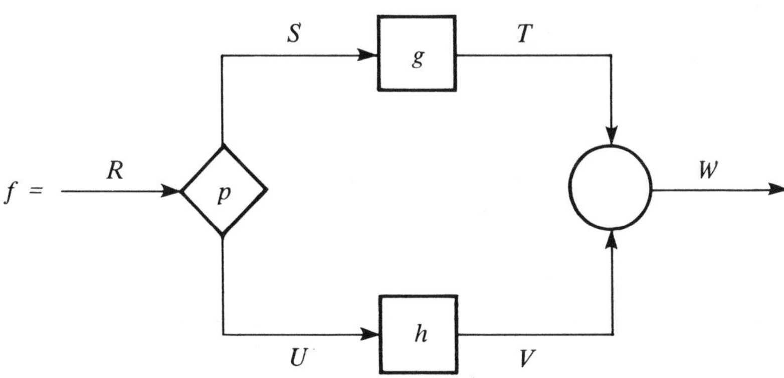

Now

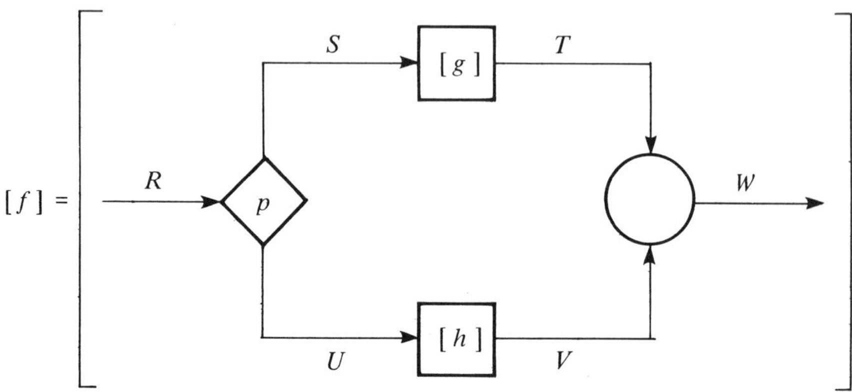

Then

$[f] = \{(r, w) \mid r \in R \wedge (((r, \text{True}) \in p \wedge r \in S \wedge (r, w) \in [g] \wedge w \in T) \wedge ((r, \text{False}) \in p \wedge r \in U \wedge (r, w) \in [h] \wedge w \in V)) \wedge w \in W\}.$

This agrees with the statement of the theorem with the data sets suppressed.

Case $f =$ **(DO-WHILE,** p, g**)**

In flowchart form,

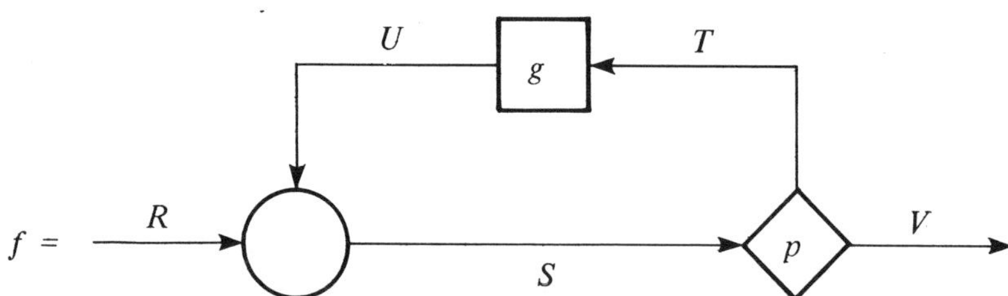

Now

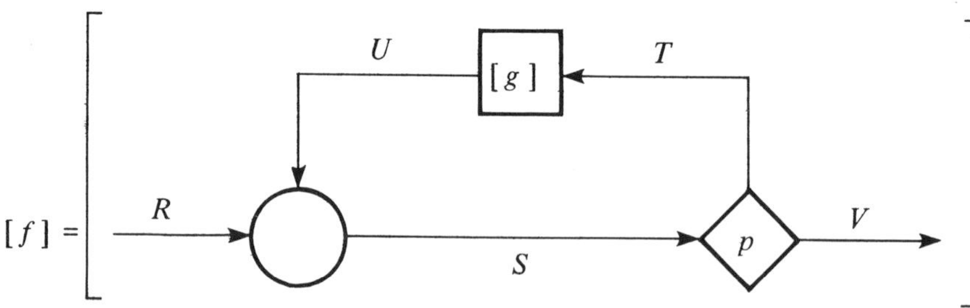

and, indeed,

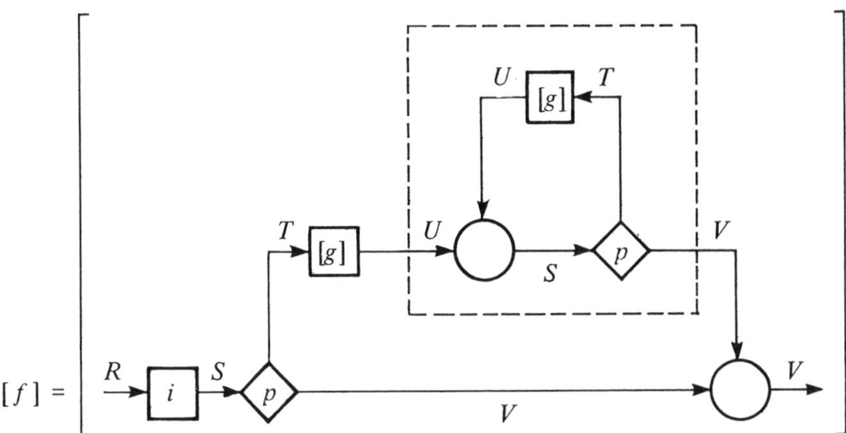

by construction and inspection, where i is an identity function. We note that if $R = U$, then the DO-WHILE subprogram in the dotted section has program function $[f]$, that is,

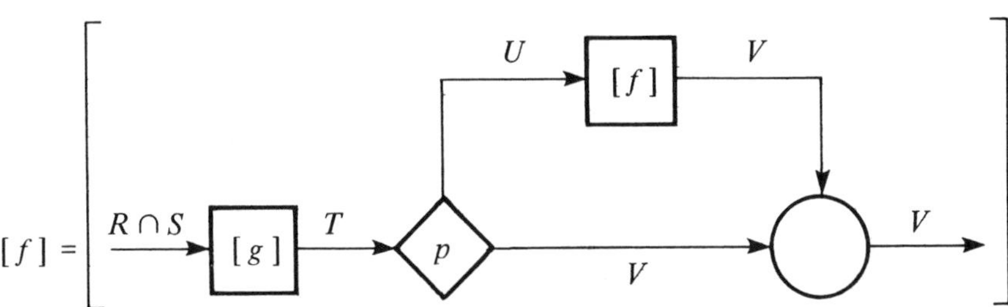

This agrees with the statement of the theorem with the data sets suppressed. We call the condition $R = U$ the *loop qualification* on f; that is, both input lines to the collecting node have identical data spaces.

Case $f =$ (DO-WHILE, p, g)

In flowchart form,

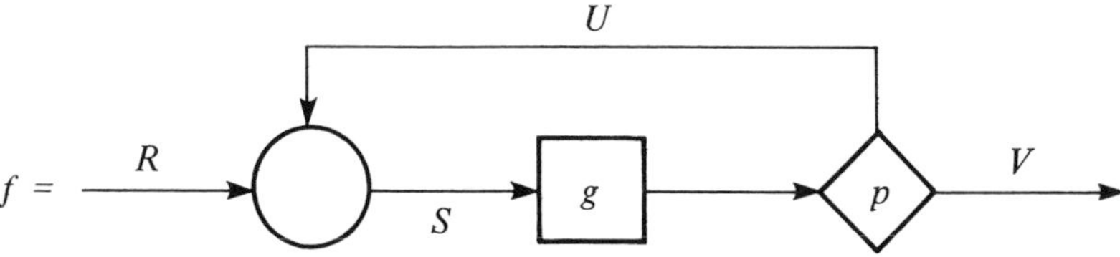

Now,

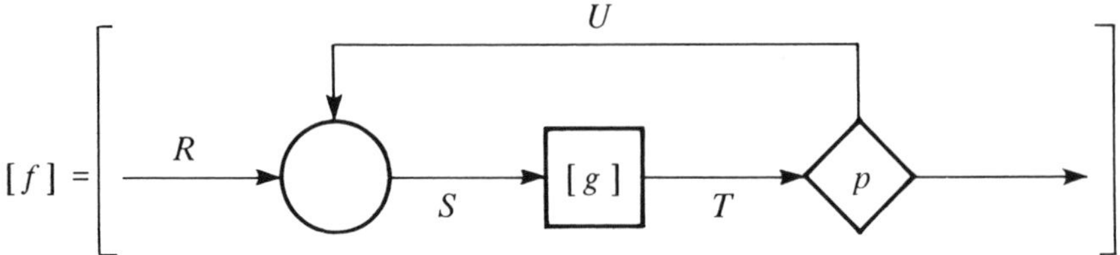

and, indeed,

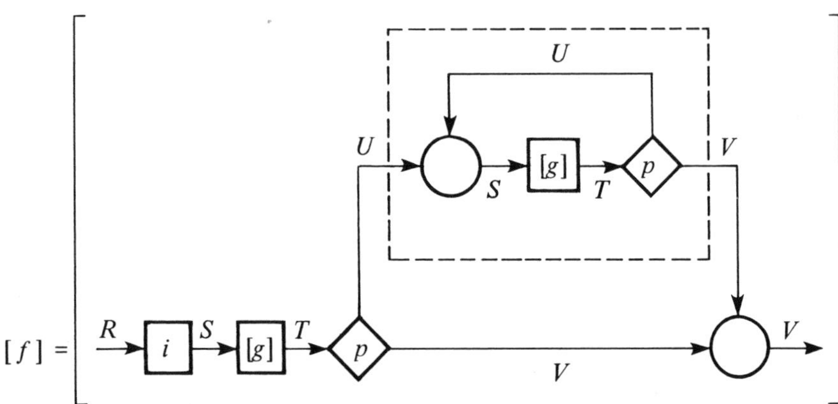

by construction and inspection. If $R = U$ (the loop qualification), then the DO-UNTIL subprogram in the dotted section has program function [*f*], that is,

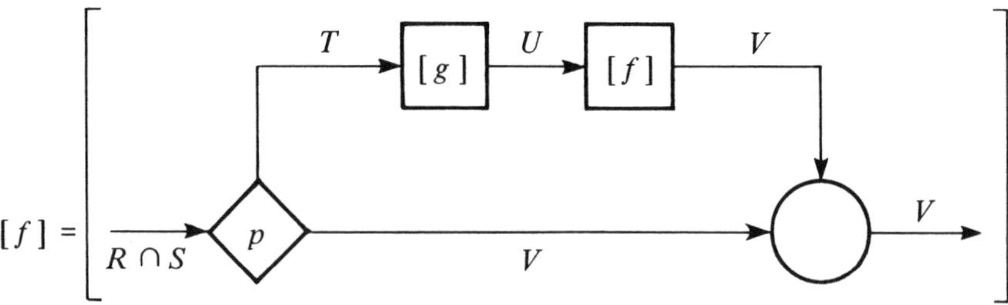

This agrees with the statement of the theorem with the data sets suppressed. With this case, the proof of the theorem is completed.

Correctness Notes. At first glance the verification conditions for DO-WHILE and DO-UNTIL seem to involve a recursive relation in program function $[f]$. But this is not the case; the verification conditions involve $[f]$ as an input, not as an unknown to be solved for.

It is also noteworthy that the top down approach to correctness avoids the problem of incomplete rules (or in other formulations, incomplete functions, for which we have no counterparts) and termination. In a program equation such as

$$f = \text{WHILE } p \text{ DO } g,$$

the functions p and $[g]$ are usually taken to be the "independent variables" and the function $[f]$ to be the "dependent variable," a "bottom up" viewpoint. Of course, even though p and $[g]$ may be given by complete rules, the new rule "WHILE p DO g" may turn out to be partial because of nontermination. However, in the top down viewpoint the function $[f]$ is the "independent variable," and the program equation defines "dependent variables" p and $[g]$ implicitly (and meaningfully). Now, since $[f]$ is a function, p and $[g]$ must be defined such that the rule "WHILE p DO g" terminates for any input in the domain of $[f]$.

The loop qualification required in the Correctness Theorem is a serious restriction with respect to the allocation and freeing of storage space. If the body of a DO loop allocates or frees space, then the loop qualification is not satisfied, and the reduction of a loop verification to the form of the theorem is not valid.

Top Down Program Expansions

Thus far, we have considered programs first and then their meanings as program functions. In top down programming we want to reverse that order of conception; that is, given a function (a program specification), we want to find some program (a rule) that has that program function. This reversal of conception allows us to avoid questions of "partial rules," "partial correctness," and the general termination problem, because they never arise. In the usual way of looking at program equations, such as

$$f = (\text{DO-WHILE}, p, g),$$

the graph label DO-WHILE, predicate p, and function or subprogram g usually taken to be the "independent variables," and program f is taken to be the "dependent variable." In this case, even though p and g are given by rules defined everywhere on their domains, the new program (DO-WHILE, p, g) may not terminate and thus be called a partial rule. One may prove properties relating p and g to f in case of termination to get partial correctness, but one must also establish termination separately to get total correctness.

We observe that if we take f to be the independent variable in the foregoing equation, then these partial rule and partial correctness problems disappear. If f denotes a complete rule, then p and g must denote complete rules in order to satisfy the equation as dependent variables. That is the essence of top down programming, regarding the constituent subprograms and predicates of an expansion as dependent variables that satisfy a prescribed equation which is inherited top down.

When this approach is taken, perhaps the most surprising result is the amount of freedom available to a programmer in writing a correct program. In the bottom up approach, programming appears to be an activity with almost unlimited freedom to improvise or solve problems in various ways. But in developing a program top down it is clear that this freedom is highly restricted. At first glance it may seem that there is less freedom in programming top down than in bottom up, but a second thought shows that is not the case. They must lead to equivalent results, and in fact what really is exhibited in the bottom up approach is a false freedom that is subsequently paid for in a painful error elimination process, following an original "gush of originality."

In order to exhibit the degree of freedom available in programming we formulate the Expansion Theorem below in both a verbal and a set theoretic version. The Structure Theorem exhibits characteristics of a completed program, while the Expansion Theorem shows how programs can look at every intermediate stage of their construction. At every such intermediate stage a program developed in a top down discipline can be guaranteed to be correct, insofar as it is developed, without the necessity of altering parts of the program already done in order to accommodate the remaining parts of the program yet to be developed. It is a familiar experience in large program development to get "90% done" and to remain at that 90% level for a lengthy period. That phenomenon occurs not because the last 10% is difficult to write, but because in order to write the last 10%, critical sections of the first 90% need to be altered. The Expansion Theorem and top down programming can guarantee that the first 90% can remain intact while the last 10% is finished on schedule.

Expansion Theorem (Verbal Version)

Theorem: In a program function expansion of the form (data sets suppressed; see below for more detail):

1. $f = [(\text{BLOCK}, \text{g}, \text{h})]$

   Any pair (g, h) whose composition is f may be chosen.

2. $f = [(\text{IF-THEN-ELSE}, p, g, h)]$

   Any predicate p with the same domain as f may be chosen; then g and h are fully determined, as the members of the partition of f defined by p.

3. $f = [(\text{DO-WHILE}, p, g)]$

   The program function f must be the identity in the intersection of its domain and range; any function g may be chosen whose completion is the varying part of f; and p is fully determined by f and g.

In short, the invention of an IF-THEN-ELSE program is equivalent to a partition of a prescribed program function, while the invention of a DO-WHILE program is equivalent to the determination of a function whose completion is a prescribed program function. That is, the only freedom in an IF-THEN-ELSE program is its predicate, and the only freedom in a DO-WHILE program is its iterative process—all other freedoms, in the THEN or ELSE clauses, or in the WHILE predicate, are illusions. THEN and ELSE clauses are frequently used for elaborating functional specifications not fully stated; but these are not freedoms of choice, but interpretations of intentions at more detailed levels. The point is that if functional specifications are sufficiently well defined to decide whether a program satisfies them, then there is no freedom beyond the choice of the predicate in an IF-THEN-ELSE program. In the case of the DO-WHILE the question is more subtle and relates to the character of the termination questions in programming top down, in contrast to bottom up. The WHILE predicate is completely determined on the domain and range of the function (specification). The DO-WHILE program must terminate on reaching any element of the range and must continue otherwise, because if not, it cannot possibly satisfy the prestated (top down inherited) function specification.

In order to formulate a more concise, set theoretic version of the

Expansion Theorem, we introduce a reinterpretation of the logical constant "True." Ordinarily, a predicate is taken to be a function, p, such that

$$\text{range}(p) = \{\text{True, False}\}.$$

We reinterpret the constant True by the statement for an associated function

$$\overline{p} = \{(x, y) \mid (x, \text{True}) \in p\};$$

that is, if $p(x)$ is true, then for any element y, $(x, y) \in \overline{p}$.

We also introduce the idea of a refinement of a function, corresponding to the ordinary idea of the refinement of a partition. (A refinement of a partition is simply a new partition, each of whose members is a subset of some member of the original partition.) We form a partition of the domain of a function, called a partition of *level sets*, or the *contour* of the function, by grouping arguments that have identical values into subsets of the domain. Then we say that one function is a refinement of another if its contour is a refinement of the others.

Finally, we define the *fixed points* of a function f, denoted as the fixed(f) subset:

$$\text{fixed}(f) = \{(x, y) \mid (x, y) \in f \land x = y\}.$$

Expansion Theorem (Set Theoretic Version)

Theorem: In a program expansion of the form (data sets suppressed; see below for more detail):

$f = [(\text{BLOCK}, g, h)]$

1. Choose function g as any refinement of program function f.
2. Then h is uniquely determined by the relation

$$f = g * h.$$

$f = [(\text{IF-THEN-ELSE}, p, g, h)]$

1. Choose predicate p such that domain(p) = domain(f).
2. Then g and h are uniquely determined by the relations

$$g = \overline{p} \cap f$$
$$h = f - g.$$

$f = [(\text{DO-WHILE}, p, g)]$

1. Verify that

$$\text{domain}(\text{fixed}(f)) = \text{domain}(f) \cap \text{range}(f).$$

2. Choose function g such that

$$* g * = f - \text{fixed}(f).$$

3. Then p is uniquely determined such that

$$p(x) = \text{True if } x \in \text{domain}(g) - \text{range}(f)$$

$$p(x) = \text{False if } x \in \text{range}(f).$$

Proof:

Case $f = [(\textbf{BLOCK}, g, h)]$

In flowchart form,

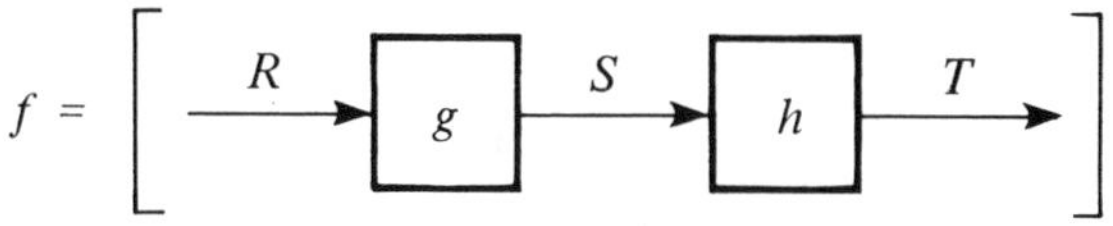

$$f = \left[\xrightarrow{R} \boxed{g} \xrightarrow{S} \boxed{h} \xrightarrow{T} \right]$$

Consider the following construction of g, h, R, S, T:

Set $R = \text{domain}(f)$.

Set $T = \text{range}(f)$.

Choose any refinement of f, say, g; then for any $x \in R$, $y \in R$,
$g(x) = g(y) \supset f(x) = f(y)$.

Set $S = \text{range}(g)$.

Set $h = \{(s, t) \mid (r, s) \in g \wedge (r, t) \in f\}$.

Now it is easy to verify by this construction that

$$[(\text{BLOCK}, g, h)] = \{(x, y) \mid (x, y) \in f),$$

as was to be shown. The function h is uniquely determined in the construction by f and g.

Case $f = $ **[(IF-THEN-ELSE,** p, g, h**)]**

In flowchart form,

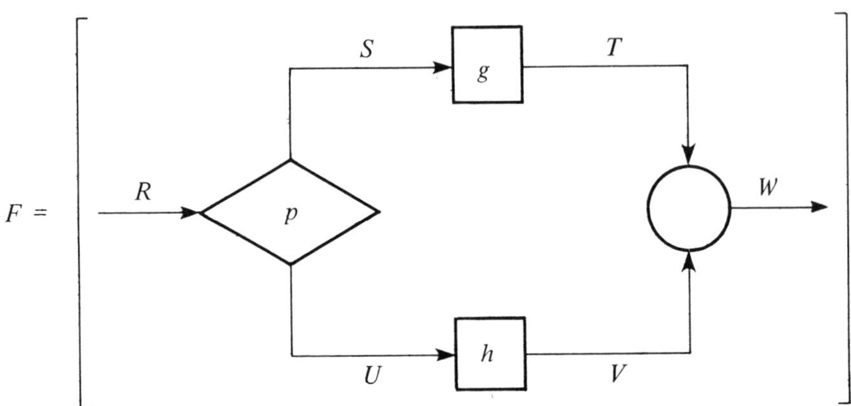

Consider the following construction of p, g, h, R, S, T, U, V, W:

Set $R = \text{domain}(f)$.

Choose any predicate p such that $\text{domain}(p) = \text{domain}(f) = R$.

Set $S = \{s \mid (s, \text{True}) \in p\}$.

Set $g = \{(s, t) \mid s \in S \wedge (s, t) \in f\}$.

Set $T = \text{range}(g)$.

Set $U = \{u \mid (u, \text{False}) \in p\}$.

Set $h = \{(u, v) \mid u \in U \wedge (u, v) \in f\}$.

Set $V = \text{range}(h)$.

Set $W = T \cup V$.

Now it is easy to verify by this construction that

$$[(\text{IF-THEN-ELSE}, p, g, h)] = \{(x, y) \mid (x, y) \in f\},$$

as was to be shown. Note that g is a subset of f defined by p, that is, $\bar{p} \cap f$, and h is the complement of g in f, that is, $f - g$.

Case $f = $ **[(DO-WHILE,** p, g**)]**

In flowchart form,

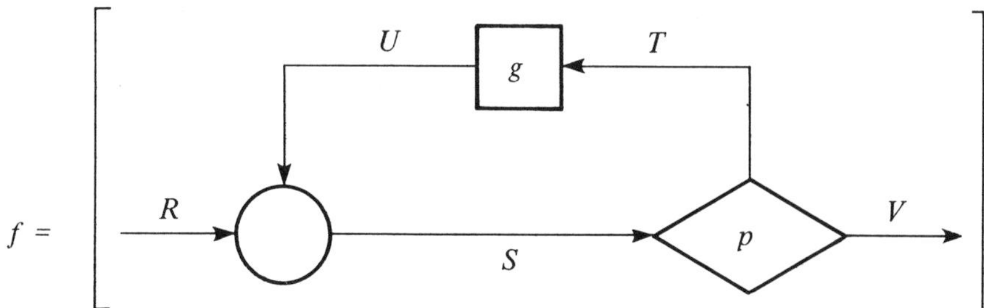

Consider $(s, v) \in f$, that is, $v \in \text{range}(f)$. We note that necessarily $p(v) = \text{False}$. Otherwise, the control path to g is taken, and the program cannot terminate with value v, which contradicts the correctness of the expansion.

Next, consider $(r, v) \in f$ such that $r \in \text{domain}(f) \cap \text{range}(f)$; then $p(v) = \text{False}$ by the foregoing remark, and the function g is bypassed, so that necessarily $v = r$ or $r \in \text{domain}(\text{fixed}(f))$. Conversely, if $r \in \text{domain}(\text{fixed}(f))$, then $r \in \text{range}(f)$ and $p(r) = \text{False}$; hence $r \in \text{domain}(f) \cap \text{range}(f)$. That is, $\text{domain}(\text{fixed}(f)) = \text{domain}(f) \cap \text{range}(f)$, as needed to be shown.

Next choose function g such that $* g * = f - \text{fixed}(f)$. At least one such choice is possible, namely, for $g = f - \text{fixed}(f)$, since the domain and range of $f - \text{fixed}(f)$ are disjoint.

Finally, we have already seen that necessarily $p(x) = \text{False}$ when $x \in \text{range}(f)$. But clearly, we must have $p(x) = \text{True}$ when $x \in \text{domain}(g)$, in order that the correct control path be taken to finally reach an output $v \in \text{range}(f)$; in addition, since $* g * \supset f$, then necessarily $\text{domain}(g) \supset \text{domain}(*g*) \supset \text{domain}(f)$, so that $x \in \text{domain}(g)$ implies $x \in \text{domain}(f)$. Thus in summary,

$$p(x) = \text{True if } x \in \text{domain}(g) - \text{range}(f)$$

$$p(x) = \text{False if } x \in \text{range}(f),$$

as was to be shown.

The data sets required are as follows:

Set $R = \text{domain}(f)$.

Set $V = \text{range}(f)$.

Set $T = \text{domain}(g)$.

Set $U = \text{range}(g)$.

Set $S = R \cup U$.

This discussion is concluded with a combinatorial characterization of g, the iterative process of a DO-WHILE program.

For function f, consider any superfunction h such that $\text{range}(h) = \text{range}(f)$. For each level set, or contour, of h, define any arbitrary set of rooted trees on its elements. If x of $\text{domain}(h)$ is a root of such a tree, then we set

$$y(x) = h(x).$$

If $x \in \text{domain}(h)$ is not a root of such a tree, let y denote the parent of x in that tree, and define

$$g(x) = y.$$

It is easily verified that any function g so defined, and no other, will satisfy the relation $* \; g \; * = f$.

With this it is clear that in all three cases the entire freedom of choice is a combinatorial one. In a BLOCK program it is the choice of a function; in an IF-THEN-ELSE program the choice is a partition of a function; in a DO-WHILE program the choice is a tree structure within the level sets of a function.

Indeterminate Programs

In certain applications, particularly those of artificial intelligence (see Nilsson [33]), it is convenient to generalize the idea of a program to a construct that permits ambiguity in execution, rather than uniqueness. For example, an algorithm may specify a selection of a member of some set for processing, without naming a specific member. In this event, intermediate and/or final results may be indeterminate. Such "indeterminate algorithms" are often useful in describing the essentials of a process without getting unduly involved with its specifics. Indeterminate algorithms are also useful for treating a person-machine computing system, in which the actions of people—say, at terminals—are indeterminate. Then an entire system can be defined to be governed by an indeterminate algorithm.

Our development of programs, which we call "determinate programs," where necessary, can be generalized to include "indeterminate programs" by a very simple extension—namely, by extending the idea of function throughout to the idea of relation. A *relation* is defined to be a set of ordered pairs, without the additional qualification required of a function to provide unique values for given arguments. As with functions, relations inherit set properties. In fact, not only the intersection and difference of two relations are new relations (as in the case of functions), but the union of two relations is also a relation (not generally so for functions). Domains and ranges of relations are defined as for functions.

Next we define an *indeterminate program* to be a finite set of relations, called *indeterminate instructions,* each of whose domains is included in a data space, and each of whose ranges is included in the Cartesian product of the data space and the indeterminate program, again called the state space. An *indeterminate program execution* is, again, a sequence of state values

$$s = (d_i, r_i),\ i = 0, 1, \ldots$$

such that

$$(d_i, s_{i+1}) \in r_i,\ i = 0, 1, \ldots$$

which terminates, if ever, when $d_i \notin \text{domain}(r_i)$. Precisely as before, all executions that terminate define a set of ordered pairs, now a relation instead of a function, which we call the *indeterminate program relation;* that is, in retrospect an indeterminate program is a (nonunique) rule for calculating the members of its relation, using other relations in so doing.

At this point we leave it to the reader to observe that every construction and theorem goes through for indeterminate programs and their relations, just as for determinate programs and their functions.

References

1. Allen, C. D. "The Application of Formal Logic to Programs and Programming." *IBM Systems Journal* 10, No. 1 (1971): 2–38.
2. Ashcroft, E. A. "Program Correctness Methods and Language Definition." In *Proceedings of the ACM Conference on Proving Assertions about Programs,* pp. 51–57. Las Cruces, N. M.: New Mexico State University, 1972.
3. Ashcroft, Edward A., and Manna, Zohar. "The Translation of 'GO TO' Programs to 'WHILE' Programs." Stanford Artificial Intelligence Project Memo AIM-138, Computer Sciences Department Report STAN-CS-71-188, Jan. 1971.
4. Baker, F. T. "Chief Programmer Team Management of Production Programming." *IBM Systems Journal* 11, No. 1 (1972): 56–73.
5. Böhm, Corrado, and Jacopini, Giuseppe. "Flow Diagrams, Turing

Machines and Languages with Only Two Formation Rules." *Comm. ACM* 9 (1966): 366–371.

6. Burge, W. H. "Some Examples of Programming Using a Functional Notation." Paper presented at Second Symposium of Special Interest Group Association for Computing Machinery on Symbolic and Algebraic Manipulation, Los Angeles, March 1971.
7. Burstall, Rod M. "An Algebraic Description of Programs with Assertions, Verification and Simulation." In *Proceedings of the Association for Computing Machinery Conference on Proving Assertions about Programs.* Las Cruces, N. M.: New Mexico State University 1972.
8. Church, A. *Introduction to Mathematical Logic.* Vol. 1. Princeton, N. J.: Princeton University Press, 1956.
9. Dijkstra, E. W. "A Constructive Approach to the Problem of Program Correctness." *BIT* 8, No. 3 (1968): 174–186.
10. Dijkstra, E. W. "Notes on Structured Programming," *Technische Hogeschool Eindhoven* (THE), (1969).
11. Dijkstra, E. W. "Structured Programming." In *Software Engineering Techniques,* edited by J. N. Burton and B. Randell, pp. 88–93. Nato Science Committee, 1969.
12. Floyd, R. W. "Assigning Meanings to Programs." In *Proceedings of the Symposium in Applied Mathematics,* vol. 19, edited by J. T. Schwartz, pp. 19–32. Providence, R. I.: American Mathematical Society, 1967.
13. Floyd, R. W. "Nondeterministic Algorithms." *ACM* 14, No. 4 (Oct. 1967): 636–644.
14. Good, D. I. "Toward a Man-Machine System for Proving Program Correctness." Ph.D. thesis, University of Wisconsin, 1970.
15. Halmos, Paul R. *Naive Set Theory.* Edited by J. L. Kelley and P. R. Halmos. Princeton, N. J.: D. Van Nostrand, 1960.
16. Hoare, C. A. R. "An Axiomatic Approach to Computer Programming." *Comm. ACM* 12, No. 10 (Oct. 1969): 576–580, 583.
17. Hoare, C. A. R. "Proof of a Program: FIND." *Comm. ACM* 14, No. 1 (Jan. 1971): 39–45.
18. Horning, J. J., and Randell, B. "Structuring Complex Processes." IBM T. J. Watson Research Center Report RC 2459, May 1969.
19. Ianov, Iu. "The Logical Schemas of Algorithms." *Problems of Cybernetics* 1 (English translation (Pergamon Press)) (1960).
20. Jones, C. B. "Formal Development of Correct Algorithms: An example based on Earley's recognizer." In *Proceedings of the Association for Computing Machinery Conference on Proving Assertions about Programs,* pp. 51–57. Las Cruces, N. M.: New Mexico State University, 1972.

21. King, J. C. "A Program Verifier." Ph.D. thesis, Carnegie-Mellon University, Pittsburgh, 1969.
22. Landin, P. J. "A Correspondence between ALGOL 60 and Church's Lambda-Notation," *Comm. ACM* 8 (Mar. 1965).
23. London, R. L. "Certification of Algorithm 245 Treesort 3: Proof of Algorithms—A New Kind of Certification." *Comm. ACM* 13 (1970): 371–373.
24. London, R. L. "Proving Programs Correct: Some Techniques and Examples." *BIT* 10, No. 2 (1970): 168–182.
25. London, R. L. "Correctness of a Compiler for a LISP Subset." In *Proceedings of the Association for Computing Machinery Conference on Proving Assertions about Programs,* pp. 51–57. Las Cruces, N. M.: New Mexico State University, 1972.
26. McCarthy, J. "Towards a Mathematical Science of Computation." In *Proceedings of the IFIP Congress.* Amsterdam: North-Holland, 1962.
27. Mendelson, E. *Introduction to Mathematical Logic.* Princeton, N. J.: D. Van Nostrand, 1964.
28. Mills, H. D. "Syntax-Directed Documentation for PL360." *Comm. ACM* 13, No. 4 (April 1970): 216–222.
29. Mills, H. D. "Top Down Programming in Large Systems." In *Debugging Techniques in Large Systems, Courant Computer Science Symposium 1.* Edited by Randall Rustin, pp. 41–55. Englewood Cliffs, N. J.: Prentice-Hall, 1971.
30. Nahikian, Howard M. *Topics in Modern Mathematics.* Edited by C. B. Allendoerfer. London: The MacMillan Co., Collier-MacMillan Ltd., 1966.
31. Naur, P. "Proof of Algorithms by General Snapshots." *BIT* 6 (1966): 310–316.
32. Naur, P. "Programming by Action Clusters." *BIT* 9 (1969): 250–258.
33. Nilsson, N. J. *Problem-Solving Methods in Artificial Intelligence.* New York: McGraw-Hill, 1971.
34. Scott, D. "The Lattice of Flow Diagrams." Programming Research Group report, Oxford University, 1970.
35. Scott, D. "An Outline of a Mathematical Theory of Computation." Programming Research Group report, Oxford University, 1970.
36. Snowdon, R. A. "PEARL: An Interactive System for the Preparation and Validation of Structured Programs." University of Newcastle Upon Tyne, Computing Laboratory Tech. Report No. 28, edited by Dr. B. Shaw, 1971.
37. Strachey, Christopher. "Towards a Formal Semantics." In *Formal*

Language Description Languages, edited by T. B. Steel, pp. 198–220. Amsterdam: North-Holland, 1966.

38. Wilder, Raymond L. *Evolution of Mathematical Concepts—An Elementary Study,* New York: John Wiley and Sons, 1968.
39. Wirth, Niklaus. "Program Development by Stepwise Refinement." *Comm. ACM* 14, No. 4 (April 1971): 221–227.
40. Zurcher, F., and Randell, B. "Iterative Multi-Level Modelling—A Methodology for Computer System Design." In *Proceedings of the IFIP Congress,* pp. D138–D142. Amsterdam: North-Holland, 1968.

ARTICLE 14

Reading Programs as a Managerial Activity

(1972)

It is standard business practice for managers to measure the quantity and quality of the production of their organizations. But to a great extent there has been an exception in programming, where the work has been of mysterious and specialized origin. This exception was necessary in the past because producing computer programming was an ad hoc process whose results were more visible in their execution than in themselves. But as technical foundations emerge and programming becomes a more manageable process, this condition will change.

As human endeavors go, programming is a very young activity. It has seen a succession of machines, beginning some 25 years ago. At the start, machines had very simple operations, necessarily done sequentially and related to only a single set of data storage elements. But up to the present we have gone through three major generations of hardware, each with increasing sophistication. There are new complexities in concurrent data processing operations, which involve not only several processors but, for each processor, many channels (which are themselves special processors), operating out of the same memories as the main central processing units. Extensive data storage and addressing techniques have been developed, in terms of based and indexed addressing in main storage, multiple register addressing for multiple high-speed processing, and a variety of mass storage and input/output units, each of which has a peculiar kind

Reprinted from *Defense Systems Management Review,* Robert Wayne Moore, Ed., Summer 1980, Vol. 3, No. 3, pp. 140–144.

of data storage and transfer linkage with the main storage. These changes in hardware architecture have had the effect of keeping the programming state of the art "off balance," making obsolete much of the knowledge of earlier machine generations (for example, IBSYS in the 7094, insofar as the 360 is concerned) and keeping programming the mysterious, black art that it often seems to be today.

As painful as hardware development has been in terms of software adaptation and the programming state of the art, that hardware development has produced spectacular results in terms of processing and storage capabilities. Machines can now process and store several orders of magnitude more data for the same cost as could be done at the beginning of computing. Hardware has proliferated complexity in software, but this very economy has also made certain simplifications in software development possible, by permitting inefficiencies in hardware usage. For example, high-level languages such as Fortran or PL/I are possible and practical in today's machines, where they would not have been reasonable for the efficiencies required of the early machines. The machines today can be used to help supervise their own activities and the activities of programmers, where they were too scarce and expensive a resource for that purpose in the early days of computing.

These economic and technical influences are converging to a new mode of operation in which the baseline for programming and software development is a "virtual machine" composed jointly of hardware, software, and often some firmware (that is, microprogramming). As a result the software management problem is seeing a more stable platform from which to develop. This more stable platform includes languages such as PL/I, Fortran, and Jovial, in which it is practical to carry out the main sections of large programming systems and in which the idiosyncracies of this or that machine are largely hidden by the translation from high-level language to machine language automatically and in a practically error-free way. This stable platform introduces a new possibility for managing programming and for the development of large programming systems that has not been present before. Until now there has been no good reason for managers to learn to read programs written in one machine code or another, since that ability would be obsolete by the next project, when a new machine architecture was implemented. But the stability of the present software platform at programming language levels above individual machines makes programming reading a skill and resource for managers that is worth acquiring and, in fact, is necessary for the effective development of large programming systems or the evaluation of programmers in development projects.

Programs are imperative statements to machines to accomplish purposes of some set of users. These imperative statements are phrased in programming languages, and their authorship is called programming. But as in any written language, it is usually easier to learn to read the language than to write it, and in fact a great deal can be accomplished in the acquisition of information or the critical review of documents in the language with a reading-only capability. Ordinarily, in reading a language, one picks up automatically a certain ability to write it, but not necessarily the ability to accomplish particular objectives in such writing.

For these reasons it seems that the time has come for managers to begin reading programs in a systematic way, even though the writing of such programs is not, and never will be, part of their responsibility. The advent of structured programming makes the reading of programs more easily accomplished than was ever before possible because it permits the reader to enjoy a special privilege in the reading, namely, that of reading in a sequential, systematic way, as in an ordinary English text, in order to follow the imperative requirements being laid down by the program. In programs that are not structured, program reading requires a great deal of jumping back and forth in the sequence of the text and keeping track mentally of many contingencies at which branches might be taken and special or different conditions handled. Structured programming forces the writer of programs to organize the language statements so that they can be read sequentially. The main beneficiaries of this discipline are the programmers themselves, but anybody else who has an occasion to read the code benefits in even greater individual ways because of the problem of familiarity with the program. Quite often a programmer writing an unstructured program will have in mind some pattern of operations that permits jumping back and forth in an efficient way. But just as often, the jumping back and forth even ends up confusing the original programmer, and the result is that program errors may go as far as system integration or even into user operation before being detected. For someone unfamiliar with the program, structured programming has an even more dramatic effect because this person does not have the problem of determining which jumps to look at first or how to keep track of the various jumps in some pattern of thinking that must be developed ad hoc during the reading process.

In time, it is expected that we will get the horse before the cart and teach program reading to anyone before program writing. In fact, our present programming courses are patterned along those of a "course in French dictionary." In such a course we study the dictionary and learn what the meanings of French words are in English (that corresponds to learning what PL/I or Fortran statements do to data). At the completion of such a course in French dictionary we then invite and exhort the graduates to go forth and write French poetry. Of course, the result is that some people can write French poetry and some not, but the skills critical to writing poetry were not learned in the course they just took in French dictionary. For example, the ones who could write English poetry will probably end up as the best writers of French poetry. This corresponds in programming to the fact that the people taking the programming course who end up doing the best programming are those who came into the course with certain algorithmic and analytical skills, quite independent of anything they learned in the course itself.

But it is a fact that one may read programs for quite different reasons than one might have for writing them, and that skills of verification or of translation may be quite different than the algorithmic and analytical skills required in writing programs.

With the wholesale reading of programs by managers, other anomalies of programming can be expected to fall into place. It is curious that in programming, the typical programmer never expects to see anyone else read the program. The programmer will be judged by execution and judged in highly superficial ways at that. When machines do a million multiplies a second, a factor of ten in inefficiency is not even detectable unless the program is a well-worn set of problems that many other people have done for comparison. Similarly, the use of core is difficult to judge unless there are well-worn standards of comparison around. We know from experience and spot sampling that programs can be very inefficient in both throughput and core, and we also know that program logic can be very tortured, difficult to maintain, and practically impossible to build on or extend; yet programs with such gross deficiencies pass "the inspection of execution" successfully every day. It is small wonder that programmers have psychological problems at times because they are deprived of a very human need in their work—the need to be appreciated or the need to be commended for work well done. As long as no one reads their code and as long as everyone concerned knows that the inspection of execution is such a gross measurement tool, there is not a great deal of incentive or reward for doing a very good job.

It is surprising sometimes to think of how fast a society can become inflexible. Programming is less than 20 years old; as a management activity, it is less than 10 years old. It has already developed some sacred cows, such as seeing the reading of code as a sign of mistrust or the judgment of code by anything but the gross inspection by execution an impertinence of management. These sacred cows were born easily, and they will be slain easily as well. Any experience at all with managers who read code intelligently shows that the programmers are more motivated and proud of their work in a way not possible otherwise.

The reading of programs by managers will also introduce a new level of precision in programming that is made possible, but not made inevitable, by new technical developments in programming. Structured programming and results in program correctness give programmers a technical foundation for writing nearly error-free code, but this potential will not be realized without a psychological transformation as well. We go back to the problem of a 20-year-young activity groping its way into a systematic process, moving from a frustrating trial-and-error, highly "creative" activity in which cleverness and obfuscation are virtues to a systematic engineering-like process in which the emphasis is on precision, logic, and repeatability. This psychological transformation is not a process that is reserved for a very few gifted individuals. It is a process that we have seen begin to happen on a broad scale from junior up to senior personnel. It simply amounts to this. When a programmer knows that what is in his or her head is correct, it becomes more important all of a sudden to get it on paper in exactly that correct form, to look up past data definitions in order to be sure that they are precisely compatible, and to examine every special case with more care in order to make sure that they treat the subject in exactly the right way. This psychology of precision moves from that understanding of the programmer's own logical capability clear through to the development of machine-readable material, however it is accomplished. On the other hand, if a programmer thinks that what is in his or her mind is correct but is subconsciously counting on debugging runs to iron out small errors in logic, then concentration is lost here and in the entire process, and small errors are made that later torment the programmer and others in the debugging process. The critical matter is not simply for a programmer to be able to program correctly. The programmer must *know* that he or she is able to program correctly. For it is this latter knowledge of the ability to program correctly that affects the psychological transformation and makes possible the concentration that is necessary to write the correct programs. This difference between being able to program correctly and knowing it is a distinction that is available to a programmer only after considerable education in questions of mathematics and logic that allow a person to regard programming as a logical activity similar in form to a game such as tic-tac-toe, and differing from the game only in the degree of complexity, but not in any inherent requirement that transcends the programmer's human capabilities.

Programmers with this kind of psychological transformation will be disappointed indeed if their code is not read and if the reasoning that they formulate for their code is not appreciated.

The question of documentation has plagued programming management for a long time. In the mathematical theory behind structured programming, documentation turns out to have a natural home. The documentation of a program and the proof that it is correct are synonymous. In fact, anything beyond that is superfluous. This proof of correctness may be at several levels: at the user level, the program maintenance level, or even in some cases at a machine level. But the correctness problem gives the rationale and a basis for judgment of the relevance and quality of documentation that we have not had before.

In the proofs of program correctness, documentation appears as an adjunct of the program itself. It is easy to point to documentation that attempts to replace the code. When this occurs, there is a frequent danger that the code gets changed without the documentation being changed; the result is that documentation loses its currency. When programs are maintained in a visibly correct form, the standards of correctness are themselves standards for maintaining documentation in a current and relevant form.

ARTICLE 15

How to Buy Quality Software

(1974)

Some Lessons Learned—and Some Not!

Software procurement has many similarities to and analogies with hardware procurement, but a blind transfer of concepts and procedures has led to monumental disasters. And a strange thing about these disasters is that they are usually hidden by both buyer and seller. The buyer does not want to look dumb or taken in, so the reaction to the disaster usually takes the form "Look how much we learned in phase 0; we're in good shape to begin phase 1 development"—when in truth the term "phase 0" came into being only some six months ago, when something seemed amiss; three years ago the project had no phases—it was the real thing! The seller does not want to look dumb either, or to have the disaster known and affect the seller's reputation. So disasters are often hidden, and chances to learn important lessons are missed.

Admitting that there are similarities to hardware procurement, we also note crucial differences in software procurement [4].

1. More flexibility to engineering changes is required. "Everyone knows that hardware has to be fixed for manufacturing, but software has a trivial manufacturing process—duplicating a tape, and that sort of thing, so why can't the software respond?"

© 1974 IEEE. Reprinted, with permission, from *EASCON 1974 Record,* IEEE Electronics and Aerospace Systems Convention, October 7–9, 1974, Washington, D.C.

2. Hardware deficiencies need to be made up in software. "So the memory packaging didn't work out and only half the planned memory is available, but some clever programmers ought to be able to work around that."
3. Sheer complexity has to be taken into account. Hardware function is typically provided in an instruction set of small, independent operations, each of which can be designed and tested in relative isolation. Software function is typically provided in the user interface that calls complex interdependent sets of operations that are difficult to design and test.

A Pragmatic Conclusion

It is not possible to adequately accept a software system "pitched over the wall" without exorbitant expense. Why? Because what needs to be tested is the design of the software itself. In hardware the design is relatively simple, but the manufacturing is critical, so tests of hardware function confirm manufacturing to relatively simple design. In software the design is relatively complex, and the manufacturing is trivial, so tests of software function depend critically on design.

Even more crucial, the most important thing about a software system is the integrity of its design—but that integrity cannot be specified except in qualitative terms. Yet it is just that integrity that makes the software system easy or hard to maintain and modify, impossible or not to use as a platform for a follow-on capability. A software system can pass its performance and capability acceptance tests and still be an internal nightmare of ad hoc designs put together as a tour de force in the short-term memories of a team of programmers that is disbanded and scattered as soon as the tests are completed.

The basic problem in buying software is that complexity still defies measurement in pragmatic terms [7]. We can measure whether a software system requires too much memory, or too much time, and react accordingly. But we do not have practical, objective ways to tell a well-designed system of deep simplicities from a brute force bowl of spaghetti. Structured programming has made a quantum jump in addressing the design problem [5, 6, 9], but there is still need for the practical measurement of complexity within structured systems.

One way around this is not to buy software systems at all, but to rent them. In this case there are significant incentives for the supplier to provide a system that works after acceptance testing, as well as through acceptance testing, and the burden of maintaining a bowl of spaghetti falls on the supplier. For one-of-a-kind systems, renting may not be feasible, but providing incentives for the post-acceptance performance and maintenance may still be possible.

A Pragmatic Proposal

Stop accepting software systems "pitched over the wall." Instead, require two conditions for systems development, which are observable during the development process: (1) *top down structured programming* [6] to provide better visibility of system integrity during its construction and (2) *development accounting* [8] in order to better assess the quality of the development process itself.

In top down structured programming, a systematic discipline permits a continuous, orderly review of development progress, as systems specifications are translated into design and functional software. This is in sharp contrast with traditional bottom up development, in which little effective review is possible until the integration phase late in the development. Top down structured programming requires more design skill and thinking at the beginning of a development but pays off in management visibility during development [1]. Top down development also makes development accounting feasible, which is not feasible in bottom up development because of the sheer amount of rework and finger pointing at integration time.

The idea of development accounting is to record enough data on development history, including the fate of every line of code created, that meaningful management statistics can be generated and studied. There may be resistance to recording the fate of every line of code—every programmer mistake—in some projects, but it has already been done [1, 3] and represents minor growing pains in an adolescent profession. There will be costs associated with such recording, but at most 5% in projects where 20% overruns are the rule and 100% overruns occur more often than anyone cares to admit.

It is to be expected that many new ideas and uses for such data will arise when it becomes available for study and use. Just as in financial accounting, management standards of integrity, objectivity, and judgment need to be developed. But with so much at stake and so little to risk, development accounting seems first-order business for systems management in learning better "how to buy quality software."

Development Accounting

Software development is a new activity for the human race, dealing with complexity and logical precision never required of humans before. So frustrations and subsequent improvements can be expected. As a consequence of its infancy and adolescence, software development has been practiced as a black art—not maliciously, but because it never seemed possible or necessary to make a public practice out of it. But software development technology is coming of age and moving from private art to public practice [1, 3].

The young (people or industries) are never much interested in history, but they learn. Theoretically, a software system exists at any moment independent of its historical development, and any other history arriving at the same system will produce the same subsequent usage history. But the practical chance of two different development histories producing an identical software system is near zero. The systems may look alike to the user, each may have "no known errors," and so on, but their internals will be different, and their design integrity and future error properties will be different. Suppose two such systems, called A and B and developed to the same specifications, produced the statistics in Table 15-1. After acceptance, each system has "no known errors." In fact, system A may have more errors left in it than system B. But the evidence points to system B, which was hard to put together, with apparently subtle interface errors that took considerable time to find, and therefore has the likelihood of more such errors not yet turned up. From a practical standpoint these are not the same systems, and usually A will turn out to be better designed (fewer old errors) and more reliable.

TABLE 15-1

	A	*B*
Development		
Lines of Code	50,000	50,000
Errors Fixed		
day old	500	500
week old	10	50
month old	5	50
year old	5	100
Known Errors	0	0
Acceptance		
Errors Fixed	10	50
Known Errors	0	0

The foregoing statistics are not kept, of course, in the typical black art software development process, because of the notion that it is a private matter how a system gets to a state of "no known errors." But it does indeed matter how a system gets to such a state because it foretells how the system will fare in the future.

Development Statistics

A well-designed system of deep simplicities has a development history that is sharply distinguished from the brute force bowl of spaghetti. The most noticeable difference is the debugging history. A well-designed system can be put together with few errors during its code and integration phases [1, 2]. A bowl of spaghetti will have a history of much error discovery and fixup.

So one critical accounting parameter is the number of errors found and fixed—all errors from the coding pad or terminal on. It is state-of-the-art procedure today to track errors from unit test on, but not state-of-the-art procedure to track errors from lines of code on.

Another difference is in the age of the errors found. In a well-designed top down structured programming development [6], testing under actual system conditions begins early, with system errors found in typically a day or so. In the brute force approach, code is frequently unit tested with drivers, and system errors are often found later in integration—weeks or months later.

The number and age of errors lead to the idea of *error days* as probably the best single statistic we could measure for estimating the quality of an otherwise accepted system. It indicates probable future error incidents, but also indirectly indicates the effectiveness of the design and testing process. High error days indicate either many errors (probably due to poor intermediate design products) or long-lived errors (probably due to poor integration and testing procedures).

With experience, other statistics will prove useful in evaluating system development quality. Reasonably objective classifications of all program additions, deletions, and modifications into various categories are possible, such as the following.

Planned Work

1. Normal production
2. Scaffolding
3. Drivers

Unplanned Rework

1. Specification changes
2. Design improvements
3. Design errors
4. Logic errors
5. Syntax errors

For example, syntax errors are found during assembling/compiling, logic errors are found in test execution, and design errors are found in coding, and so on. Such ratios as

$$\frac{\text{Design errors}}{\text{Logic errors}}, \quad \frac{\text{Logic errors}}{\text{Syntax errors}}, \quad \frac{\text{Design errors}}{\text{Normal Production}}$$

will describe different aspects of the development process and provide quality indicators and standards with programming management and procurement experience.

References

1. Baker, F. T. "Chief Programmer Team Management of Production Programming." *IBM Systems Journal* 11, No. 1, (1972): 56–73.
2. Baker, F. T. "System Quality Through Structured Programming." In *AFIPS Conference Proceedings.* 1972 Fall Joint Computer Conference, vol. 41, part I, pp. 339–343. Arlington, Va.: AFIPS Press, 1972.
3. Baker, F. T., and Mills, H. D. "Chief Programmer Teams." *Datamation* (Dec. 1973): 58–61.
4. Boehm, B. W. "Software and Its Impact: A Qualitative Assessment." *Datamation* (May 1973): 48–59.
5. Dahl, O. J., Dijkstra, E. W., and Hoare, C. A. R. *Structured Programming.* London: Academic Press, 1972.
6. Mills, H. D. "Top Down Programming in Large Systems." In *Debugging Techniques in Large Systems, Courant Computer Science Symposium 1.* Edited by Randall Rustin, pp. 41–45. Englewood Cliffs, N. J.: Prentice-Hall, 1971.
7. Mills, H. D. "The Complexity of Programs." In *Program Test Methods.* Edited by W. C. Hetzel, Englewood Cliffs, N. J.: Prentice-Hall, 1972.

8. Mills, H. D. "On The Development of Large Reliable Programs." In *1973 IEEE Symposium on Software Reliability,* pp. 155–159. Silver Spring, Md.: IEEE, 1973.
9. Wirth, N. *Systematic Programming: An Introduction.* Englewood Cliffs, N. J.: Prentice-Hall, 1973.

ARTICLE 16

How to Write Correct Programs and Know It

(1975)

Abstract

There is no foolproof way ever to know that you have found the last error in a program. So the best way to acquire confidence that a program has no errors is never to find the first one, no matter how much it is tested and used. It is an old myth that programming must be an error-prone, cut-and-try process of frustration and anxiety. The new reality is that you can learn to consistently write programs that are error free in their debugging and subsequent use. This new reality is founded on the ideas of structured programming and program correctness, which not only provide a systematic approach to programming but also motivate a high degree of concentration and precision in the coding subprocess.

Key Words and Phrases

structured programming
program correctness
programming practices

Introduction

An Old Myth and a New Reality

It is an old myth that programming must be an error-prone, cut-and-try process of frustration and anxiety. The new reality is that you can learn to consistently write programs that are correct *ab initio* and prove to be error free in their debugging and subsequent use.

By practicing principles of structured programming and its mathematics you should be able to write correct programs and convince yourself and others that they are correct. Your programs should ordinarily compile and execute properly the first time you try them, and from then on. If you are a professional programmer, errors in either syntax or logic should be extremely rare because you can avoid them by positive actions on your part. Programs do not acquire bugs as people do germs—just by hanging around other buggy programs. They acquire bugs only from their authors.

There is a simple reason that you should expect your own programs to be completely free of errors from the very start, for your own peace of mind. It is that you will never be able to prove that such a program has no errors in it in a foolproof way. This is not because programs are so complex that it isn't worth the effort; it is because there simply is no human way—logical or mathematical—to prove it, no matter how much effort you might put into it.

The ultimate faith you can have in a program is in the thought process that created it. With every error you find in testing and use, that faith is undermined. Even if you have found the last error left in your program, you cannot prove it is the last, and you cannot know it is the last. So your real opportunity to know you have written a correct program is to never find the first error in it, no matter how much it is inspected, tested, and used.

Now the new reality is that professional programmers, with professional care, can learn to consistently write programs that are error-free from their inception—programs of 20, 50, 200, 500 lines, and up. Just knowing that it is possible is half the battle. Learning how to write such programs is the other half. And gaining experience in writing such programs, small ones at first, then larger ones, provides a new psychological basis for sustained concentration in programming that is difficult to imagine without direct personal experience. Professional programmers today are producing code at the rate of one error per year in their finished work; that performance is not possible by cut-and-try programming. The professional programmer of tomorrow will remember, more or less vividly, every error in his career.

What is a Correct Program?

Cut-and-try programming faces three kinds of difficulties:

1. Specification changes
2. Programming errors
3. Processor discrepancies

A correct program defines a procedure for a stated processor to satisfy a stated specification. If you do not know what a program is supposed to do, or do not know how the processor is supposed to work, you cannot write a correct program. So we presume a known specification and a known processor throughout. Even so, a practicing programmer must be prepared to deal with incomplete and changing specifications and with processors that behave differently than their manuals say. For those difficulties we have no systematic remedy, except for radical reductions of programming errors that can help isolate difficulties in these other areas. Nevertheless, the usual experience in programming often fails to separate these three sources of difficulty, so that programming errors—lumped in with everything else—seem much more inevitable than they really are.

Writing correct programs does not mean that you can write programs once and for all. It means that you can write programs to do exactly what you intend them to do. But as intentions change, program changes are required as well. The same opportunities and principles apply to these program changes. You should be able to modify programs correctly, if they are well designed and explained, as well as write them correctly to begin with.

This distinction between correctness and capability is critical in understanding this new reality. Determining what a program should do is usually a much deeper problem than writing a program to do a predetermined process. It is the latter task that you can do correctly. For example, you might wish to program a world champion chess player; that is a matter of capability, and a problem you may or may not be able to solve. Or you could wish to program a chess player whose move has been determined for every situation that can arise. You can write such a program correctly, but whether or not it becomes a world champion is another matter.

The Difficulty with Correctness Proofs

We begin with a fundamental difficulty, which may seem fatal to our objective but which paradoxically tells us what to do. There is no foolproof way to prove that a program is correct. This fundamental difficulty is not in programming, but in mathematics—because the schoolboy idea of mathematics (or logic) as a body of supernatural verities and infallible procedures is simply not so. Mathematics is a human activity subject to human fallibility. It has no basic secrets of truth or reason. One simple example is in what we call the "natural numbers," which are not natural at all. Everyone learns to count in the "natural numbers" from someone else, who learned to count from someone else. But reaching back far enough, nobody knew how to count! The natural numbers are conscious human inventions, just as radios, Hamlet, and airplanes are. They have survived because they work. And so it is with what school children learn of fractions, quadratic equations, calculus, and so on, as though they were "the truth, the whole truth, and nothing but the truth," when nothing could be further from the truth.

Even so, mathematics is very useful, and we believe it to be largely correct in most of its development. It is correct enough to conduct business, design computers that run, and send men to the moon and back. And that is pretty good. It just is not foolproof. Indeed, you should use all the mathematics you can to help convince yourself that your programs are correct. But you should do so knowing the limitations of mathematics yourself, and not looking for some magic to replace your own responsibility.

What is a Mathematics Proof?

If there is no infallible road to a mathematics proof, what is it, and why bother anyway?

A mathematics proof is a repeatable experiment, just as an experiment in a physics or chemistry laboratory. But the main subject in each experiment is another person. The intended result of the experiment is a subjective conviction on the part of this other person that a given hypothesis leads to a given conclusion. The experiment may be carried out in a conversation, collectively in a lecture, or in writing. In a lecture or in writing, many people may be involved. A successful experiment ends in a subjective conviction by a listener or reader. The conviction may be incorrect. The conviction may be correct but based on a faulty conversation. Any human fallibility may be present, because it is a human activity.

The conversation deals with a proof that the hypothesis leads to the conclusion. The proof may consist of a single claim, "It is obvious," or a sequence of such claims for a succession of intermediate conclusions, each of which serves as a hypothesis for the next conclusion. At each claim the subject agrees or disagrees; in the first case the experiment continues, and in the second case the experiment terminates. If the final conclusion is reached, the experiment terminates in success; otherwise, it ends in failure.

Mathematical notation plays no role in the proof, except in its effect on the experimental subject. What mathematical notation does is to facilitate human communication and memory. It permits a succession of claims to be stated and agreed to rapidly, so that more ground can be covered for the same human effort. It permits, by pencil and paper, a person to extend memory for details (for example, doing long division or simplifying an algebraic expression). It even permits humans to agree on rules for agreeing about proof claims (mathematical logic).

What is a convincing proof? Clearly, that depends on the experimental subject. But for a given subject there are many conversations possible about the same hypothesis and conclusion. If there are too few steps, the leap in intuition may be too large. If there are too many steps, human exhaustion or lack of interest may set in. So there is a balance needed, which depends on the subject. But it is a typically human problem, whose resolution requires human experience and judgment.

Why bother with mathematics at all, if it only leads to subjective convictions? Because that is the only kind of reasoned conviction possible, and because the principal experimental subject of your conversation is yourself! Mathematics provides language and procedure for your own mental security.

Acquiring Confidence in Programs

As we have noted, our ultimate confidence in a program is subjective, whether we realize it or not. If we believe a program is correct because of a formal proof of its correctness, our subjective confidence is in the proof methodology and in the further belief that this methodology applies to the full scope of the program.

More often, our subjective confidence in a program is based on a combination of experience from its inspection (including formal proofs of correctness), testing, and usage.

If programming is practiced as a cut-and-try activity, a certain number of errors are expected in syntax and logic, and the compiling, testing, and debugging phase is further expected to uncover most of these errors. But even in a cut-and-try activity, if the number of errors found in testing and debugging is excessive, a thoughtful programmer becomes uneasy. Instead of being grateful for finding so many errors, the programmer begins to doubt the thought processes that produced them. Many programmers recommend starting all over when this occurs.

On the other hand, as happens occasionally even in a cut-and-try activity, if a program is free from error in all its testing and usage—with no debugging required—the subjective confidence of the programmer is remarkably affected. It will never be possible to prove that such a program has no errors. But each new hurdle it passes in more testing and usage improves the plausibility that this is so and that the thought processes that produced the program are holding up.

Thus when you think about it, the real objective in programming should be to write correct programs from the start—not merely to emerge from debugging with no errors. The new reality is that writing such correct programs from the start is a very possible human activity. And so it is that the very impossibility of foolproof proofs of the correctness of programs tells us what we must do. If no error ever occurs in a program, then a proof of correctness can tell us no more.

The personal discovery of this new reality changes the life of a programmer by introducing an entirely new psychological awareness of the power and benefits of concentration in program design and coding. There is little motivation to concentrate in a cut-and-try activity; one more error to discover among many is of little consequence. But in a precision mental activity the difference between no errors and one is profound. When a programmer discovers the power of his or her own mental capabilities, what goes into the program as a reflection of the programmer's thinking becomes much more important.

If a child knows how to play a perfect game of tic-tac-toe but does not know what he knows, he still loses games occasionally from a lack of concentration but does not recognize his lapses. If asked to play an important game (say, for a candy bar), his attitude is "I hope I win," but if he loses, he says "Tough luck." If that same child discovers that he knows how to play tic-tac-toe perfectly, his whole attitude is changed. Instead of saying, "I hope I win," he says. "It's up to me!" He may lose, but instead of "Tough luck," he says, "I goofed!", and he has discovered his own lack of concentration. And if he likes candy bars, he soon learns to concentrate during important games and to relax later. It is the same with the programmer who discovers that it is important to know "how to write correct programs and know it."

Programming Fundamentals

Functions as Expressions of Essential Program Logic

A program operates on data, some of it intentional, some of it often a byproduct of doing something else. For example, a program may operate on an array to recalculate its elements but will at the same time calculate subscripts in order to identify specific elements of the array during execution. In particular, the last values for subscripts will be left lying around in memory. Ordinarily, one will be interested in the array elements and whether they are correctly computed, and not in the last values various subscripts happened to have. But in some cases computed data not central to the intention of the program may find a use in another program if its condition is known.

This picture of programs that operate on data, whether of central interest or not, arises naturally from viewing data as it occurs in machine storage. It is well known that such usage of data is one of the principal pitfalls in making larger and larger systems of programs work. It is the question of side effects, where some data not immediately visible at a program interface is altered or used.

The idea of a mathematical function allows one to be precise about the intentional effect of programs on data. For example, in the array case its elements can be mapped into new elements using a functional description. Nothing is said about subscripts or even if subscripts are used in the computation of its elements. In this form anyone else is forewarned that any assumptions about subscripts are made at one's own peril and are probably untrue.

A typical first encounter with the idea of a function is one that relates two variables, say, a function f that relates y to x in the form

$$y = f(x),$$

where

$$f(x) = x^2 + 3x + 2.$$

For our purposes in dealing with finite but complex combinatorial objects another definition of a function, as a set of ordered pairs, is more useful. For example, we may write $(x, y) \in f$ instead of $y = f(x)$ to emphasize the set aspect. Since a function is a set, the ordinary set operations apply to functions. The expression $x^2 + 3x + 2$ is a part of a rule that defines which ordered pairs belong to f; in fact, it is only one of many possible rules. In programming, functional specification corresponds to function, and program corresponds to rule.

For the example above, we can use set notation to describe f as

$$f = \{(x, y) \mid y = x^2 + 3x + 2\}.$$

The variables x and y are dummy variables, since

$$g = \{(u, v) \mid v = u^2 + 3u + 2\}$$

or

$$h = \{(u, v) \mid v = (u + 1)\ (u + 2)\}$$

are both sets identical to f. In this context we see that the three rules correspond to three different programs (different operations and different variables) that realize the same functional specification.

Structured Programming and Program Correctness

You can write programs with correct function logic by using principles of structured programming and program correctness that are applied in your line-by-line program construction. The task of the programmer begins with a functional specification that describes what the program-to-be is to do. In the traditional process the programmer somehow converts that specification into program statements and then verifies that the statements created in fact do what the program was intended to do. In structured programming there is a precise description of the results of this mental activity. It begins with the functional specification and repeatedly divides it, a step at a time, into new functional subspecifications, connected by program statements, until the program is complete. It does not consist of a large leap in faith and hope from a functional specification to a loose collection of program statements that are fitted piece-by-piece into a program. The structured programming process analyzes functional specifications rather than synthesizing program statements. One brief way of understanding structured programming and how to prove the correctness of programs written in this way is as follows.

a. Any functional specification can be defined in terms of a mathematical function that maps inputs into outputs without regard to its internal construction. We show such a function (functional specification) as

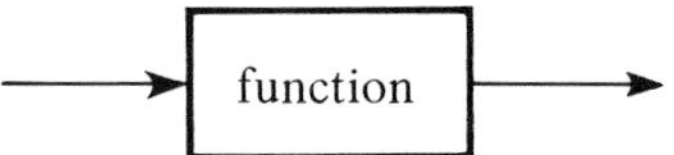

b. Any flowchartable program realizes a function that can be expressed by the repeated use of only the three basic program figures shown in Figure 16-1.

Each IF-THEN-ELSE, SEQUENCE, and DO-WHILE on the left-hand side is a function realized in a new way on the right-hand side. Each THEN part, . . . , DO part on the right-hand side is just a new function and can be replaced by another IF-THEN-ELSE, SEQUENCE, or DO-WHILE figure in a subsequent expansion step.

The structured programming process proceeds from an original functional specification as a series of design decisions that specify which figure and what resulting new tests and functions are required to expand the original and any intermediate functions required. When the functions required can be written directly as program statements, the expansion process is completed.

In a language such as PL/I these expressions can be written di-

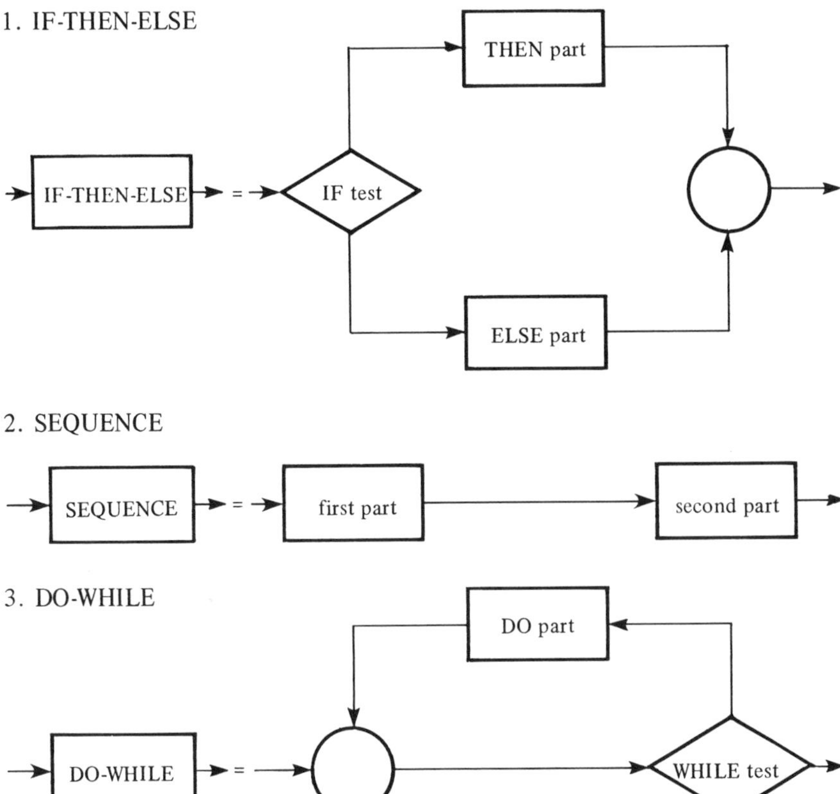

FIGURE 16-1

rectly in matching statements, without labels or GO TO's to result finally in a GO TO–free program. Such a GO TO–free program can be read sequentially, without jumping around. The relationship between program text and execution thus becomes especially clear.

c. At each expansion step the correctness of that step can be decided by answering a standard question that goes with that type of expansion. If the answer is yes, the step is correct, and the program expansion can proceed. If the answer is no, the step is not correct, and a new one should be defined right then. The questions are:

1. IF-THEN-ELSE: Whenever the IF test is true, does the THEN part do the IF-THEN-ELSE, and whenever the IF test is false, does the ELSE part do the IF-THEN-ELSE?
2. SEQUENCE: Does the first part followed by the second part do the sequence?

3. DO-WHILE: (a) Is termination guaranteed? (b) Whenever the WHILE test is true, does the DO part followed by the DO-WHILE do the DO-WHILE, and whenever the WHILE test is false, does the identity function (no-op program) do the DO-WHILE?

The questions for the IF-THEN-ELSE and SEQUENCE expansions are self-evident. The question for the DO-WHILE becomes self-evident by observing this sequence of equivalent expansions: Expand the execution of the DO-WHILE into an IF-THEN (no ELSE part), and then observe that the DO-WHILE reappears as the second part of the sequence making up the THEN part (see Figure 16-2).

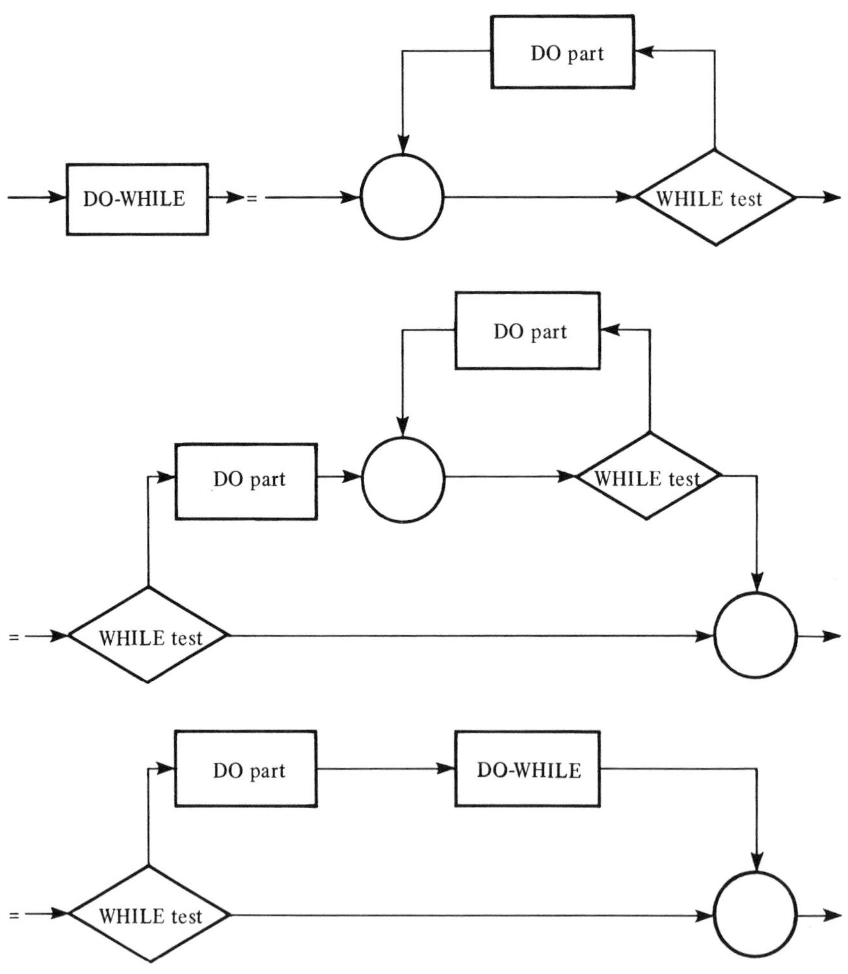

FIGURE 16-2

d. When steps b and c are carried out to the point where no subspecifications remain, the result is a complete program, and the proof of its correctness has been completed as well.

Some illustrations of individual steps with their correctness questions are:

1. IF-THEN-ELSE: $z = \max(x, y)$

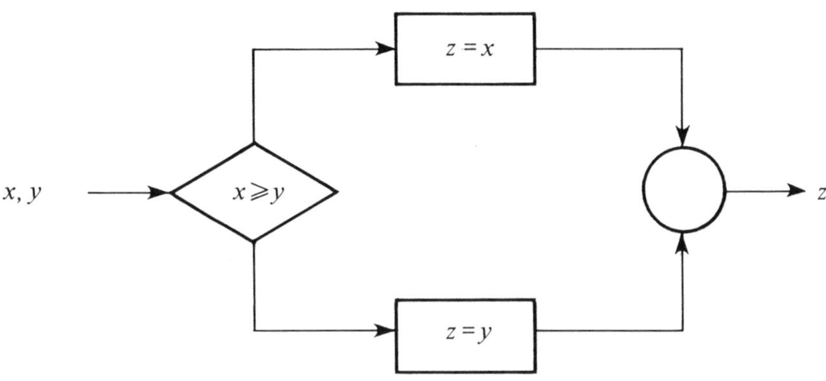

Whenever $x \geq y$ does $z = x$ do $z = \max(x, y)$ and whenever $x < y$ does $z = y$ do $z = \max(x, y)$?

2. SEQUENCE: $z = \max(x, \text{abs}(y))$

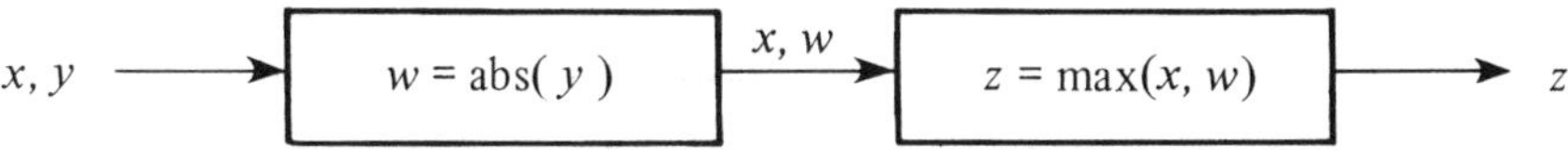

Does $w = \text{abs}(y)$ followed by $z = \max(x, w)$, do $z = \max(x, \text{abs}(y))$?

3. DO-WHILE: remove leading zeroes (from a positive decimal integer)

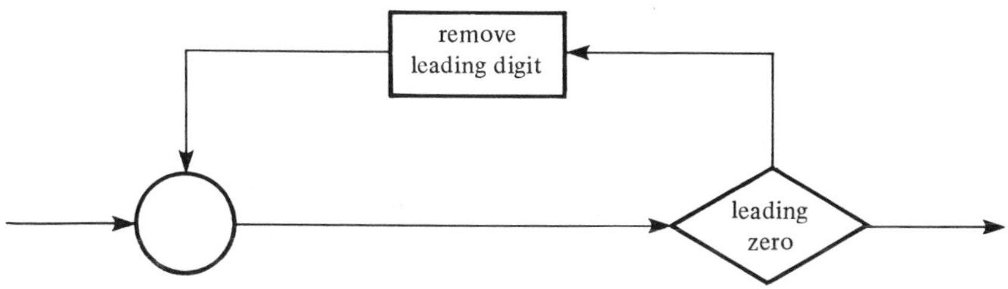

(a) Is termination guaranteed? (b) Whenever there is a leading zero, does remove leading digit followed by remove leading zeros do remove leading zeros; and whenever there is no leading zero, does doing nothing do remove leading zeros?

The Disease of Syntax Errors

The problem of writing correct program logic is more difficult than that of writing correct syntax, and most of this article is about the latter problem. Our concern with correct syntax is to identify an attitude of precision that will carry over with good effect into the problem of program logic. In fact, this emphasis on syntax is based on the reverse experience that when programmers get program logic correct from the start, the attitude of precision carries back into the coding, and they begin to get program syntax right from the start, with no special effort.

With the advent of compilers and other debugging aids, it has been easy to adopt an attitude of "let the compiler do it" in finding errors of syntax. But in the long run this is a devastating attitude because it fosters ignorance and carelessness that slides over to program logic that the compiler cannot uncover.

If your programming is a vocation rather than an avocation, there is no reason for you to take errors of syntax lightly in writing a program. Syntax errors are errors of either ignorance or carelessness. If they are errors of ignorance, you need to do more homework on the syntax of your programming languages. If they are errors of carelessness, you need to learn how to concentrate and take what you are doing more seriously.

Writing correct syntax is like playing a perfect game of tic-tac-toe, not like sawing a board exactly in half, which requires perfect precision. It is a combinatorial process that requires only a fixed and humanly possible degree of precision for correctness. For example, a complicated expression may end with five (or six) parentheses; but it will never end with 5.37521 . . . parentheses. The difference between five and six is distinguishable in writing and reading, and whether it should be five or six depends only on previous characters of discrete kinds and locations in the expression.

Writing Some Searches

Search 1

In order to see these principles in action, consider the problem of searching for an item called KEY in a list called TABLE, with a total of N elements, denoted TABLE(1), . . . , TABLE(N), respectively; we are to display the results of the search in an item called I, which is to satisfy the relation

TABLE(I) = KEY, if possible

I = 0, otherwise.

Note that we have defined a function in words. The argument is N + 2 items, namely N, TABLE(1), . . . , TABLE(N), KEY, and the value is I, as diagrammed

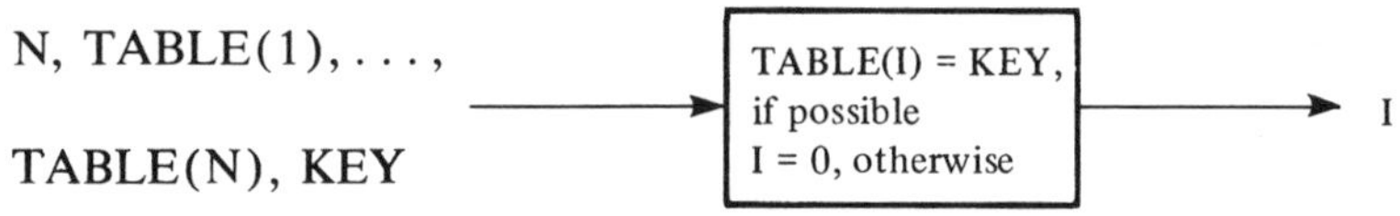

```
N, TABLE(1), . . . ,          ┌──────────────────┐
                              │ TABLE(I) = KEY,  │
              ───────────────►│ if possible      │──────────────► I
TABLE(N), KEY                 │ I = 0, otherwise │
                              └──────────────────┘
```

It is easy to invent a program, say in PL/I, for this function.

```
SEARCH1:PROCEDURE;
        I = 0;
        DO J = 1 TO N;
               IF TABLE(J) = KEY THEN
                     I= J;
        END;
END SEARCH1;
```

It is not an efficient program, to be sure, but it seems to be correct. Why? First, it is a sequence of two subprograms whose functions are

1. first part: set I to zero.
2. second part: find, if possible, a value for I for which TABLE(I) = KEY; otherwise, leave I unchanged.

The sequence question above asks if first part followed by second part does the sequence. It is believed so. Next, the second part above is itself a loop, but not a DO-WHILE figure. Instead, it is the familiar indexed loop, which we will call DO loop for short. It is worth our attention as an extra convenience beyond the three basic figures given above, under an extra point of discipline. This extra discipline is that the index of the DO loop is not altered in any way by the DO part of the DO loop. Then the DO loop becomes an extended sequence, with a first part, second part, . . . , *n*th part. The corresponding correctness question is a simple extension of the sequence question as well. The DO part in this case is

DO part: if TABLE(J) = KEY then set I to J;
otherwise, leave I unchanged

and it is easy to see that the sequence of such DO parts, for J = 1, . . . , N indeed does the DO loop (second part above). Finally, the DO part is itself an IF-THEN (IF-THEN-ELSE with null ELSE) figure, and it is easy to see that it satisfies its functional requirement.

In summary, we have articulated an analysis a programmer does at a glance to illustrate the building blocks of a skilled observer. In this case they are structured in a tree of the form shown in Figure 16-3.

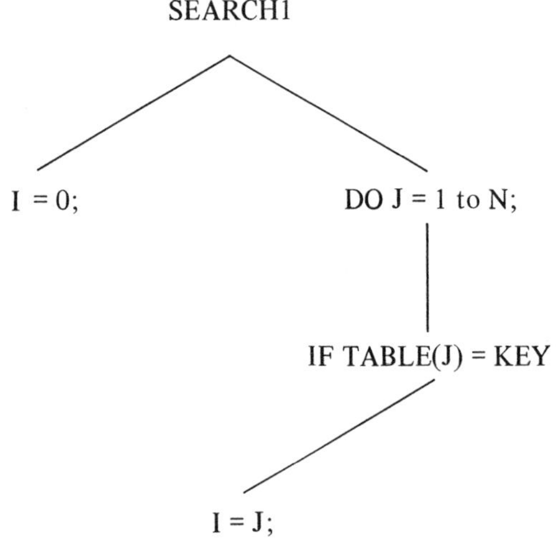

FIGURE 16-3

Each node defines a subfunction and subprogram simultaneously. A skilled pianist has learned to play scales and arpeggios with little attention to the individual notes, and a skilled programmer also learns to put small combinations of statements together in almost the same way. Even so, the basic questions are valid and need consideration explicitly. If the answers are obvious, they will not take much time to verify; if not obvious, they are worth looking into.

Search 2

It is easy to see how to improve SEARCH1 to SEARCH2 as follows:

```
SEARCH2:PROCEDURE;
        I = 0;
        DO J = 1 TO N WHILE(I = 0);
              IF TABLE(J) = KEY THEN
                    I = J;
        END;
END SEARCH2;
```

Whereas SEARCH1 looked at every item in TABLE, whether successful or not part way through, SEARCH2 has enough sense to stop looking at the first success in TABLE. The only change in SEARCH2 is the WHILE clause. The effect is a DO loop with a conditional termination, which can be rewritten as:

```
J = 1;
DO WHILE(J <= N & I = 0);
        IF TABLE(J) = KEY THEN
              I = J;
        J = J + 1;
END;
```

That is, the DO loop WHILE becomes a sequence of a first part for initialization and second part of DO-WHILE, whose DO part includes incrementing the index. In this form the DO-WHILE question applies; it asks:

> whenever $J \leq N$ and $I = 0$, does the DO part followed by the DO-WHILE (with $J = J + 1$ now) do the DO-WHILE; and whenever $J > N$ or $I \neq 0$, does doing nothing do the DO-WHILE?

We can see that it does. If KEY has not yet been found in TABLE, and we have not looked at every item, then we can look at the next item and set I, J accordingly and still complete the task required of the DO-WHILE.

Looking back to the functional idea in programming discussed earlier, note also that the improved SEARCH2 leaves an unpredictable value for J, whereas SEARCH1 left $J = N + 1$ always. If a programmer took the program, rather than the functional specification, as definitive, there could be trouble depending on a value for J.

Search 3

If the elements of TABLE are sorted (say, in ascending order), then a possibly more efficient search can be defined as a binary search. By examining an element near the middle of the table, either we find KEY or we then know that KEY is to be found only in one half or the other of the remaining table. That basic step can be repeated in the half indicated and continued until a table of only one element is reached. If KEY is not found by that step, it does not exist in the table. We put the foregoing in a program, as follows, introducing variables LO and HI, which define the lower and upper subscript of the table being searched at each step.

```
SEARCH3:PROCEDURE;
        I = 0;
        LO = 1;
        HI = N;
        DO WHILE(LO <= HI & I = 0);
                J = (LO + HI)/2;
                IF TABLE(J) = KEY THEN
                       I = J;
                ELSE
                       IF TABLE(J) < KEY THEN
                              LO = J + 1;
                        ELSE
                              HI = J - 1;
        END;
END SEARCH3;
```

The tree of questions about SEARCH3 is given by Figure 16-4. There are five nonterminal nodes in this tree, corresponding to two sequences, one DO-WHILE, and two IF-THEN-ELSE's. (Note that we regard a sequence of assignments as simply one generalized assignment for our purposes here.) Each node defines a function which in turn serves as a component in the next function.

The function for SEARCH3 is the same as that stated already, namely, given N, TABLE(1), . . . , TABLE(N), KEY, find I that satisfies the relation

$$\text{TABLE(I)} = \text{KEY}, \quad \text{if possible, } \text{I} = 0, \quad \text{otherwise.}$$

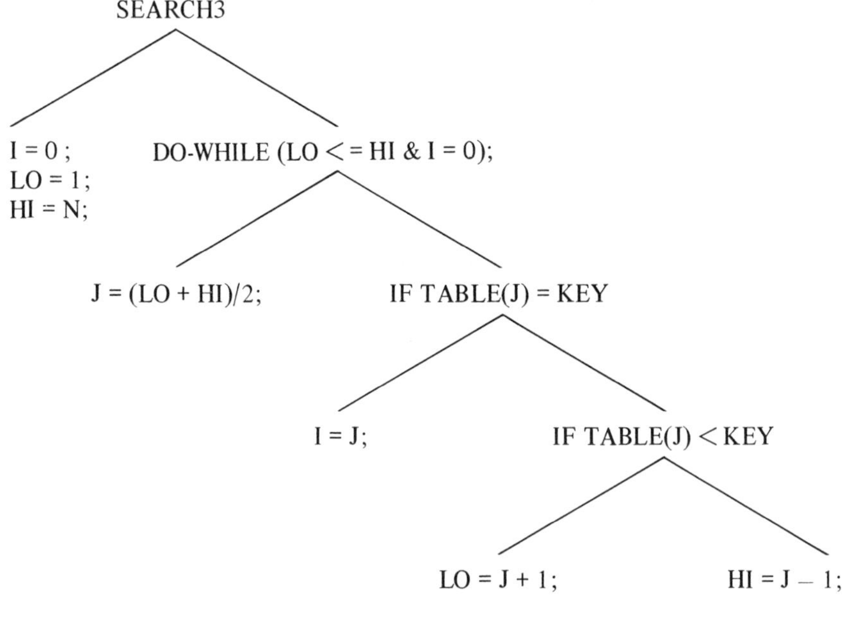
SEARCH3
I = 0 ;
LO = 1;
HI = N;
DO-WHILE (LO < = HI & I = 0);
J = (LO + HI)/2;
IF TABLE(J) = KEY
I = J;
IF TABLE(J) < KEY
LO = J + 1;
HI = J – 1;

FIGURE 16-4

The function for the DO-WHILE is, given N, TABLE(1), . . . , TABLE(N), KEY, LO $\geq$ 1, HI $\leq$ N, find I which satisfies:

TABLE(I) = KEY and LO $\leq$ I $\leq$ HI, if possible, I unchanged otherwise.

It is clear, with the three initialization assignments, that this sequence (of initialization and the DO-WHILE) does SEARCH3.

Next, the DO part of the DO-WHILE is a sequence. The function of this DO part is, given N, TABLE(1), . . . , TABLE(N), KEY, LO, HI, find I, LO, HI so that:

I = (LO + HI)/2 and TABLE(I) = KEY, if possible or I is unchanged and

LO is changed to (LO + HI)/2 + 1 if TABLE((LO + HI)/2) < KEY

and HI is changed to (LO + HI)/2 −1 if TABLE((LO + HI)/2) > KEY

In order to see that the DO-WHILE is accomplished by this WHILE test and this DO part, two principal considerations are needed. First, doing the DO part once without finding KEY cannot prevent the DO-WHILE finding KEY if it is possible; second, doing the DO part sufficiently many times (finitely) guarantees the ultimate failure of the WHILE test. For the first consideration the assumption of a sorted TABLE must be invoked, with the verification that each failure to find KEY in the TABLE ensures that KEY will not be found above or below that point as the case may be. For the second consideration it is sufficient to consider the algebraic difference HI − LO and to observe that when I remains 0 (otherwise, the WHILE test is false), then either LO or HI is changed so that

$$(\mathrm{HI} - \mathrm{LO})_{\mathrm{after}} < (\mathrm{HI} - \mathrm{LO})_{\mathrm{before}} - 1,$$

so that eventually,

$$\mathrm{HI} - \mathrm{LO} < 0,$$

and the WHILE test will fail.

We will not elaborate the arguments for the two IF-THEN-ELSE's. But note that their functions are defined by the preceding arguments for the DO-WHILE. Note also the essential difference in the argument for a DO-WHILE and for an indexed DO loop.

To Dig Deeper

In Structured Programming

The first name in structured programming is Edsger W. Dijkstra, who early recognized the problem of complexity in the programming process and identified the need for mental discipline in functional abstractions and control logic. In a famous letter, "GOTO Statement Considered Harmful" [7], Dijkstra set off a controversy that has rocked computer science. In the chapter, "Notes on Structured Programming" of *Structured Programming* [5], he gave the motivation and method for structured programming as a systematic process of divide and conquer by abstraction and refinement.

The first proof that structured programs were sufficiently powerful to represent any flowchartable program logic was due to Giuseppe Jacopini in the paper, "Flow Diagrams, Turing Machines, and Languages with

Only Two Formation Rules" [4], coauthored with Corrado Böhm. As Dijkstra points out [7], the mindless conversion of general flowcharts into structured programs is not to be recommended, but Jacopini shows that you can design structured programs for any logic requirements to begin with.

The correctness of structured programs is given an elegant treatment by C. A. R. Hoare in "An Axiomatic Approach to Computer Programming" [12], which introduced a new systematic approach for proving structured programs correct. This approach is illustrated by N. Wirth in *Systematic Programming: An Introduction* [22] and by J. R. Kelley and C. L. McGowan in *Top-Down Structured Programming* [14]. The approach of Hoare et al. is somewhat different for loops than the approach we gave above. It stems from ideas of Naur [19] and Floyd [11], which address the loop iteration directly by means of discovery of an *invariant condition,* which is satisfied in every iteration and can be used to deduce the loop exit condition. In contrast, the approach we gave above converts an iteration into a recursion, after ideas that go back to McCarthy in "A Basis for a Mathematical Theory of Computation" [16].

The stepwise expansion of specifications into structured programs was discussed early by Dijkstra in "A Constructive Approach to the Problem of Program Correctness" [8], by Wirth in "Program Development by Stepwise Refinement" [21], and by Mills in "Top Down Programming in Large Systems" [17].

In Programming Practices

A major application of structured programming (in conjunction with certain organizational techniques) is described by F. T. Baker in "Chief Programmer Team Management of Production Programming" [2] and in "System Quality Through Structured Programming" [3]. Baker reports a substantial increase in productivity and an even more remarkable decrease in error incidence over industry norms in the development of a large conversational information system.

In a special issue on programming of the ACM Computing Surveys [1], edited by P. J. Denning, authors P. J. Brown, J. M. Yohe, N. Wirth, D. E. Knuth, and B. W. Kernihan and P. J. Plouger discuss various aspects of programming practice. Dijkstra gives special insights into good mental practices in programming in an early paper, "Programming Considered as a Human Activity" [6], and a later one, "The Humble Programmer" [9].

The stepwise refinement approach to program development can be identified as a system design methodology as well, as discussed in an early paper by F. Zurcher and B. Randell, "Iterative Multi-Level Modelling —A Methodology for Computer System Design" [23]. In "A Design Methodology for Reliable Software Systems" [15], B. H. Liskov combines principles of structured programming and program correctness into a systematic approach to software development.

In Mathematics

It is said that war is too important to be left to the generals, and so it is that clear thinking in programming is too important to be left to the mathematicians. Dijkstra, in "Programming as a Discipline of a Mathematical Nature" [10], expresses the needs and opportunities for incorporating mathematical thinking into programming very well. Mills, in "The New Math of Computer Programming" [18], discusses structured programming and why it works in algebraic terms. W. Huggins has observed [13] that "algebra is the natural tool to study things made by man, and analysis is the natural tool to study things made by God." That apt remark seems to apply to man-made programs, indeed.

R. L. Wilder, in *Evolution of Mathematical Concepts—An Elementary Study* [20], points out (pp. 196f) that "it appears to be a universal phenomenon in the evolution of culture, that when a culture has evolved sufficiently to achieve a certain degree of maturity, there then arises a need among its participants for an 'explanation' of its origin . . . the mathematical subculture of modern western culture furnished no exception . . . the faith in the 'truth' of mathematical theories that has been sustained in the general culture is shared to a considerable extent by the mathematical subculture." Professor Wilder then goes on to conclude that mathematics will continue to evolve just as any other human activity—on the basis of its value to the human condition.

Acknowledgment

It is a pleasure to acknowledge stimulating discussions in "How to Write Correct Programs and Know It" in theory and practice with R. C. Linger.

Bibliography

1. *ACM Computing Surveys* 6, No. 4 edited by P. J. Denning, (December 1974): 209–321.

2. Baker, F. T. "Chief Programmer Team Management of Production Programming." *IBM Systems Journal* 11, No. 1, (1972): 56–73.
3. Baker F. T. "System Quality Through Structured Programming." In *AFIPS Conference Proceedings*. 1972 Fall Joint Computer Conference, vol. 41, part I, pp. 339–343. Arlington, Va.: AFIPS Press, 1972.
4. Böhm, Corrado, and Jacopini, Giuseppe. "Flow Diagrams, Turing Machines, and Languages with Only Two Formation Rules." *Comm. ACM* 9, No. 5 (May 1966): 366–371.
5. Dahl, O. J., Dijkstra, E. W., and Hoare, C. A. R. *Structured Programming,* London: Academic Press, 1972.
6. Dijkstra, E. W. "Programming Considered as a Human Activity." In *Proceedings of the IFIP Congress 1965,* pp. 213–217. Amsterdam: North-Holland, 1965.
7. Dijkstra, E. W. "GOTO Statement Considered Harmful." *Comm. ACM* 11, No. 3 (March 1968): 147–148, 538, 541.
8. Dijkstra, E. W. "A Constructive Approach to the Problem of Program Correctness." *BIT* 8, No. 3 (1968): 174–186.
9. Dijkstra, E. W. "The Humble Programmer." *Comm. ACM* 15, No. 10 (October 1972): 859–866.
10. Dijkstra, E. W. "Programming as a Discipline of a Mathematical Nature." *Amer. Math. Monthly* 81, No. 6 (June/July 1974): 608–611.
11. Floyd, R. W. "Assigning Meanings to Programs." In *Proceedings of the Symposium in Applied Mathematics,* vol. 19, edited by J. T. Schwartz, pp. 19–32. Providence, R. I.: American Mathematical Society, 1967.
12. Hoare, C. A. R. "An Axiomatic Approach to Computer Programming." *Comm. ACM* 12, No. 10 (October 1969): 576–580, 583.
13. Huggins, W. Personal communication. Johns Hopkins University. 1973.
14. Kelley, J. R., and McGowan, C. L. *Top-Down Structured Programming.* New York: Petrocelli, 1975.
15. Liskov, B. H. "A Design Methodology for Reliable Software Systems." In *AFIPS Conference Proceedings.* 1972 Fall Joint Computer Conference, vol. 41, part I, pp. 191–199. Arlington, Va.: AFIPS Press, 1972.
16. McCarthy, J. "A Basis for a Mathematical Theory of Computation." In *Computer Programming and Formal Systems.* Edited by P. Braffort and D. Hirschberg, pp. 33–70. Amsterdam: North-Holland, 1967.
17. Mills, H. D. "Top Down Programming in Large Systems." In *De-*

bugging Techniques in Large Systems. Edited by Randall Rustin, pp. 41–55. Englewood Cliffs, N. J.: Prentice-Hall, 1971.

18. Mills, H. D. "The New Math of Computer Programming." *Comm. ACM* 18, No. 1 (January 1975): 43–48.
19. Naur, P. "Proof of Algorithms by General Snapshots." *BIT* 6 (1966): 310–316.
20. Wilder, R. L. *Evolution of Mathematical Concepts—An Elementary Study.* New York: John Wiley and Sons, 1968.
21. Wirth, N. "Program Development by Stepwise Refinement." *Comm. ACM* 14, No. 4 (April 1971): 221–227.
22. Wirth, N. *Systematic Programming: An Introduction.* Englewood Cliffs, N. J.: Prentice-Hall, 1973.
23. Zurcher, F., and Randell, B. "Iterative Multi-Level Modelling—A Methodology for Computer System Design." In *Proceedings of the IFIP Congress,* pp. D138-D142. Amsterdam: North-Holland, 1968.

ARTICLE
17

The New Math of Computer Programming

(1975)

Abstract

Structured programming has proved to be an important methodology for systematic program design and development. Structured programs are identified as compound function expressions in the algebra of functions. The algebraic properties of these function expressions permit the reformulation (expansion as well as reduction) of a nested subexpression independently of its environment, thus modeling what is known as stepwise program refinement as well as program execution. Finally, structured programming is characterized in terms of the selection and solution of certain elementary equations defined in the algebra of functions. These solutions can be given in general formulas, each involving a single parameter, which display the entire freedom available in creating correct structured programs.

Key Words and Phrases

structured programming	stepwise refinement
algebra of functions	program correctness

CR (ACM Computing Reviews) Categories: 4.6, 5.21, 5.24

In honor of Alston S. Householder

© 1975, Association for Computing Machinery, Inc. Reprinted, with permission, from *Communications of the ACM,* January 1975, Vol. 18, No. 1.

Computer Programming

History

Computer programming as a practical human activity is some 25 years old, a short time for intellectual development. Yet computer programming has already posed the greatest intellectual challenge that mankind has faced in pure logic and complexity. Never before has man had the services of such logical servants, so remarkable in power, yet so devoid of common sense that instructions given to them must be perfect and must cover every contingency, for they are carried out faster than the mind can follow.

The practical electronic computer was the invention of some of our best minds in mathematics and engineering [7], e.g. von Neumann, Goldstine, Burks, Bigelow, Williams, Eckert, Mauchly, Atanasoff, Pomerene. Many people from the world's best universities and laboratories came into its development early, in both hardware design and programming, e.g. Wilkes [17], Forrester, Alexander, Forsythe, Rutishauser, Hopper. In the beginning, the emphasis was on numerical computation, and a new mathematics for numerical analysis emerged, spearheaded by the classic studies of von Neumann and Goldstine [16], Householder [10], Wilkinson [18], Henrici [8], et al. Later an additional emphasis developed in symbolic computation, and another new mathematics for symbolic analysis emerged, spearheaded by McCarthy [13], Newell and Simon [15], Minsky [14], et al. The hallmark of numerical computation is iteration and real analysis, and the main conceptual problem is the approximation of iterative algorithms for the reals in floating point numbers. The hallmark of symbolic computation is recursion and combinatorial analysis, and the main conceptual problem is the representation of complex objects in flexible recursive data structures.

The foregoing required computer programming of mathematical processes. But it is only recently that a new mathematics of computer programming itself has begun to emerge, in works of Dijkstra [6], Hoare [9], Wirth [19], et al. In this case, the mathematics models the mental processes of programming—of inventing algorithms suitable for a given computer to meet prescribed logical specifications. Bauer [2], Dijkstra [5], and Knuth [11] have summarized much of this development and its unique characteristics under the term structured programming.

A Mathematical Perspective

We discuss structured programming in mathematical form to illustrate the relevance and power of classical mathematical concepts to simplify and describe programming objects and processes. It is applied mathematics in the classic tradition, providing greater human capability through abstraction, analysis, and interpretation in application to computer programming.

Our principal objective is to model the mental process of structured programming with the selection and solution of certain function equations which arise as a natural abstraction of concrete programming processes. Before these function equations can be abstracted, however, we need to develop the idea of structured programming, and the corollary that structured programs can be viewed as compound function expressions in the algebra of functions. It is the algebraic properties of structured programming that provide its practical power—in the natural nesting of algebraic expressions—and the ability to consider a nested expression independently of its environment in a compound expression.

In illustration, we can all remember from elementary mathematics classes that the problem wasn't simply to get the right answer, but to find the right process for getting the answer. Frequently we got only part credit for a correct answer because we didn't show how we got it. There was a reason. If we do simple mathematical problems by guessing the answers, then when we get to the harder problems we won't be able to guess the answers. That is exactly the role of the new math in computer programming—to go from programming as an instinctive, intuitive process to a more systematic, constructive process that can be taught and shared by intelligent people in a professional activity.

Structured Programming

Flowchart Theorems

Flowcharts are graphical rules for defining complex state functions[1] in terms of simpler state functions known to a computing device. More precisely, let X be a finite set of possible states of a computation; a flowchart is an oriented, directed graph with three kinds of nodes (see Figure 17-1).

A function node is labeled with a finite state function, say, $f \subset X \times X$. A predicate node is labeled with a finite state predicate, say, $p \subset X \times \{T, F\}$, and directs control to one of the two out-lines of the

[1] A *function* is a set of ordered pairs, say f, with all first members unique. If $(x, y) \in f$ we may write $y = f(x)$ instead, and call x an *argument*, y a *value* of f. The set of all arguments, values is called the *domain, range* of f, denoted by $D(f)$, $R(f)$, respectively.

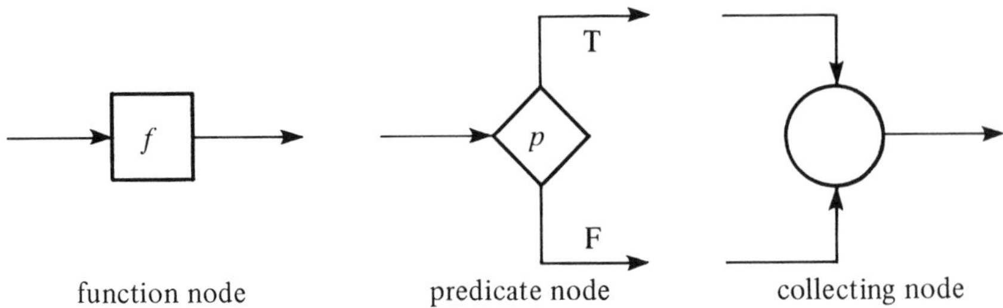

FIGURE 17-1

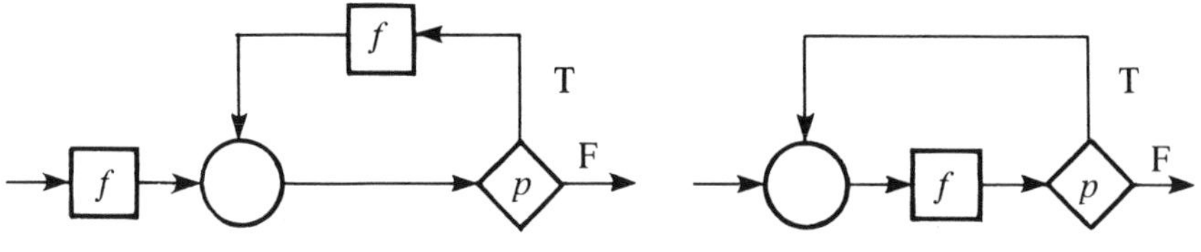

FIGURE 17-2

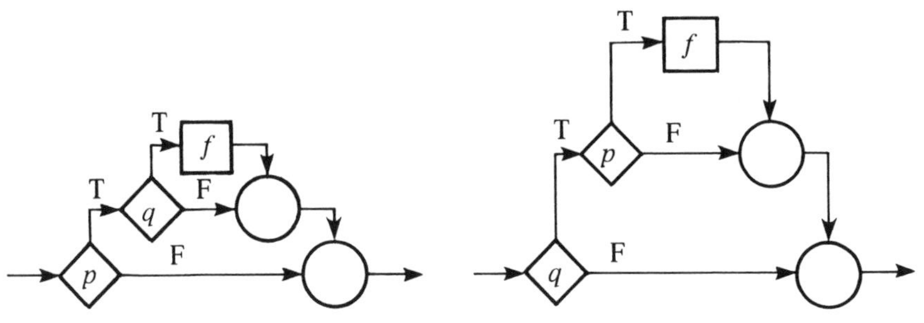

FIGURE 17-3

node. A collecting node is not labeled, and merely passes control from the two in-lines to the out-line.

Different flowcharts may define the same calculations and same functions; for example, the forms in Figure 17-2 define identical calculations. Different flowcharts may define different calculations, but the same function (see, for example, Figure 17-3).

Thus, several levels of flowchart equivalence can be defined, which preserve calculations, function, etc. In particular, Böhm and Jacopini [3], Cooper [4], and others have studied the expressive power of various classes of flowcharts in defining calculations and functions. The principal outcome of these studies is that relatively small, economical classes of flowcharts can define the calculations and functions of the class of all flowcharts, possibly at the expense of extra calculations outside the original description of the state set.

The foregoing motivates a more formal treatment, as follows. Define a class of D-*charts* (D for Dijkstra [5]) over a set of state functions $F = \{f_1, \ldots, f_m\}$ and a set of state predicates $P = \{p_1, \ldots, p_n\}$ as follows:

1. If $f \in F$, then

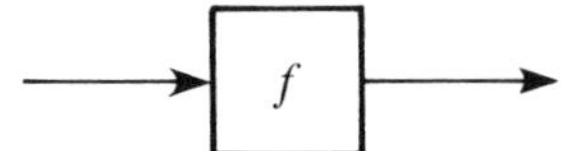

is a D-chart.

2. If $p \in P$ and

are D-charts, then

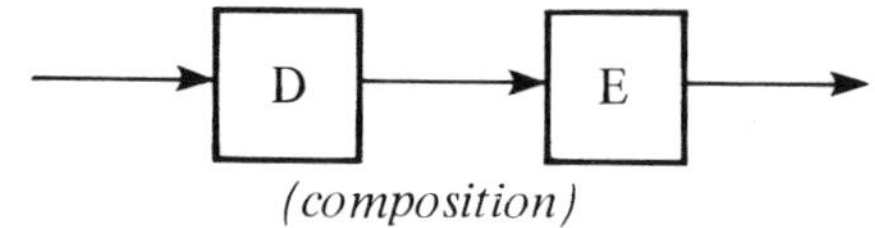

(composition)

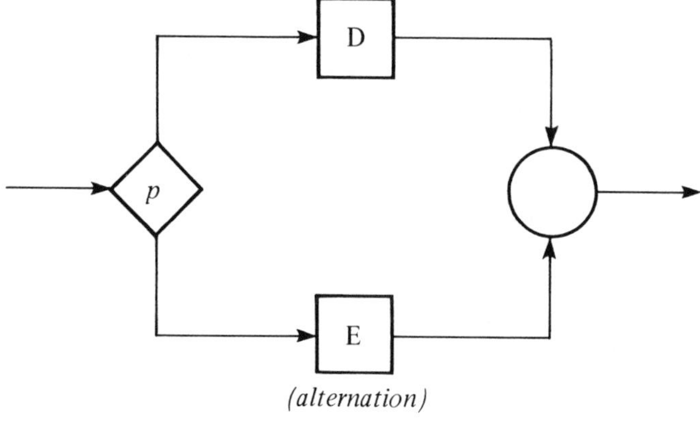

(alternation)

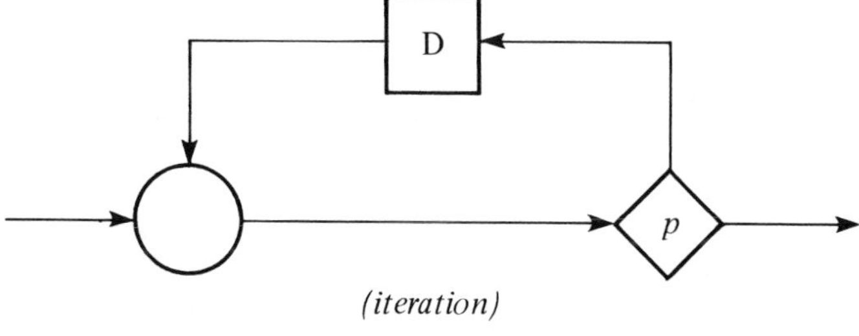

(iteration)

are D-charts.

A Structure Theorem. Consider any flowchart whose functions form a set *F* and predicates form a set *P*. Augment sets *F* and *P* with functions and predicates which set and test variables outside the state set of the given flowchart. Then there exists a D-chart in the augmented sets which simulates the calculations of the given flowchart.

In illustration, following Cooper [4], consider any given flowchart, and label each of its lines uniquely. Then the flowchart in Figure 17-4, using a new variable *L* (for label), will simulate the calculations of the original flowchart.

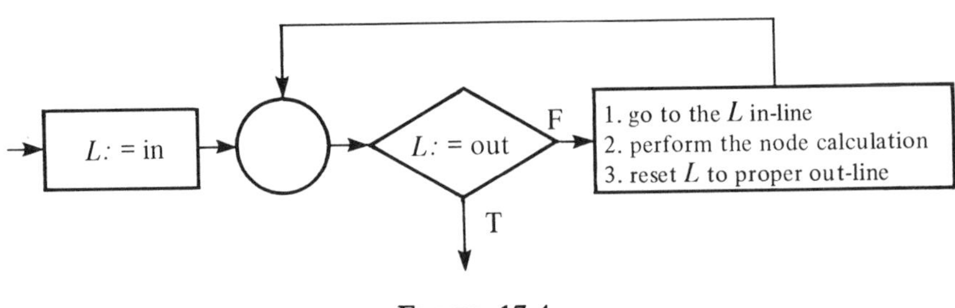

FIGURE 17-4

The operation inside the loop can be expanded into a loop-free D-chart of tests on *L,* leading to the various nodes of the original flowchart, as a set of nested alternations. In brief, this flowchart shows that, at the expense of setting and testing a single variable *L* (outside the original state set), the calculations of any flowchart whatsoever can be simulated as a subsequence of the calculations of a D-chart with a single loop.

Böhm and Jacopini [3], Ashcroft and Manna [1], and Kosaraju [12] have sharper results, which preserve more of the structure of the original flowchart. Böhm and Jacopini preserve the loops of the original flowchart, with a more efficient simulation of its calculations. Kosaraju has found a hierarchy of expressive capabilities among several classes of flowcharts. In particular, Kosaraju has discovered the precise conditions under which a D-chart can simulate a given flowchart without augmenting its functions and predicates.

Theorem (Kosaraju [12]). Consider any flowchart *A* whose functions form set *F,* and whose predicates form set *P.* Then, there exists a D-chart over *F* and *P* which preserves the calculations of the given flowchart *A* if and only if every loop of *A* has a single exit line.

Function Expressions

The algebra of functions inherits function expressions from the algebra of sets, e.g., if g, h are functions, then so are $g \cap h$ (set intersection) and $g - h$ (set difference); of course $g \cup h$ may or may not be a function, but will be a relation in any case.

Basic flowchart programs of common use, such as defined for D-charts, are conveniently represented as additional function expressions, e.g.,

composition

for write

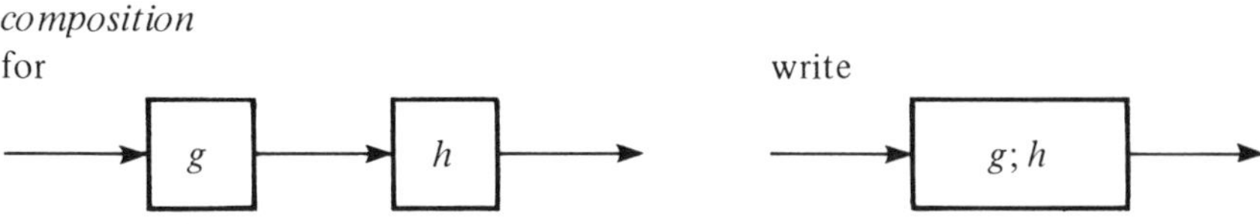

where

(1) $$g\,;h = \{(x, z) \mid (\exists y)(y = g(x) \wedge z = h(y))\}$$

(note that the operator ; reverses the operands of the ordinary function composition operator *, e.g., $g\,;h = h * g$).

alternation

for write

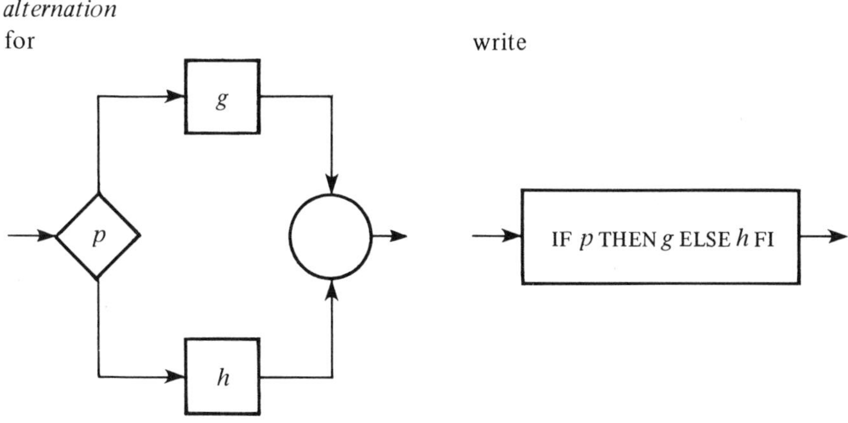

where

(2) $$\text{IF } p \text{ THEN } g \text{ ELSE } h \text{ FI} = \{(x, y) \mid (p(x) \wedge y = g(x)) \vee (\neg p(x) \wedge y = h(x))\}.$$

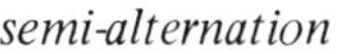

semi-alternation
for

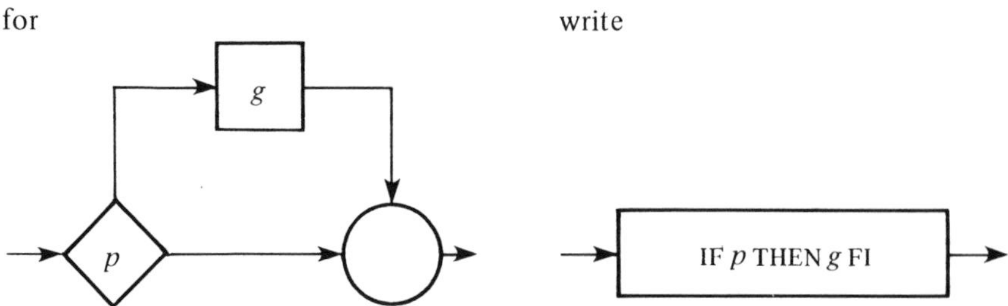

where

(3) $\text{IF } p \text{ THEN } g \text{ FI} = \{(x, y) \mid (p(x) \wedge y = g(x)) \vee (\sim p(x) \wedge y = x)\}.$

iteration
for

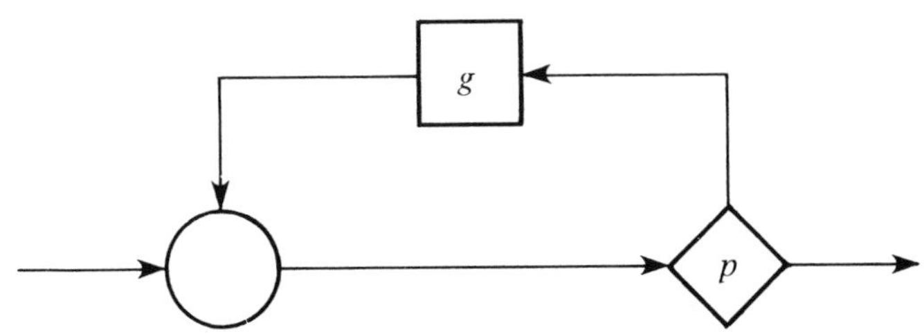

which defines the same calculations as

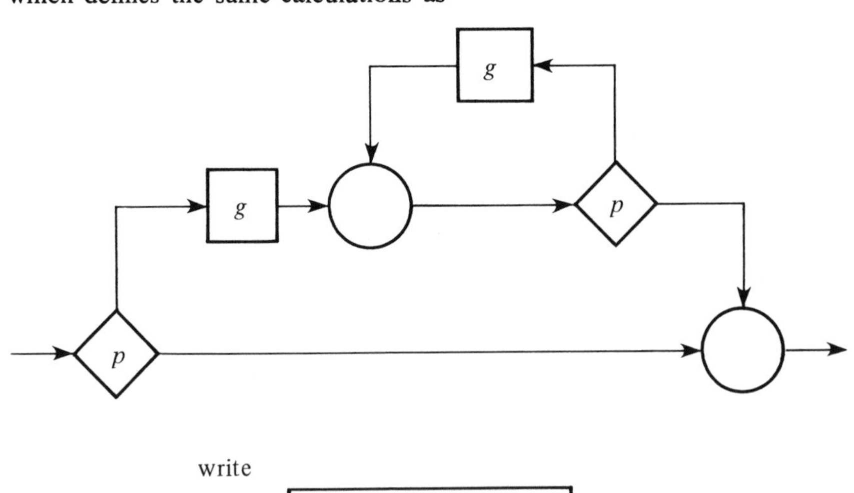

write

WHILE p DO g OD

where

(4) WHILE p DO g OD = IF p THEN g ; WHILE p DO g OD FI

The iteration expression is defined by recursion in terms of semi-alternation and composition.

As a consequence of these definitions, any D-chart can be represented as a *compound function expression,* and the calculations of any flowchart can be simulated by such an expression.

Additional expression types may be useful and efficient for certain processors, e.g., define

(5) DO g UNTIL p OD = g ; WHILE $\sim p$ DO g OD,

(6) CASE k OF $g_1, g_2, \ldots, g_n$ FO = IF $k = 1$ THEN g_1 ELSE
IF $k = 2$ THEN g_2 ELSE

. . .

IF $k = n$ THEN g_n FI . . . FI FI.

We define a *structured program* to be a compound function expression in any prescribed set of expression types. The D-charts are structured programs in the set of types {composition, alternation, iteration} as defined above.

Stepwise Function Refinement

The powerful properties of structured programming are rooted, finally, in algebraic properties of function expressions; e.g., arithmetic expressions,[2] logic expressions, etc., permit their evaluation, manipulation, etc., a step at a time in innermost subexpressions, independently of their outer environment. We add 2 + 4 the same way whether we later multiply the result by 9 or divide it by 3, in 9 * (2 + 4) or (2 + 4)/3. Alternately, a number such as 6 can be expanded as (2 + 4), if useful, or (2 * 3), irrespective of the operations being performed on it. Similarly, function expressions can be formulated and contemplated independently of their environments in more complex compound function expressions.

As noted by Dijkstra [6], Wirth [19], et al., the creative, iterative mental process of structured programming is the *stepwise refinement* of a function into an expression in intermediate functions, until functions available in the computer at hand are reached. Thus, not only is the final expression involved, but also the intermediate mental steps for reaching it are recorded. For example, the sequence of flowcharts labeled 1 and 2 in

[2] Exact, not approximate, arithmetic is meant here.

Figure 17-5 lead to the same final (structured) program. But sequence 2 does not follow stepwise refinement.

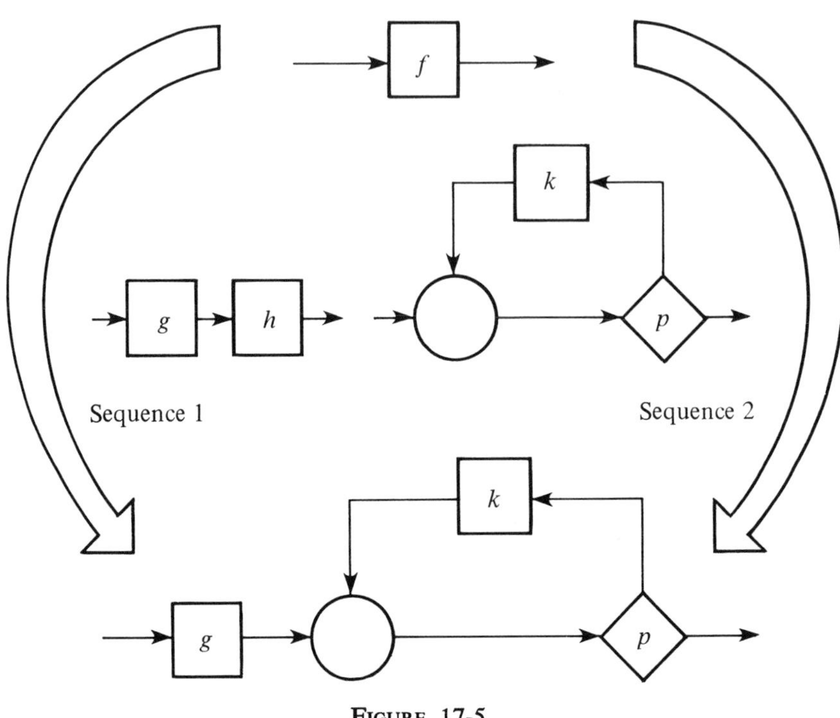

FIGURE 17-5

The difference is critical, because sequence 2 contains a mental discontinuity (two, in fact), which requires additional mental processing outside the sequence. In sequence 1, each of the three members are equivalent compound expressions, i.e.,

$$f = (g\ ;h) = (g\ ; \text{WHILE } p \text{ DO } k \text{ OD})$$

But in sequence 2, the first and third members are equivalent, as above, but the middle member is different from either of the others. Thus, from *f* in sequence 2, by some unrecorded insight, the function called *h* in sequence 1 is defined as an iteration. This expression equals no other object in sequence 2, and requires that unrecorded insight for validation. Then, at last, this expression is fixed up by putting *g* in front of it, still needing that unrecorded insight to get *g* right. When such functions get complex, and many such unrecorded insights need to exist over days, weeks, and months, it is no wonder that programming can be complex and frustrating.

The Correctness of Function Expressions

The verification of correctness of function expressions can proceed with stepwise refinement. In fact they are better practiced jointly than separately and sequentially. Each stage in stepwise refinement identifies a compound expression in intermediate functions, each of which may be later expressed in other functions. These intermediate functions are critical in validating correctness. They serve two roles—first, as functions in expressions being validated, and second as functions by which their replacement expressions are validated.

During stepwise refinement, a standard validation procedure can be defined for each expression type. These procedures state what is to be proved—the function description determines how such a proof should be carried out in detail.

Theorem (Correctness). The Correctness of an Alternation Expression. To prove $f =$ IF p THEN g ELSE h FI it is necessary and sufficient to show, for every $(x, y) \in f$, that either $p(x) = T$ and $y = g(x)$ or $p(x) = F$ and $y = h(x)$.

The Correctness of a Composition Expression. To prove $f = g ; h$ it is necessary and sufficient to show, for every $(x, y) \in f$, that $y = h(g(x))$.

The Correctness of an Iteration Expression. To prove $f =$ WHILE p DO g OD it is necessary and sufficient to show, for every $(x, y) \in f$, that the iteration terminates and that either $p(x) = T$ and $y = f(g(x))$ or $p(x) = F$ and $y = x$.

The proof of this theorem follows directly from the definitions of (1), (2), (3), and (4).

Function Equations and Their Solutions

The Computation Problem and the Programming Problem

In stepwise refinement, members of a finite set of prescribed function equations arise, one for each expression type, of the forms

(7) $f =$ IF p THEN g ELSE h FI (alternation)

(8) $f = g\,;h$ (composition)

(9) $f =$ WHILE p DO g OD (iteration)
etc.

When p, g, h are taken as the independent functions, and f as the dependent (unknown) function, these equations represent the *computation problem;* i.e., given a compound function expression, the problem is to evaluate it by stepwise evaluations of innermost expressions.

However, the *programming problem* begins with a function to be expressed, with f as the independent function, and p, g, and h as the dependent (unknown) functions. This motivates the study of these prescribed function equations, with f given, to characterize the solutions in p, g, h. With a little analysis we can write the solutions down directly, and exhibit, thereby, the entire freedom of a programmer in a correct stepwise refinement.

The Alternation Equation

The general minimal solution for the alternation equation can be given in terms of a single parameter, any subfunction (subset) of f, say u. Then (p, g, h) solves the alternation eq. (7), where[3]

(10) $g = u,$

$h = f - u,$

$p = (D(u) \times \{T\}) \cup (D(f - u) \times \{F\}).$

Note that $\{g, h\}$ is a partition of f.

The Composition Equation

The general minimal solution for the composition equation can be given in terms of a single parameter, any function, say, u, with domain $D(f)$

[3] The solution (p, g, h) is minimal, in the sense that, for any other solution (p_0, g_0, h_0), $p \subseteq p_0$, $g \subseteq g_0$, $h \subseteq h_0$. In this case, (p_0, g_0, h_0) must satisfy the additional conditions $\{x \mid p_0(x)\} \cap D(g_0) = D(g)$, $\{x \mid \sim p_0(x)\} \cap D(h_0) = D(h)$. Nonminimal solutions exist similarly for the other equations, as well.

whose level sets[4] refine the level sets of f; i.e., every level set of u is a subset of some level set of f. Then (g, h) solves the composition eq. (8), where[5]

$$(11) \qquad \begin{aligned} g &= u, \\ h &= u^{-1} ; f \text{ where } (u^{-1} = \{(x, y) \mid (y, x) \in u\}) \end{aligned}$$

Thus, whereas the solution set of the alternation equation has precisely the freedom of a binary partition of the function f, the solution set of the composition equation has the freedom of any system of partitions on the level sets of f, a much richer choice.

The Iteration Equation

The iteration equation is more complex and interesting than the alternation and composition equations. First, whereas any function can be expressed in an alternation or composition, this is not so for an iteration expression; it turns out that an existence condition is required for a solution. Second, whereas all functions p, g, h vary over the solution set in the alternation and composition equations, it turns out that only the function g varies over the solution set in the iteration equation; that is, the predicate p is fixed entirely by f alone. In other words, p is a derivative of f, just as the slope of a differentiable function is a derivative of that function. We call p the *iteration derivative* of f.

Consider the iteration equation, given f, to find (p, g) such that (eq. (9)) $f =$ WHILE p DO g OD. For the moment, suppose g is restricted to functions for which $D(g) \subset D(f)$; we show below that this involves no loss of generality.

Then we will see that if the existence condition $(x \in D(f) \cap \mathrm{R}(f)) \supset f(x) = x$ holds (otherwise there is no solution), the general minimal solution for the iteration equation can be given in terms of a single parameter, a function u which defines any system of trees on the level sets of f in $D(f) - R(f)$, i.e.,[6]

$$u = \{(x, y) \mid y \text{ is the parent of } x\}.$$

---

[4] A level set $D_y(f) = \{x \mid (x, y) \in f\}$, i.e., all arguments with the same value of f. More directly u must satisfy the predicate $D(u) = D(f) \wedge (f(x) \neq f(y) \supset u(x) \neq u(y))$.

[5] In general u^{-1} will be a relation, not a function, but the composition $u^{-1} ; f$ will be a function due to the restriction on u.

[6] More directly, the condition on u is
$u \subset (D(f) - \mathrm{R}(f)) \vee (y = u(x) \supset f(y) = f(x)) \vee u$ acyclic.

Then (p, g) solves the iteration eq. (9), where

$$(12)\qquad \begin{aligned} p &= ((D(f) - R(f)) \times \{T\} \cup (R(f) \times \{F\}), \\ g &= u \cup (f - D(u) \times R(f)). \end{aligned}$$

In order to see the foregoing, it is easiest to get the formula for p first, then the existence condition, and then the formula for g.

First, for any solution (p, g), p must have value F at every point in $R(f)$, for otherwise the iteration program cannot terminate at that value; conversely, p must have value T at every point in $D(f) - R(f)$, for otherwise the iteration program will not reach a value in $R(f)$. This gives the formula above for p in domain $D(f) \cup R(f)$.

Next, consider any point in $D(f) \cap R(f)$. By the foregoing, p has value F at such a point, and the iteration program never invokes g, but simply exists without altering the state. This gives the existence condition above, i.e., that f must be the identity function on $D(f) \cap R(f)$.

Finally, consider the graph of the state function g in $D(f) \cap R(f)$. It is apparent that the graph of the subset of g in $D(f) - R(f)$ can have no cycles—must be a tree—since otherwise the iteration program would not terminate in such a cycle. It is also apparent that all points of a connected subtree in the graph of g must be in the same level set of f, since the iteration program will terminate at the same value in $R(f)$. Thus the graph of the subset of g contained in $D(f) - R(f)$ must be a system of trees in the level sets of f. Now consider the arcs of the graph of g which originate in $D(f) - R(f)$ and terminate in $R(f)$. The originating points are roots of the trees in $D(f) - R(f)$. Since p is F in $R(f)$, the iteration program terminates with each such arc. Thus, for each such originating point, say x, we must have $g(x) = f(x)$. This gives the formula for g, above, with parameter u, a function defining a system of trees on the level sets of f in $D(f) - R(f)$.

Now we remove the restriction that $D(g) \subset D(f)$ as follows. Suppose $D(g) \not\subset D(f)$; then pick any (x, y) such that $x \in D(g) - D(f)$, $y = g(x)$. If for no $z \in D(f)$ and integer k, $g^k(z) = x$, then (x, y) is superfluous for g and $g - \{(x, y)\}$ is also a solution; otherwise let $g^k(z) = x$, and adjoin $(x, f(z))$ to f, and g remains a solution. In either case the number of elements in $D(g) - D(f)$ is reduced by one; this can be continued until $D(g) \subset D(f)$.

Equations in Compound Function-Expressions

It is direct, but possibly tedious, to extend solutions to function equations in elementary expressions to equations in arbitrary compound expressions of the form f = compound function expression, where no function variable occurs more than once. For each level of nesting an additional parameter is involved, and is effective only within the scope of that nesting. Thus, the parameters of the solution can be associated with the nesting tree of the compound expression.

In particular, the solutions above provide existence predicates on the parameters for each type of function equation, and the formulas for the stepwise refined solutions. These predicates and formulas can be invoked iteratively to describe the set of all solutions to a compound function equation of any complexity. Since there are only a finite number of compound function equations in a fixed number of functions, these formulas permit the explicit formulation of all correct D-chart programs of any size.

References

1. Ashcroft, E., and Manna, Z. "The Translation of 'Go To' Programs to 'While' Programs," *Information Processing* 71. Amsterdam: North-Holland, 1972, pp. 250–255.
2. Bauer, F. L. "A Philosophy of Programming." University of London Special Lectures in Computer Science, Oct. 1973. Lecture notes published by Math. Inst., Tech. U. Munchen.
3. Böhm, C., and Jacopini, G. "Flow Diagrams, Turing Machines, and Languages with Only Two Formation Rules," *Comm. ACM* 9, 5 (May 1966), 366–371.
4. Cooper, D. C. "Böhm and Jacopini's Reduction of Flow Charts," *Comm. ACM* 10, 8 (Aug. 1967), 463.
5. Dahl, O. J., Dijkstra, E. W., and Hoare, C. A. R. *Structured Programming*. London: Academic Press, 1972.
6. Dijkstra, E. W. "A Constructive Approach to the Problem of Program Correctness," *BIT* 8 (1968), 174–186.
7. Goldstine, H. H. *The Computer from Pascal to von Neumann*. Princeton University Press, 1972.
8. Henrici, P. *Discrete Variable Methods in Ordinary Differential Equations*. New York: Wiley, 1962.
9. Hoare, C. A. R. "An Axiomatic Basis for Computer Programming," *Comm. ACM* 12, 10 (Oct. 1969), 576–580, 583.
10. Householder, A. S. *The Theory of Matrices in Numerical Analysis*. New York: Blaisdell, 1964.
11. Knuth, D. E. "A Review of Structured Programming," Stanford Comput. Sci. Dept. Rep. Stan-CS-371, June 1973, 22 pp.

12. Kosaraju, S. R. "Analysis of Structured Programs," *J. Comput. Syst. Sci.* (Dec. 1974) to appear.
13. McCarthy, J. "A Basis for a Mathematical Theory of Computation." In *Computer Programming and Formal Systems,* P. Brafford and D. Hirschberg (Eds.). Amsterdam: North-Holland, 1963, pp. 33–70.
14. Minsky, Marvin. *Computation: Finite and Infinite Machines.* Englewood Cliffs, N.J.: Prentice-Hall, 1971.
15. Newell, Allen, and Simon, Herbert. *Human Problem Solving.* Englewoods Cliffs, N.J.: Prentice-Hall, 1971.
16. von Neumann, J., and Goldstine, H. H. "Numerical Inverting of Matrices of High Order," *Bull. Amer. Math. Soc.* 53 (1947), 1021–1099.
17. Wilkes, M. V. *Automatic Digital Computers.* London, 1956.
18. Wilkinson, J. H. *The Algebraic Eigenvalue Problem.* Oxford: Clarendon Press, 1965.
19. Wirth, N. *Systematic Programming: An Introduction.* Englewood Cliffs, N.J.: Prentice-Hall, 1973.

ARTICLE 18

Software Development

(1976)

Abstract

Software development has emerged as a critical bottleneck in the human use of automatic data processing. Beginning with ad hoc heuristic methods of design and implementation of software systems, problems of software maintenance and changes have become unexpectedly large. It is contended that improvement is possible only with more rigor in software design and development methodology. Rigorous software design should survive its implementation and be the basis for further evolution. Software development should be done incrementally, in stages with continuous user participation and replanning, and with design-to-cost programming within each stage.

Key Words and Phrases

design-to-cost programming
software design
software development
software maintenance
top-down development

Twenty-Five Years of Data Processing

The Data Processing Explosion

In the past twenty-five years a whole new data processing industry has exploded into a critical role in business and government. Every enterprise

© 1976 IEEE. Reprinted, with permission, from the *IEEE Transactions on Software Engineering,* Vol. SE-2, No. 4, December 1976.

or agency in the nation of any size, without exception, now depends on data processing hardware and software in an indispensable way. In a single human generation, several hardware generations have emerged, each with remarkable improvements in function, size, and speed. But there are significant growing pains in the software which connects this marvelous hardware with the data processing operations of business and government.

Had this hardware development been spaced out over 125 years, rather than just 25 years, a different history would have resulted. For example, just imagine the opportunity for orderly industrial development with five human generations of university curriculum development, education, feedback for the expansion of useful methodologies and pruning of less useful topics, etc. As it is, we see a major industry with minimal technical roots, because almost no one in a responsible position has an original university education in the subject, and the universities have no experience in even knowing what to teach. In comparison, it is worth noting just how many years and how much give and take has gone into the development of the current mathematics curriculum to support engineering and the physical sciences—at least the 125 years imagined earlier.

Even so, from ground zero, the technical and industrial progress of society in 25 years of data processing is impressive. But the needs and frustrations are so great that some perspective is in order to better understand how we got here and where we might be going.

Data Processing Then

Before the last 25 years, these same enterprises and agencies conducted their operations without automatic data processing, while still processing data in sufficient amounts to manage their affairs. But the data processing was done by people. Even if desk calculators, or tabulators, were used here and there, people still inspected intermediate results, and applied their common sense, where necessary, to correct obvious mistakes. If data processing instructions were faulty, or missing, people used common sense, again, to make the operations work. In other words, data processing systems were forgiving systems, because of the intelligence used in their execution.

Such forgiving systems permit the evolution and natural selection of data processing improvements in an orderly way. If an improvement is proposed, it is easily adopted with little risk, because unforeseen side effects will usually be noticed and suppressed by people. As a result, data processing is done, in large part with little self-consciousness, as implicit parts of other activities, such as billing, inventory control, etc.

Alexander, in *Notes on the Synthesis of Form* [1] discusses the notion of "goodness of fit" in architecture between design and a problem context. In primitive cultures, architectural design is frequently "unselfconscious," and design principles are transmitted in the form of tradition and custom. Variation in design is discouraged by the very nature of its recording in cultural terms. But small changes in response to ill fit, e.g., to the shape of terrain, etc., are easy and natural. There is a striking correspondence here with data processing in previous generations. It was unselfconscious in just this sense discussed by Alexander.

In retrospect, it is also clear that our previous enterprises and agencies got by with less data processing than is done now. With industrialization accelerated, physical operations are controlled more closely than before (e.g., compare the logistic management of food stuffs through present-day grocery chains compared to previous grocery systems) and administrative activities have mushroomed (e.g., compare tax reporting requirements of business today and 50 years ago). It is not clear which is father and which is child—the needs for data processing or the ability to do data processing. But in any case, an entirely new age of automatic data processing has replaced those days when people did it all (or, at least, most of it).

Data Processing Now

The automatic data processing of today is done by computers with no common sense at all. As a result, faulty or missing instructions wreak such wholesale havoc that an entirely new emphasis on the correctness and completeness of the processing instructions is required. In institution after institution, the transition from manual to automatic data processing has been of mixed benefit; while remarkable new capabilities have been wrought, they have also been traumatic and disruptive.

This new automatic data processing is the beginning of self-conscious design. Alexander [1] goes on to discuss the emergence of self-conscious design in architecture in Samoa, where ". . . custom demands that guest houses be built exclusively by carpenters. Since these carpenters need to find clients, they are in business as artists; and they begin to make personal innovations and changes for no reason except that prospective clients will judge their work by its inventiveness," [1, p. 57]. Again, the correspondence with programmers and designers of these first 25 years in data processing is very telling.

But Alexander goes on to describe in architecture a general point of relevance to data processing as well [1, pp. 58–59].

> In the unselfconscious system the individual is no more than an agent . . . All that is required is that he should recognize misfits and respond to them by making minor changes. It is not even necessary that these changes be for the better. As we have seen, the system, being self-adjusting, finds its own equilibrium . . . The selfconscious process is different . . . To achieve in a few hours at the drawing board what once took centuries of adaptions and development, to invent a form suddenly which fits its context—the extent of the inventions necessary is beyond the average designer.

It is small wonder that shock and frustration appear in converting data processing operations from informal manual, self-correcting activities to formal, mechanical, explicit forms. The new, self-conscious data processing designers have hardware to control and exploit which none of their teachers ever heard of. In architecture, it is as though nails, bricks, and mortar were suddenly invented, unheard of before. One could expect some rather strange structures to come out!

And in this new environment of frustration and fear, even small improvements and changes are viewed with suspicion and distrust. In fact, the computer programs which serve our institutions are both incredibly correct, and hopelessly incorrect. They are incredibly correct compared to the manual procedures they have replaced. They represent a level of precision and completeness unheard of 25 years ago. But they are hopelessly incorrect because they are the result of 25 years of amateur system development efforts by people who are entirely new to the problems. As a result, the programs which support our institutions are frequently mysterious, incommunicative with other programs which deal with similar subjects and data, and beyond rational understanding and change.

Human Fallibility—From Grand to Grandiose

In this first 25 years, the major software inventions have been programming languages and operating systems. These are good starts in permitting the development of data processing applications. But they have a side effect; since programmers are the only people who know the programming languages and operating systems, the programmers become a priesthood between people and computers. The arrogance, power, and impotence of this priesthood can be seen in the way system development is carried out today, in the way large systems are conceived and produced. A large system development may involve several hundred people for several years in a sequence of stages, called requirements analysis, specification, design, implementation, testing, operation. It is necessary and useful to break this much work into parts such as these. But there are dangers, too, particularly in the conduct of these stages in sequence, and not in iteration—i.e., that development is done open loop, rather than in a closed loop with user feedback between iterations. The danger in the sequence is that the project moves from being grand to being grandiose, and exceeds our human intellectual capabilities for management and control.

In illustration, consider a software system needed for inventory control in an enterprise, say to be developed over a three-year period. Right off, there is a conflict. The people who know what inventory control is really required in the enterprise are too busy doing it to spend much time on requirements analysis, so surrogate experts with more time available (guess why!) are found. After some time (but not much help from the key people) a software specification is developed, probably incomplete, probably inconsistent, and almost certainly based on a set of amateur opinions about how to do the inventory control. And at this point the software specification begins a life of its own—frozen except for strict change control. The specification is a marvelous shield for programmers during implementation. They can hide behind it, while the users-to-be wonder what is going on. In the meantime, the inventory control department has to operate as best it can, with all the new ideas and procedures it can think up. But left alone for three years, the programmers finally complete the implementation and testing, and the system is ready for initial operation. However, there remain a few difficulties. The people doing inventory control are suspicious and skeptical of the new system, especially when it produces idiotic results now and then, and requires idiotic instructions to operate. Furthermore, few of the new ideas of the past three years have been incorporated in the new system, so that these new ideas must be abandoned if the system is to be used. But most critical of all, the software project has been conceived and managed as a terminal three-year project, with all the tradeoffs and compromises that implies, while the inventory control operation goes on indefinitely.

This example may seem a bit overdone. In fact, compared with reality it may be underdone. But if that is so, why do enterprises tolerate the frustrations and difficulties of such development? Two reasons are economics and ignorance. The economics is that automatic data processing is cheap, if it is repetitive enough, and the administrative data processing done today in the country could not be done manually—there are not enough people. The ignorance is due to our adolescence in a 25-year-old industry. The next 25 years will see much more effective system development, and system evolution beyond initial development, carried out in units of small competent teams, rather than casts of hundreds or thousands. But that is easier said than done, and in order to see where we can go, we need to better understand where we are.

From Development to Maintenance

In the beginning of application developments in data processing, it was commonly supposed that development was the main problem. But in only 25 years, some 75 percent of data processing personnel are already taken up with maintenance, not development. And unless radical new methods are found, maintenance will go even higher in its demands and will very nearly stifle further development. Why is that?

There are two reasons, one of simple but often overlooked logistics, one of a deeper technical nature. The logistic reason is that an application system is maintained indefinitely after a definite period of development, and with every completed development some fraction of the development team (or its equivalent) must be deleted from development and added to maintenance. For example, with a constant work force, if a fraction x of each development team must stay behind for maintenance; then in an average development period, the fraction of all personnel devoted to development goes from D to $D(1-x)$. At the end of k periods, starting at $D=1$ (all development), the fraction of development is $(1-x)^k$, and the fraction of maintenance M is $1-D$ or

$$M = 1 - (1-x)^k.$$

In illustration, if $x = 0.2$, $k = 6$ (say a dozen years of 2-year projects for an enterprise), then

$$M = 1 - (0.8)^6 = 0.737856,$$

i.e., just about the 75 percent which is typical today. There is only one stable point in this ecology—100 percent maintenance. Only the purging or replacement of applications brings this stable point below 100 percent.

The technical reason for this high level of maintenance is that it has turned out to be more difficult to develop good systems than commonly supposed. By "good" is meant both correctness and capability. First, the difficulty of integrating and debugging systems has been severely underestimated time after time. And a large work force is used today in corrective maintenance, simply to fix software that "could have" been built correctly to begin with. Note the misuse of the words "debugging" and "maintenance." Debugging connotes the removal of errors which have been inserted by some natural process beyond control of the programmers —but it was the programmers who inserted the bugs! Maintenance connotes restoring a device to its original correct state—but the program was not correct to begin with! In both cases, these are kind euphemisms for a bewildered society of programmers. Second, there has been a consistent underestimation of the uncertainties and change facing data processing applications. For example, tax laws change, and differ from state to state —users get better ideas—operations change. So a considerable work force is required in adaptive maintenance, adding to and modifying the basic system, often until the basic system can no longer be found in the confusion caused by the modification process.

From Interaction to Integration

In the beginning of automatic data processing, every application was an isolated, stand-alone operation. It had to be. Such a single application would encompass data entry, computation, report generation, etc., as a self-sufficient system. However, as more and more applications are developed, common elements of data, computations, and reporting emerge. The same personnel information shows up in payroll, engineering cost estimating, and personnel profiles. The same sort of operations are required for all files against which transactions are updated periodically. The same executives need information from different applications for decision-making purposes. So data and programs become interrelated, and an integrated data base emerges for every enterprise or agency, whether consciously planned or not. The integration may not be physical, or even logical, but the more different copies and formats used for the same data, the more extra work and hardship occurs for users.

In the beginning, data processing applications were cost-displacing luxuries. But today, many data processing applications are embedded necessities for staying in business. Airline reservation systems, manufacturing process control systems, insurance underwriting and claim systems are examples of systems whose costs in down time or limited function are not found in the machine room, but in the profit and loss sheet of the business.

Software Design Methodology

Conceptual Integrity

The principal lesson of the first 25 years of data processing is that software development is harder to manage and control than it appeared to be at the outset. Without a clean and compelling design, a large application system soon becomes a jumble of confusion and frustration. Local details may be easily understood and checked, but the system gets beyond intellectual control anyway.

Fred Brooks, in *The Mythical Man-Month,* states that "conceptual integrity is *the* most important consideration in system design" [4, p. 42] and backs it up with a dramatic recollection of his experience in managing the development of OS/360, as follows [4, pp. 47–48].

> It is a very humbling experience to make a multimillion-dollar mistake, but it is also very memorable. I vividly recall the night we decided how to organize the actual writing of external specifications for OS/360. The manager of architecture, the manager of control program implementation, and I were threshing out the plan, schedule, and division of responsibilities.
>
> The architecture manager had 10 good men. He asserted that they could write the specifications and do it right. It would take ten months, three more than the schedule allowed.
>
> The control program manager had 150 men. He asserted that they could prepare the specifications, with the architecture team coordinating; it would be well-done and practical, and he could do it on schedule. Furthermore, if the architecture team did it, his 150 men would sit twiddling their thumbs for ten months.
>
> To this the architecture manager responded that if I gave the control program team the responsibility, the result would not in fact be on time, but would also be three months late, and of much lower quality. I did, and it was. He was right on both counts. Moreover, the lack of conceptual integrity made the system far more costly to build and change, and I would estimate that it added a year to debugging time.

Heuristics and Rigor

The principal basis for maintaining conceptual integrity in software development is rigorous design. It was imagined, to begin with, that heuristic design methods were sufficient. And, indeed, the possibility of rigorous design methods was hardly considered. After all, it seemed a simple, but tedious, matter for clever people to think up all the data processing pieces that had to be done, and make sure that nothing was left out. As Brooks points out, we now know better. But we have a legacy of heuristic thinking in software development that will still be painful to cure.

The difference between heuristics and rigor in design of data processing systems is in the integrity and stability of the design. A heuristic design almost always works—the trouble is in "almost always." When it fails, the system must be fixed and patched up. After a succession of such failures and fixes the design will become highly idiosyncratic, based on the particular failure history that has occurred. This dependence on failure histories takes place before actual system operations in a heuristic design process in the imagination of the designers. If designers mentally test and fix a heuristic design by thinking up cases and discovering deficiencies, then the design becomes idiosyncratic based on the imaginary history of failures.

A rigorous design will take more creativity and thought than a heuristic one, but, once created, a rigorous design is more stable. A rigorous design should survive its implementation, not be swamped by it, and provide a framework for the intellectual control of changes to the implementation as requirements change.

The difference between heuristics and rigor in design can be illustrated in constructing a tic-tac-toe playing program, say, to commence play from any feasible situation (e.g., to sit in at any point of any game). Anyone with a pad and pencil can readily figure out what to do next in any such situation. But writing all such possibilities down may be impractical. So the next step might be a heuristic approach, based on introspection on the analysis process imagined above with pad and pencil. The beginning of such a process (oversimplified for illustration) might be "play in priority order, if possible, center, any corner, any side." This will account for some reasonable moves, but will fail in many situations, and an analysis of these situations will suggest additional criteria of play. But with each addition, a less obvious situation may still lead to a failure. After many such additions, the program may indeed be capable of perfect tic-tac-toe. But it will be difficult to prove it, except for an exhaustive analysis, which itself will be hard to prove complete, etc. As noted before, such a heuristically developed design, even though possibly correct, will be highly idiosyncratic based on the history of imagined (or real) failures encountered in play.

In contrast with such a heuristic design process, a rigorous treatment of tic-tac-toe is possible, using a recursively defined function, namely, a function defined over tic-tac-toe boards (partial games) with values "win, draw, lose" (or 1, 0, −1) called "best outcome which can be guaranteed from here on," say "best," for short, e.g., best has values

best (board) = best outcome guaranteed starting with "board."

Then, by using the symmetry of the game for both players, the function best can be defined recursively, as follows,

$$\text{best (board)} = \text{IF board end THEN outcome of board}$$
$$\text{ELSE } \max_{\text{move}} (-\text{best } (-(\text{board} + \text{move})))$$

where "−board" reverses ×'s and O's in "board," and "move" is any choice of a present blank space. With a little study this can be seen to guarantee the best play possible. How this design is to be programmed is quite another, but quite straightforward, logical matter. The programming must take account of whether recursive functions are available in the programming language to be used, storage and computation strategies best suited to evaluating the function best, etc. But the logical design for the program is expressed in a concise and complete way for examination and criticism at the outset, and as an unambiguous requirement for what is to be programmed.

There are powerful tools in mathematics for expressing and validating logical design on a rigorous basis. In the first 25 years programmers have largely ignored them, in part because the tools themselves have not been particularly tailored to software design, and in part because the problems solved in software design have been simple enough (or seemed simple enough) to permit bare-minded, ad hoc approaches. But there are key ideas in set theory, mathematical logic, axiomatic systems, automata theory, mathematical linguistics, recursive functions, etc., for use in rigorous logical expression. One problem today is that the usual treatment of these ideas of logical expression is often embedded in larger mathematical subjects, which go much deeper than programmers need or have time for. But the use of effective logical expression in software design is bound to break through these barriers as benefits of their power become better known, and as better expository writing makes them more available to programmers. Liskov and Zilles illustrate several techniques of logical expression for data abstractions in [12].

Program Design

Jackson begins his book *Principles of Program Design* with the following statement [11, p. 1].

> The beginning of wisdom for a programmer is to recognize the difference between getting his program to work and getting it right. A program which does not work is undoubtedly wrong; but a program which does work is not necessarily right. It may still be wrong because it is hard to understand; or because it is hard to maintain as the problem requirements change; or because its structure is different from the structure of the problem; or because we cannot be sure that it does indeed work.

Structured programming, as introduced by Dijkstra [5], addresses this problem. But there is a great deal of oversell and confusion about structured programming, primarily because an adolescent data processing community is anxious to find simple answers to complex problems. Although structured programming began with a famous letter to the CACM editor "GOTO Statements Considered Harmful" [7], the essence of structured programming is the presence of rigor and structure in programming, rather than absence of GOTO's in programs. As in logical design, the idea of a rigorous rather than a heuristic program design method is new, and is still largely unknown in programming as practiced today.

As Jackson says so well, getting a program to work is not sufficient, but getting it designed right is the important thing, not only to operate correctly in all circumstances required, but to be understandable and modifiable. There is a powerful discipline available for getting programs designed right: the constructive approach to program correctness, as advocated early by Dijkstra, given in axiomatic form by Hoare [9], and more recently described and illustrated in a landmark book *A Discipline of Programming,* where Dijkstra states his case as follows [6, p. 216].

> The first message is that it does not suffice to design a mechanism of which we hope that it will meet its requirements, but that we must design it in such a form that we can convince ourselves—and anyone else for that matter—that it will, indeed meet its requirements. And, therefore, instead of first designing the program and then trying to prove its correctness, we develop correctness proof and program hand in hand. (In actual fact, the correctness proof is developed slightly ahead of the program; after having chosen the form of the correctness proof we make the program so that it satisfies the proof's requirements.) This, when carried out successfully, implies that the design remains "intellectually manageable." The second message is that, if this constructive approach to the problem of program correctness is to be our plan, we had better see to it that the intellectual labour involved does not exceed our limited powers . . .

Where this discipline is followed, getting programs to work is a by-product of getting them right. In fact, as pointed out in the paper "How to Write Correct Programs and Know It" [13], well-designed programs can be expected to run correctly ab initio. Since it is well known that no foolproof methods exist for knowing that the last error in a program has been found, there is much more practical confidence to be gained in never finding the first error in a program, even in debugging. Ten years ago such an objective would have been dismissed as unreal. But it is happening regularly among good programmers today.

The reason program correctness is key to good program design is that a discipline of rigor is imposed in place of the currently widespread heuristics. Structured programming is marked by a stepwise refinement design process, in which programs are derived and validated as successive function expansions into simpler, more primitive functions. At first glance, stepwise refinement may simply look like an orderly, top down sequence for inventing program statements, but there is more at stake in going from heuristic invention to rigorous derivation. What is at stake is a visible design structure that survives the coding, for use in maintenance and modification as well as implementation. Each refinement marks the top of a hierarchy which can serve later as a new intermediate starting point for verifying correctness or adding capability to a program. The paper "The New Math of Computer Programming" [14] develops a rigorous treatment of stepwise refinement in mathematical terms, in which correctness is guaranteed by closed formulas for correct expansions. In another landmark book, *Algorithms + Data Structures = Programs* [18], Wirth gives many excellent examples of rigorous stepwise refinement.

Jackson [11] develops a special synergism between logical design and program design, based on the following idea. A structured program based only on control logic of composition (SEQUENCE), alternation (IF-THEN-ELSE), and iteration (DO-WHILE) produces execution strings of processing statements which are described by regular expressions. On the other hand, file structures used in data processing can also be frequently described by regular expressions. Given such a file structure and its regular expression, what is more natural than a program structure which produces the same regular expression? For example, with file structure given by

A(B | *(CD))

the corresponding program structure is

```
process A
IF B THEN
   process B
ELSE
   WHILE C DO
        process C
        process D
   OD
FI
```

Thus, in processing a single file, there is a rigorous connection between file and program. The very structure of the program guarantees that any possible file realization will be processed completely. A more extensive illustration of the connections between logical design and program design is given by Noonan [15].

The Basis for Software Reliability Is Design, Not Testing

It is well known that you cannot test reliability into a software system. If programs are well designed in both data structure and control structure, there is no contest between a programmer and a computer in finding errors; the programmer will win hands down (this is not necessarily true for a bowl of spaghetti). So the first defense against errors is well-designed programs and preventative proofing by authors themselves.

But effective design can do far more than make errors easy to discover. Design can reduce the size of a system, reduce its interconnections, reduce the complexity of its program specifications. In short, good design makes correct systems possible out of correct programs. Parnas illustrates this principle in [16].

Is ultrareliable software possible? Given double the budget and schedule (to test the sincerity of a requirement for ultrareliability) do not spend the extra on testing, spend it in design and inspection. Start with a design competition and plan to keep the simplest one. Continually recompete subdesigns at major stages of stepwise refinement. Seed "secret errors" into the design to exercise and calibrate the inspection process. Create the "need to read" where possible, say, by requiring independent documentation and user guides out of the inspection process. Software systems with error-free operation are coming into existence today, and will be more common tomorrow.

Software Development Methodology

The Problem of Scaling Up

Logically, there seems little difference between a small program and a large one. They both use the same instruction sets, the same compilers. So with ten times the effort, why cannot a program of ten times the size be built? The difficulty is that scaling up goes faster than linearly in effort, as a little thought substantiates. The number of possible connections among n items is $n(n-1)/2$, and it seems reasonable to expect program interactions to tend to such an n^2 law. So there is more logical designing and checking to do per unit of program developed. Further, as this work goes up, more people are required to do it; and to coordinate their efforts, they must communicate with one another. This means the n^2 law again. So, as more people are added, each spends more time communicating and less time producing.

In these problems of scaling up, the difficulties show up at system integration time. There is seldom difficulty in providing a suitable design of noteworthy promise, and there is seldom difficulty in programming the pieces, the modules; the main difficulty is that the modules seldom all run together as designed. An additional difficulty (as if integration were not enough!) is often that when the system does finally run all together as designed, it does not do what the users had imagined it would. So an additional problem of specifications and requirements analysis that should have been handled at the outset, but was not, shows up.

Top Down Development

The necessity of top down development in large software systems is born out of bitter experience with top down design and bottom up development. In top down development, the control programs that integrate functional modules are written and tested first, and the functional modules are added progressively. In fact, the development proceeds on an incremental basis, level by level, with testing and integration accomplished during the programming process, during stepwise refinement, rather than afterwards, as discussed by Baker [2] and Basili and Turner [3].

In a software system, top down development typically starts with a logical design for the harmonious cooperation of several programs through access to several shared data sets. For example, a financial information system may include a file maintenance program, several data entry programs, which produce transaction files for the file maintenance program, and several data retrieval/report programs which access the main file. Although each such program can be developed top down independently, top down system testing requires coordination between them, e.g., data entry programs providing input for the file maintenance program, which in turn creates files for data retrieval programs, etc.

In top down development, design performance is crucial. It represents thinking and problem solving before integration, rather than afterwards. Conversely, top down development forces design evaluation by the ongoing integration process. In bottom up development, poor design is often hidden until late in integration, after much functional code has been written and tested, only to be discarded.

In retrospect it is easy to see that the advantage of top down development over bottom up development is the advantage of a closed-loop management feedback process over an open-loop process. In a bottom up development, the modules are not tested as part of the final system until the end of the development; in top down development, they are tested in their system environment the next day. If there are program errors of system-wide effect, top down development discovers them early, when freshly programmed (and the original programmer is on hand). If there are design errors, top down development forces their discovery and correction during stepwise refinement, whereas bottom up development often leaves them undiscovered until integration time, when original programmers have often departed.

Top down development is more difficult to design for than bottom up development, but the extra effort in design is made up in integration and testing. The problem of design in top down development is not only how the final system will look, but also how the system under development will look at every stage of its construction. Building a bridge illustrates this idea. In drawing a bridge on paper, a spanning girder can be drawn first, to hang in midair until other members are drawn later to support it. But to actually construct that same bridge, a construction plan is needed, which allows girders to be placed and pinned one by one, in support of one another, until the bridge is completed.

Building a software system bottom up is like building a paper bridge: no construction plan is needed, only the final design, and everyone hopes it all goes together as planned. If people were infallible, especially designers, no construction plans would be needed, but people are fallible.

Building a software system top down is like building a real bridge. Finding a proper top is a significant technical task. A proper top is one that executes as a partial system early in the development, and which provides the basis for adding intermediate and final modules in a continuous code/integrate/test iteration process.

Development Tools

At first glance one would wish for the most powerful set of development tools possible. That is true, but it is not the whole truth. It is even more important for development tools to be dependable. A simple language with a good compiler is better than a powerful one with a poor compiler. A dependable two-hour turnaround is better than an average one-hour turnaround with high variability. Good work habits can accommodate dependable tools at whatever level available. But undependable tools promote helter-skelter work habits.

One form of dependability in tools is the rigor of their specifications and implementations. A programming language cooked up haphazardly as a collection of brilliant ideas is a menace to good programming methodology. It is also more difficult to implement, so the odds favor an unreliable compiler, whose unreliable parts programmers learn to avoid through bitter experience, and then, of course, some of those brilliant ideas are effectively excised. Almost all of the programming languages devised in this first 25 years fall into this category; very few have benefited from a rigorous syntactic and semantic analysis at their inception. Pascal is such an exception, as axiomatized by Hoare and Wirth [10]. A programming language designer faces a terrible temptation in all the seemingly good ideas around. In this case, Wirth's advice is especially valuable about the need for rigor and simplicity, namely [17, p. 29], "The [programming] language must rest on a foundation of simple, flexible, and neatly axiomatized features, comprising the basic structuring techniques of data and program." Gannon and Horning [8] also discuss the need for good language constructs in terms of human factors.

A good number of debugging tools have been devised to take the place of good programming, but they cannot. Programs should be written correctly to begin with. Debugging poorly designed and coded software systems is veterinary medicine for dinosaurs. The real solution is to get rid of the dinosaurs, even though they pose interesting questions indeed for veterinarians. The best debugging tool, given a properly specified and implemented programming language, is the human mind. Forgiving compilers aid and abet sloppy programmers. If programmers can be precise and demanding, so should compilers.

Library systems may seem mundane as tools, compared with compilers, analyzers, etc., but they are critical and important as discussed by Baker [2]. Library systems should first of all be tools of project management; as a by-product they will be tools for programmers. But if they start out as tools for programmers, it is much more difficult to ensure that they meet the needs for project management. Library systems should record and archive the entire software development process, from the coding pad, or keystroke, on.

The Error Day

Theoretically, a software system exists at any moment, independent of its historical development, and any other history arriving at the same system will produce the same subsequent usage history. But the practical chance of two different development histories producing an identical software system is near zero. The systems may well look alike to the user, each have "no known errors," etc., but their internals will be different, and their design integrity and future error properties will be different. A well-designed system of deep simplicities has a development history which is sharply distinguished from a brute force bowl of spaghetti. The most noticeable difference is the debugging history. A well-designed system can be put together with few errors during its implementation. A bowl of spaghetti will have a history of much error discovery and fixup. So, one difference is the number of errors found and fixed, all errors from the coding pad or keystroke on. (It is usual today to track errors from module release on, but unusual to track errors from lines of code on.) Another difference is in the age of the errors found. In a well-designed top down development, testing under actual system conditions begins early, with system errors found in typically a day or so. In the brute force approach, code is frequently unit tested with drivers, and system errors are often found later in integration, weeks, months, or years later.

The number and age of errors lead to the *error day* (i.e., for each error removed, the sum of the days from its creation to its detection) for estimating the quality of an otherwise acceptable system. It indicates probable future error incidents, but also indirectly indicates the effectiveness of the design and testing process. High error days indicate either many errors (probably due to poor design) or long-lived errors (probably due to poor development).

In illustration, imagine that two such systems, called *A* and *B*, developed to the same specifications and acceptance conditions, produced the statistics in Table 18-1. After acceptance, each system has "no known errors." But system *B* was harder to put together, with more subtle interface errors that took considerable time to find, and thus there is a strong

TABLE 18-1. *Same Specifications, Same Acceptance Testing*

During Development	*A*		*B*	
Lines of code	50,000	Error	50,000	Error
errors fixed		Days		Days
day old	100	100	500	500
week old	10	50	50	250
month old	5	100	50	1000
year old	5	1250	20	5000
Known errors	0		0	
error days		1500		6750
During Acceptance				
Errors fixed	10		50	
Known errors	0		0	

likelihood of more such errors not yet turned up. The statistics in Table 18-1 are not kept, of course, in the typical software development process, under the notion that it is a private matter how a system gets to a state of "no known errors." But it does, indeed, matter how a system gets to such a state because it foretells how the system will fare in the future. From a practical standpoint, these are not the same systems, even though each has no known errors at the moment. The error day gives a way to distinguish them by how they got here.

Design-to-Cost Programming

One of the most vexing problems of software development is meeting cost and schedule commitments. Overruns in time and money are usual. In fact, underruns are highly unusual. On the surface, those problems arise from the problems of specification and estimation. Loose and unstable specifications certainly prevent timely development. But the programming estimation problem is difficult, even with good specifications for a new capability or a new development environment.

One way to get around this programming specification and estimation problem is to reinterpret cost estimates desired as design-to-cost requirements and to apply a design-to-cost methodology in software development. If cost is to be fixed, a new look at specifications is required. Software, for practically any function needed, can be defined over a wide variety of costs. The basic functions of an item of software are usually a small fraction of the total software finally built. The remainder of the software deals with being friendly to users, handling errors automatically, etc., all of which are important things to do, but all of which can be prioritized with respect to the funds and time available to do them. A typical split of basic to exception code in software is 20–80, e.g., 20 percent of the code handles 80 percent of the functions required. If the basic code is misestimated even by 100 percent, that 20 percent becomes 40 percent, and a 40–60 split results. It is probably a tolerable split (at least temporarily) because it still deals with 75 percent (60/80) of the exceptions required. But the critical programming management job is to make sure that the basic 20 percent (or 40 percent) is up and running within schedule and cost, at the expense, if necessary, of the 80 percent (or 60 percent).

Design-to-cost is not a new idea. Society practices it in industry and government in many ways. A basic methodology comes from simple multilevel budgeting. For example, a city government begins with a budget of a certain size and allocates that budget into several parts; one for overall executive control, the remainder into such functions as police, fire, sanitation, etc. Each function is, in turn, rebudgeted similarly: the police department will allocate one part to its overall control, the remainder to subfunctions, such as precinct operations, patrol car operations, special investigations, etc. This budgeting process finally reaches individual performance where no further subunits are created.

As simple and old as this kind of design-to-cost methodology seems, we can apply it in practically full effect to the software development problem. Top down development can proceed like a budgeting exercise in a design-to-cost activity. Given a budget for an item of software, an appropriate fraction can be allocated to its overall design. A critical part of this overall design is the allocation of the remaining funds to the software yet to be done. Another critical part is the construction of the control program which will execute and control the software yet to be developed. Thus, the design-to-cost methodology forces the actual costs of construction of the control program at the top of the software to be taken out of the funds before the remainder is allocated to the rest of the software; i.e., the problem of the system designers and architects includes the problem of allocation between control and subsequent function.

The incorporation of a design-to-cost methodology into the planning and budgeting operations of a using organization can also bring important benefits in converting software development for termination-oriented projects to more normal ongoing activities of the organization. The evolution of large systems in small stages, with user feedback and participation in goal refinements at each step is a way of going from grandiose to grand software system development. There is much yet to learn on how to accomplish such design-to-cost programming in a larger setting of incremental software development. But we are 25 years wiser and closer to realizing the dream of even more remarkable benefits of automatic data processing to society.

References

1. Alexander, C. *Notes on the Synthesis of Form.* Cambridge, Mass.: Harvard University Press, 1970.
2. Baker, F. T. "Structured Programming in a Production Programming Environment." In *Proc. Int. Conf. Reliable Software,* Los Angeles, Apr. 1975, *ACM SIGPLAN Notices* 10 (June 1975): 172–185.
3. Basili, V. R., and Turner, A. J. "Iterative Enhancement: A Practical Technique for Software Development." *IEEE Trans. Software Eng.* 1 (Dec. 1975): 390–396.

4. Brooks, F. P. *The Mythical Man-Month: Essays on Software Engineering.* Reading, Mass.: Addison-Wesley, 1975.
5. Dahl, O. J., Dijkstra, E. W., and Hoare, C. A. R. *Structured Programming.* New York: Academic, 1972.
6. Dijkstra, E. W. *A Discipline of Programming.* Englewood Cliffs, N. J.: Prentice-Hall, 1976.
7. Dijkstra, E. W. "GOTO Statements Considered Harmful." *Comm. ACM* 11 (Mar. 1968): 147–148.
8. Gannon, J. D., and Horning, J. J. "The Impact of Language Design on the Production of Reliable Software." In *Proc. Int. Conf. Reliable Software,* Los Angeles, Apr. 1975, *ACM SIGPLAN Notices* 10 (June 1975): 10–22.
9. Hoare, C. A. R. "An Axiomatic Basis for Computer Programming." *Comm. ACM* 12 (Oct. 1970): 576–583.
10. Hoare, C. A. R., and Wirth, N. "An Axiomatic Definition of the Programming Language PASCAL." *Acta Informatica* 2 (1973): 335–355.
11. Jackson, M. A. *Principles of Program Design.* New York: Academic, 1975.
12. Liskov, B., and Zilles, S. "Specification Techniques for Data Abstractions." In *Proc. Int. Conf. Reliable Software,* Los Angeles, Apr. 1975, *ACM SIGPLAN Notices* 10 (June 1975): 72–87.
13. Mills, H. D. "How to Write Correct Programs and Know It." In *Proc. Int. Conf. Reliable Software,* Los Angeles, Apr. 1975, *ACM SIGPLAN Notices* 10 (June 1975): 363–370.
14. Mills, H. D. "The New Math of Computer Programming." *Comm. ACM* 18 (Jan. 1975): 43–48.
15. Noonan, R. E. "Structured Programming and Formal Specification." *IEEE Trans. Software Eng.* 1 (Dec. 1975): 421–425.
16. Parnas, D. L. "The Influence of Software Structure on Reliability." In *Proc. Int. Conf. Reliable Software,* Los Angeles, Apr. 1975, *ACM SIGPLAN Notices* 10 (June 1975): 358–362.
17. Wirth, N. "An Assessment of the Programming Language PASCAL." In *Proc. Int. Conf. Reliable Software,* Los Angeles, Apr. 1975, *ACM SIGPLAN Notices* 10 (June 1975): 23–30.
18. Wirth, N. *Algorithms + Data Structures = Programs.* Englewood Cliffs, N. J.: Prentice-Hall, 1976.

ARTICLE
19

Software Engineering Education

(1980)

Abstract

In a field as rapidly growing as software engineering, the education problem splits into two major parts—university education and industrial education (some of which is given at university locations, as short courses, but considered industrial education here). Both parts draw on the same underlying disciplines and methodologies. But the people involved—both teachers and students—have different objectives and characteristics. At the university level students are young, inexperienced, and relatively homogeneous in background and abilities. At the industrial level, students are older, more experienced, and vary considerably in background and abilities.

In this paper, we discuss the underlying commonalities and the overlaid differences of university and industrial education in software engineering. The commonalities in disciplines and methodologies involve the study and understanding of the software process, as discussed in Section 2 of this special issue, and of the "tools" and "know-how" discussed in Section 3. The differences are due to the characteristics and objectives of students, and show up on curricula content and structure and in course definition.

© 1980 IEEE. Reprinted, with permission, from *Proceedings of the IEEE,* Vol. 68, No. 9, September 1980.

Software Engineering Education in Flux

University Education and Industrial Education

In a field as rapidly growing as software engineering, the education problem splits into two major parts—university education and industrial education. (Short courses given at university locations without degree credits are considered industrial education here.) Both parts draw on the same underlying disciplines and methodologies. But the people involved —both teachers and students—have different objectives and characteristics.

University students are young, inexperienced, and relatively homogeneous in background and abilities. Industrial students are older, more experienced, and vary considerably in background and abilities. University teachers are oriented toward a transient student population (in 2–4 years they are gone) and to their own publications. Industrial teachers are oriented to a more stable student population and to improved industrial performance of students due to their education. In brief, university students are "supposed to be learning," while industrial students are "supposed to be working."

In a field more stable than software engineering, university education plays a dominant role in shaping the principles and values of the field, while industrial education consists of refresher and updating courses in fringe and frontier areas. But university education in software engineering was not available to the majority of people who practice and manage it today. Therefore the principles and values of software engineering are being shaped jointly by university and industrial influences.

A Serious Problem

The United States finds itself far ahead in computer hardware but also heading for a serious problem in software. In a recent object lesson, our electronics industry was strengthened significantly by the shortfall of our missile boosters compared to those of the Soviet Union 20 years ago. As a partial result of the severe discipline of power, space, and weight limitations in our boosters, our electronics was miniaturized and improved in dramatic ways. And we lead in electronics today because of this history.

In reverse, we have seen an astonishing growth in computer power and availability. And our software industry has suffered from the lack of enforced discipline thereby, even while developing the largest software systems known today. Simply put, we are used to squandering computer power. This bad habit pervades industry, government, and the very sociology and psychology of the bulk of the computer programming today. Since information processing has become an essential part of the way society manages its industries and thereby a key to industrial power, the inertia of several hundred thousand undisciplined programmers in the United States is real reason for future concern.

We can also be sure that this causality will work in reverse. The lack of computing scarcity provides temptations every day in every way to excuse and condone poor performance in the software sector. Indeed, the software industry has already bungled its way into a predominate share of the costs of data processing.

Unless we address this problem with exceptional measures, we are on the way to a "software gap" much more serious and persistent than the famous "missile gap" which helped fuel the very growth of our electronics industry.

The Problem Perpetuated

As a result of this history, the educational background and discipline of the vast majority of computer programmers is seriously low. But, as a natural human trait, most of these programmers would rather be comforted than educated. "After all, if I'm as good as the next person, I'm good enough."

Fortunately for these programmers, there are any number of industrial short courses which will comfort, rather than educate. They are "practical," "easy to understand," "the latest techniques." On attendance, programmers discover various new names for common sense, superficial ideas, and thereby conclude, with much comfort and relief, that they have been up to date all the time. But unfortunately for the country, these programmers have not only learned very little, but have been reinforced in the very attitude that they have little to learn!

To make matters worse, many of these comfortable and comforting short courses make liberal use of the term "software engineering" as a buzzword. Such a typical "education" in software engineering consists of three days of listening, no exams, but a considerable feeling of euphoria.

This accident of history poses critical problems for universities, as well. The great demand for software engineering provides many temptations for lowered academic standards. The solid mathematical bases for software analysis and design are just emerging and are not easy to package for classroom use at this stage. But since software touches so many broad issues, there is no problem in filling a semester course, or even a curriculum, with all the latest buzzwords and proposals of the field.

What Is Software Engineering?

Computer Science, Computer Programming, and Software Engineering

It is fashionable to relabel all computer programming as software engineering today, but we will not do that here. Our definition of software engineering requires both software and engineering as essential components. By software we mean not only computer programs, but all other related documentation including user procedures, requirements, specifications, and software design. And by engineering we mean a body of knowledge and discipline comparable to other engineering curricula at universities today, for example, electrical engineering or chemical engineering.

We distinguish software engineering from computer science by the different goals of engineering and science in any field—practical construction and discovery. We distinguish software engineering from computer programming by a presence or not of engineering-level discipline. Software engineering is based on computer science and computer programming, but is different from either of them.

The full discipline of software engineering is not economically viable in every situation. Writing high-level programs in large, well-structured application systems is such an example. Such programming may well benefit from software engineering principles, but its challenges are more administrative than technical, more in the subject matter than in the software.

However, when a software package can be written for $50,000, but costs five million to fix a single error because of a necessary recall of a dangerous consumer product, the product may well require a serious software engineering job, rather than a simple programming job of unpredictable quality.

Mathematical Foundations of Software Engineering

It is characteristic of an engineering discipline to have explicit technical foundations, and software engineering is no exception. Since the content of software is essentially logical, the foundations of software engineering are primarily mathematical—not the continuum mathematics underlying physics or chemistry, of course, but finite mathematics more discrete and algebraic than analytic in character. It has been remarked[1] that "algebra is the natural tool to study things made by man, and analysis the tool to

---

[1] By Professor W. Huggins, The Johns Hopkins University.

study things made by God." Software is made by man, and algebra is indeed the natural mathematical tool for its study, although algebra appears in many forms and disguises in computer science topics. For example, automata theory, theories of syntax and semantics of formal languages, data structuring and abstractions, and program correctness are all algebraic in character, in spite of widely differing notations due to their historical origins.

In contrast, electrical engineering combines physical and logical design and therefore draws on both continuum and discrete mathematics. Software engineering uses continuum mathematics only for convenient approximation, e.g., in probability or optimization theory. The difference between the logical design of electrical engineering and the logical design of software engineering is one of scale. The logical complexity of a large software system is orders of magnitude above the logical complexity of a physically realizable processor. In fact, this ability to realize and implement logical complexity of high order is the reason for software.

Note that discrete mathematics does not necessarily imply finite mathematics. The analysis of algorithms, for example, leads to deep logical questions as to whether a computational process is finite or not, even though all operations are discrete. The theory of Turing machines provides another such example [8].

Structure and Organization in Software Engineering

The primary difficulty in software engineering is logical complexity [4]. And the primary technique for dealing with complexity is structure. Because of the sheer volume of work to be done, software development requires two kinds of structuring, algebraic and organizational. Algebraic structuring, applied in different ways, allows mental techniques of divide and conquer, with the same underlying principles, in the various phases of specification, design, implementation, operation, and evolution of software. The result of proper structuring is intellectual control, namely, the ability to maintain perspective while dealing with detail and to zoom in and out in software analysis and design.

The principal organizational technique is work structuring—between workers and machines and, further, between workers. Software tools, in the form of language compilers, operating systems, data entry and library facilities, etc., represent techniques of structuring work between workers and machines. One major dimension of work structuring among people is along the conceptual–clerical axis, which permits effective isolation and delegation of clerical work. Other dimensions are based on subject matter in software and applications. A surgical team represents a good example of work structuring, with different roles predefined by the profession and previous education. Surgery, anesthesiology, radiology, nursing, etc., are dimensions of work structuring in a surgical team. The communication between these roles is crisp and clean—with a low bandwidth at their interface, e.g., at the "sponge and scalpel" level, not the whole bandwidth of medical knowledge. A grammar school soccer team represents a poor example of work structuring—the first kid who reaches the ball gets to kick it. But the first person reaching the patient does not get to operate, and hospital orderlies do not become surgeons through on-the-job training.

Career Structures in Software Engineering

In addition to degree-level engineering skills in software, we identify the need for various grades of technician skills, and for degree-level science and administration skills as well. Within the engineering skills, we can differentiate by subject matter and further by skill level through graduate degree levels.

Just as in any other profession such as law, medicine, etc., many skill categories and skill levels go into a well-formed software engineering team. In software development, the sheer weight of precise logic dominates, and the need for precision procedures for design and control is critical. For example, in law, three judges may subdivide an opinion for a joint writing project and meet the requirements for legal precision with small variations in their individual vocabularies. But a joint software development by three programmers will not tolerate the slightest variation in vocabulary because of the literal treatment of the design text by a computer.

The software engineer is at the center of software development and computer operations in which basic algorithms and data processing may require other advanced skills for their definition, analysis, and validation. Because of this, graduate science and administrative skills are frequent partners in software development, and the software engineer needs to be at home with an interdisciplinary approach.

Within software engineering, we can identify several areas of concentration which have the depth and substance that can occupy a person through a life-long career. Those areas include such topics as compilers, operating systems, data-base systems, real-time control systems, and distributed processing systems. These specialties in software engineering usually require graduate-level education for effective team leadership and advanced technical contributions.

Software Engineering Practices

Elements of Software Engineering

The effective practice of software engineering must be based on its technical foundations just as any other engineering activity, in combining real world needs and technical possibilities into practical designs and systems. For our purposes it is convenient to classify the disciplines and procedures of software engineering into three categories.

1. Design (after Plato, Phaedrus). "First, the taking in of scattered particulars under one Idea, so that everyone understands what is being talked about . . . Second, the separation of the Idea into parts, by dividing it at the joints, as nature directs, not breaking any limb in half as a bad carver might."

2. Development. The organization of design activities into sustained software development, including the selection and use of tools and operational procedures for work structuring among different categories of personnel.

3. Management. Requirements analysis, project definition, identifying the right personnel, and the estimation, scheduling, measurement, and control of software design and development.

Software Engineering Design

The availability of useful, tested, and well-documented principles of software specification and design has exploded in the past decade, in three distinct areas, namely,

1. Sequential process control: characterized by structured programming and program correctness ideas of Dijkstra [7], Hoare [14], Linger, Mills, and Witt [17], and Wirth [26, 27].
2. System and data structuring: characterized by modular decomposition ideas of Dijkstra [9], Dahl [7], Ferrentino and Mills [11, 19], and Parnas [22].
3. Real-time and multidistributed processing control: characterized by concurrent processing and process synchronization ideas of Brinch Hansen [5], Dijkstra [10], Hoare [15], and Wirth [28].

The value of these design principles is in the increased discipline and repeatability they provide for the design process. Designers can understand, evaluate, and criticize each other's work in a common objective framework. In a phrase of Weinberg [25], people can better practice "egoless software design" by focusing criticisms on the design and not the author. Such design principles also provide direct criteria for more formal design inspection procedures so that designers, inspectors, and management can better prepare for, conduct, and interpret the results of periodic orderly design inspections.

Software Engineering Development

Even though the primary conceptual work of software engineering is embodied in design, the organization and support of design activities into sustained software development is a significant activity in itself, as discussed in [3] and [20]. The selection and definition of design and programming support languages and tools, the use of library support systems to maintain the state of a design under development, the test and integration strategy, all impact the design process in major ways. So the disciplines, tools, and procedures used to sustain software development need to be scrutinized, structured, and chosen as carefully as the design principles themselves.

The principal need for development discipline is in the intellectual control and management of design abstractions and details on a large scale. Brooks [6] states that "conceptual integrity is the most important consideration in systems design." Design and programming languages are required which deal with procedure abstractions and data abstractions, with system structure, and with the harmonious cooperation of multidistributed processes. Design library support systems are needed for the convenient creation, storage, retrieval, and modification of design units, and for the overall assessment of design status and progress against objectives.

The isolation and delegation of work between conceptual and clerical activities, and between various subactivities in both categories is of critical importance to a sustained and manageable development effort. Chief Programmer Teams [3] embody such work structuring for small and medium-size projects. In larger projects, an organization of Chief Programmer Teams and other functional units is required.

Software Engineering Management

The management of software engineering is primarily the management of a design process, and represents a most difficult intellectual activity. Even though the process is highly creative, it must be estimated and scheduled so that various parts of the design activity can be coordinated and integrated into a harmonious result, and so that users can plan on results as well. The intellectual control that comes from well-conceived design and development disciplines and procedures is invaluable in achieving this result. Without that intellectual control, even the best managers face hopeless odds in trying to see the work through.

In order to meet cost/schedule commitments in the face of imperfect estimation techniques, a software engineering manager must practice a manage-and-design-to-cost/schedule process. That process calls for a continuous and relentless rectification of design objectives with the cost/schedule required for achieving those objectives. Occasionally, this rectification can be simplified by a brilliant new approach or technique, which increases productivity and shortens time in the development process. But usually, just because the best possible approaches and techniques known are already planned, a shortfall, or even a windfall in achievable software, requires consultation with the user in order to make the best choices among function, performance, cost, and schedule. It is especially important to take advantage of windfalls to counter other shortfalls; too often windfalls are unrecognized and squandered. The intellectual control of good software design not only allows better choice in a current development, but also permits subsequent improvements of function and performance in a well-designed baseline system.

In software engineering, there are two parts to an estimate—making a good estimate and making the estimate good. It is up to the software engineering manager to see that both parts are right, along with the right function and performance.

Principles of Education in Software Engineering

Degrees in Software Engineering

A degree in software engineering should first of all be an engineering degree, dealing with engineering design and construction. It should not simply be a computer programming degree or a computer science degree. As already noted, there is much programming to be done in society, and other curricula in arts and science or business administration should be called upon to provide properly focused education for more general programming in business and science applications. The UCLA masters program in Computer Science [16] is a good model of such other curricula, which has high technology content, yet does not pretend to be software engineering.

The usual principles of university education should apply to a curriculum in software engineering, namely, that it be a preparation for a career based on topics of reasonable half-life, while producing entry-level job skills and the ability to learn later. These objectives are not incompatible because the very topics required for dealing with technically challenging software problems are generally basic topics of long life, and they do indeed prepare people for more advanced education and continued learning. It is well known that mathematics and science are more easily learned when young and so, as a rule, soft topics should be deferred for postgraduate experience and continued learning. There is real danger in overusing soft topics and survey courses loaded with buzzwords to provide near-term job entry salability. But without adequate technical foundations, people will become dead-ended in mid-career, just when they are expected to solve harder problems as individuals, as members or as managers, of teams.

In the three categories of software engineering practices listed above, studies in design practices are prime candidates for early university education; development practices should be phased in later, and management practices deferred for continued postdegree learning, after considerable experience in individual and team practice in software engineering.

Foundations and Problem Solving

This is a difficult dilemma in university curricula in balancing the needs for solid technical foundations and to learn problem solving. Of course, this dilemma is not unique to software engineering. Limiting topics to techniques allows a more efficient education process in terms of quantity, volume, and quality of techniques that are teachable. But it is frequently difficult for students to apply such techniques in problem-solving contexts. Problem solving is a great motivator and confidence builder. But too much emphasis on problem solving cuts into the amount of technique preparation possible, and produces students able to make a good first showing in their career but who are likely to drop out early because of the lack of deeper technical abilities.

It is characteristic in software engineering that the problems to be solved by advanced practitioners require sustained efforts over months or years from many people, often in the tens or hundreds. This kind of mass problem-solving effort requires a radically different kind of precision and scope in techniques than are required for individual problem solvers. If the precision and scope are not gained in university education, it is difficult to acquire them later, no matter how well motivated or adept a person might be at individual, intuitive approaches to problem solving.

We all know of experiences in elementary mathematics courses of getting little or no credit for guessing correct answers without showing the process for finding them. There was a good reason, because guessing answers to small problems cannot be scaled up to larger problems, whereas processes needed to solve smaller problems can be scaled up. That scaling up problem is the principal difference between computer programming and software engineering.

Curriculum Topics

ACM Curriculum '78 [2] is a well-accepted prescription for an undergraduate degree in computer science/programming. But there are those who believe that Curriculum '78 does not present enough, and the right kind of mathematics. In any case, this author believes that degrees in software engineering should be considerably stronger in discrete mathematics than suggested by Curriculum '78. In particular, a curriculum in software engineering should require a good working knowledge of the first-order predicate calculus; the algebras of sets, functions, and relations; and a deep enough understanding of mathematical reasoning to use it in a flexible way in large and complex problems. We are beginning to see evidence of the practical power of mathematical reasoning in mastering software complexity, for example in program verification [12], and in the development of entire software systems, such as the UCLA Unix Security Kernel [24]. With such a foundation, the curriculum can provide an understanding of algorithms [1], computer programs [17, 26, 27], data structures [13], data abstractions [18], and data bases [23] as mathematical objects.

Adult University Education

The rapid growth of software engineering means that there will be a considerable amount of adult education in university work (in contrast to short courses which may be given in universities on a nondegree basis.) Typically these will be advanced degrees for people with an already good foundation in mathematics or engineering science. It is to be expected that adult education will go on in parallel in arts and sciences, and in business administration schools for much the same reason because the whole industry is growing rapidly. But as noted before, we distinguish between programming and software engineering and we mean to discuss here adult university education in software engineering only.

Adult students in university curricula have advantages and disadvantages over younger students coming directly out of previous education. Their advantages are in their motivation and in the fact that they have a larger experience base in which to embed the ideas, techniques, etc., they receive in the education process. Their disadvantages are in being rusty in the learning process and possibly in having their education somewhat outmoded through the passage of time. On balance, people who are motivated enough to return for adult education at the university level are usually superior students and get more out of their education than their younger peers, but they should be expected to live up to the academic standards of the institution.

Laboratory Courses in Software Engineering

We know from other science and engineering disciplines that laboratory courses are usually more difficult to develop than lecture courses. In software, simply letting people learn by themselves in developing programs and systems as projects can lead to two weeks of experience repeated seven times rather than a fourteen-week laboratory course of cumulative experience. The problem with such open-loop student projects is that much of the time is spent on recovering from unwise decisions or poor executions made earlier, with little real learning going on.

A degree program in software engineering should contain a minimum sequence of laboratory courses, which is based on understanding and modifying existing programs and solving hardware/software integration problems before proceeding to program design and development and later into system specification and design. This laboratory sequence should proceed from (1) a highly structured environment in which carefully conceived programs (with carefully conceived problems) are presented to students for testing and modification to (2) less structured situations where students design and develop small, then large, software products from well-defined specifications, finally to (3) even less structured situations where they deal with informal requirements from which specifications and designs are to be developed. In this sequence there is an opportunity to identify problems, which all students encounter simultaneously, for which instructors can help develop approaches and solutions. A hardware/software integration problem early in the laboratory sequence seems especially important for software engineering students, because there are usually important interfaces between hardware and software in the high-performance systems dealt with by software engineering.

References

1. Aho, A. V., Hopcroft, J. E., and Ullman, J. D. *The Design and Analysis of Computer Algorithms*. Reading, Mass.: Addison-Wesley, 1974.

2. Austing, R., et al., eds., "Curriculum 78: Recommendations for the Undergraduate Program in Computer Science—A Report of the ACM Curriculum Committee on Computer Science," *Comm. ACM* 22, No. 3 (Mar. 1979).
3. Baker, F. T. "Chief Programmer Team Management of Production Programming." *IBM Syst. J.* 2, No. 1 (1972).
4. Belady, L. A., and Lehman, M. M. "The Evolution Dynamics of Large Programs." IBM, Yorktown Heights, NY, RC 5615 (#24294), Sept. 1975.
5. Brinch Hansen, P. *The Architecture of Concurrent Programs.* Englewood Cliffs, N. J.: Prentice-Hall, 1977.
6. Brooks, F. P. *The Mythical Man-Month: Essays on Software Engineering.* Reading, Mass.: Addison-Wesley, 1975.
7. Dahl, O. J., Dijkstra, E. W., and Hoare, C. A. R. *Structured Programming.* New York: Academic Press, 1972.
8. Denning, P., and Dennis, J. *Machines, Languages, and Computation.* Englewood Cliffs, N. J.: Prentice-Hall, 1978.
9. Dijkstra, E. W. "The Structure of 'THE' Multiprogramming System." *Comm. ACM* 11, No. 5 (May 1968): 341–346.
10. Dijkstra, E. W. "Co-operating Sequential Processes." In *Programming Languages,* pp. 43–112. London: Academic Press, 1968.
11. Ferrentino, A. B., and Mills, H. D. "State Machines and Their Semantics in Software Engineering." In *Proc. IEEE Comsac '77,* pp. 242–251, 1977. (IEEE Catalog no. 77Ch1291-4C.)
12. Gerhart, S. L. "Program Verification in the 1980's: Problems, Perspectives, and Opportunities." ISI Report ISI/RR-78-71. Aug. 1978.
13. Gotlieb, C. C., and Gotlieb, L. R. *Data Types and Data Structures.* Englewood Cliffs, N. J.: Prentice-Hall, 1978.
14. Hoare, C. A. R. "An Axiomatic Basis for Computer Programming." *Comm. ACM* 12 (1969): 576–583.
15. Hoare, C. A. R. "Monitors: an Operating System Structuring Concept." *Comm. ACM* 18 (1975): 95.
16. Karplus, W. J. "The Coming Crisis in Graduate Computer Science Education." *UCLA Comput. Sci. Dep. Quarterly* (Jan. 1977): 1–5.
17. Linger, R. C., Mills, H. D., and Witt, B. I. *Structured Programming: Theory and Practice.* Reading, Mass.: Addison-Wesley, 1979.
18. Liskov, B., Zilles, S. "An Introduction to Formal Specifications of Data Abstractions." In *Current Trends in Programming Methodology.* Vol. 1, edited by R. Yeh, pp. 1–32. Englewood Cliffs, N. J.: Prentice-Hall, 1977.
19. Mills, H. D. "On the Development of Systems of People and Machines." In *Lecture Notes in Computer Science 23.* New York: Springer-Verlag, 1975.

20. Mills, H. D. "Software Development." *IEEE Trans. Software Eng.* SE-2 (1976): 265–273.
21. Moriconi, M. *A System for Incrementally Designing and Verifying Programs.* Ph.D. dissertation, University of Texas, Austin, Nov. 1977.
22. Parnas, D. L. "The Use of Precise Specifications in the Development of Software." In *Information Processing.* Edited by B. Gilchrist, pp. 861–867. Amsterdam: North-Holland, 1977.
23. Ullman, J. *Principles of Data Base Systems.* Washington, D.C.: Computer Science Press, 1980.
24. Walker, B. J., Kemmerer, R. A., and Popek, G. J. "Specification and Verification of the UCLA Unix Security Kernel." *Comm. ACM* 23, No. 2 (Feb. 1980): 118–131.
25. Weinberg, G. M. *The Psychology of Computer Programming.* New York: Van Nostrand Reinhold, 1971.
26. Wirth, N. *Systematic Programming.* Englewood Cliffs, N. J.: Prentice-Hall, 1973.
27. Wirth, N. *Algorithms + Data Structures = Programs.* Englewood Cliffs, N. J.: Prentice-Hall, 1976.
28. Wirth, N. "Toward a Discipline of Real-Time Programming." *Comm. ACM* 20 (1977): 577–583.

ARTICLE
20

Software Productivity in the Enterprise

(1981)

Productivity Differentials in Software

There is a 10 to 1 difference in productivity among practicing programmers today—that is, among programmers certified by their industrial positions and pay. That differential is undisputed, and it is a sobering commentary on our ability to measure and enforce productivity standards in the industry.

There are two main reasons for this astonishing differential. First, programming is a problem-solving activity, and there is a great differential among people in their ability to solve problems of the kinds found in programming. Second, industry tolerates this much differential because programming productivity is extremely difficult to measure. Lines of program source code written and debugged per day are easy to measure, but they are only distantly related to real productivity. Sometimes the highest real productivity is the result of finding how to reuse programs already written—possibly for a quite different looking purpose. Another form of high productivity occurs in finding how to solve problems with past existing programs, revising them as subprograms. It is low productivity to write large amounts of program source code for the easy parts of what needs to be done, when it has been done already. And yet this leads to high code counts per day's work.

In truth, there are simply no objective ways to measure programming productivity except by results, any more than one can measure the productivity of a salesman by counting the amounts of words spoken per day. And the results need to be measured in value to the enterprise, not lines of code.

While this productivity differential among programmers is understandable, there is also a 10 to 1 difference in productivity among software organizations. This difference needs a little more explanation. At first glance it would appear that differences among programmers would tend to average out in organizations. For example, the average heights of programmers from organization to organization will differ much less than the height from programmer to programmer. Why doesn't productivity average out, too?

There are two main reasons why the differential in individual productivity does not average out in software organizations. First, individual productivity is not simply additive in a software organization: 1 module and 1 module can equal 0 system if the module interfaces and functions do not match. Making individual productivity additive in software organizations takes good technology and good management. Second, individual programmers do not join software organizations at random. In each case there is an offer and an acceptance. It turns out that those organizations with good technology and good management can attract the best programmers, and vice versa. So the better organizations have it best both ways. They attract the highest individual productivity and make this productivity most additive.

But now we come to a curious paradox. The best performing software organizations—the 10 performers—are typically held in no higher esteem by their own enterprises than the 1 performers. For how are their own enterprises to know they are 1's or 10's, when they are the only software organization they know? In fact, there is a reverse affect. The 1 performers usually make software look hard; the 10 performers usually make it look easy. How can people in an enterprise distinguish between doing hard things and making things look hard in software? Every comparison they can make is apples to oranges—different problems, different enterprises, different situations. There is just no easy, objective way to know.

This difficulty of judging the productivity of one's own software organization may seem frustrating. After all, how will the 10-performing organizations get their just rewards? They will get their just rewards in a simple way. Their enterprises will survive. Data processing, and the quality of software, is more and more a matter of survival for enterprises. The greater the dependence on data processing for survival, the greater the selectivity of productive performance in software. For example, there is not a major airline company in the world without an automated airline reservations system. They cannot survive without one. So in the long run there is no problem of identifying productive software organizations.

Seven Productivity Indicators in Software

Even though the long run mill of productivity grinds surely and finely, the essence of management is to anticipate and improve the productivity of its own enterprise in the short run, including that of its software organization. In the realization that no simple measurements will suffice we offer a set of productivity indicators in software. None of these indicators are numerical or objective. Every one of them takes management assessment and judgment. Further, these indicators do not add up, nor do they have a fixed role of importance. That takes management judgment as well. There may seem little comfort in this, but promising anything more does the reader a disservice. There is no question that management measurements of numerical and objective forms can be devised to reflect these indicators. But such measurements should be devised by enterprise management who then know their special circumstances and know by construction the limitations and fallibilities of their own measurements.

1. Good Schedule and Budget Control

Overrun schedules and budgets reflect a lack of intellectual and management control. Poor schedule and budget control denies management the real ability to exercise choice in what role software will play in the enterprise. If the programmers decide when projects will be completed after they are well under way, rather than enterprise management deciding before approving them, the programmers are making enterprise-level decisions, like it or not.

Overrun budgets are usually small prices to pay compared to the opportunity cost of the enterprise in not having the software service planned. If there is not a large opportunity cost, the software should not have been justified anyway.

2. Good Methodology

Software people should know what is going on in the university and the profession. The methodology used should be based on choice of the latest and best, and not based on ignorance. It should also be laced liberally with the old and dependable. The objective of good methodology is not productivity or quality, but management control. Once management control is attained, one can choose productivity, quality, or other objectives to meet the need of the enterprise.

3. Good People

Where do the software people come from? You should get your choice of good people from mathematics and computer science university curricula. Experience has shown that it takes more mathematical maturity to manage software than to do software. You need good material to grow your futures from. The industry is overrun with poorly educated programmers who get programs to run only by trial and error. They are the equivalent of hunt-and-peck typists, who are doing what comes naturally, while touch typists have learned to do what comes unnaturally.

4. Making it Look Easy

Orderly, systematic processes make software look easy, particularly at systems integration time. The integration crunch is not a sign of a hard problem; it is a sign of poor technology and management. It is hard to see people thinking, but easy to see them coding. The programmer whose feet are on the desk may be your most productive asset. Thinking takes time—more time than we realize.

5. Stable Population

You not only need to get good people and to educate them into your own enterprise. You need to keep them. If your population is unstable, chances are you are either 1) releasing poor people you should never have hired or 2) losing good people you cannot afford to lose. Getting higher technology than you have by hiring senior professionals loses continuity with your past and loses hope for your own people, so do it carefully. You cannot spend enough on education, but make sure it is education at a university level of methodology, with pass/fail criteria, not short course entertainment.

6. People Flexibility

The requirements for high productivity of software are amazingly like those of any other part of your enterprise—marketing, manufacturing, administration, and so on. You need orderly minds and stout hearts. Constructing a good sales presentation is surprisingly similar to writing a good program: you write a program for a prospect to execute instead of a computer. So ask yourself how your software people could help in the rest of your enterprise. If their main claim to fame is knowing how computers work, rather than how your enterprise works, get some new people. They need to know how computers work, all right, but they need to do that with less than half their effort.

7. Computer Infatuation

People who love to program computers and watch them run, who eat it up, should not be allowed to program for pay. If they are very good, there are a small number of such positions—in universities and major industrial research centers. Otherwise, they should get a home computer. Software is too serious a business to do for the fun of it. One should program a computer only as a last resort—when it has not been programmed before. Those problems are getting harder and harder to find today—and there aren't too many easy things left to do.

Secrets of Exceptional Productivity

We can summarize the secrets of exceptional productivity in three steps. First, minimizing reinvention; second, minimizing rework; and third, working smart when necessary, rather than working hard.

Exceptional performance begins with minimizing reinvention and developing new software only as a last resort; but when new software is required, exceptional performance finds the simplest and most direct ways of producing that software. Minimizing reinvention applies not only to the final products, but also to the tools used in the development of software.

The most cost effective way to get a new software system up and running is to discover that it already exists. It may take some effort, and there is some risk of putting in the effort only to discover that no such system exists; but in exceptional performance, one minimizes reinvention. The next most effective way to get a new software system up and running is to discover large components that can be integrated with minimal effort into the required system.

It may seem incredible at first, but exceptional performance reduces the work required in software development by large factors. In fact, entering each of the phases of requirements, design, implementation, and operation, exceptional performance can reduce the work required in the subsequent phases by a factor of three or more. That is, a good requirements analysis can reduce the design job by a factor of three, a good design can reduce the implementation job by a factor of three, and a good implementation can reduce the operations and maintenance job by a factor of three.

In short, the opportunities for productivity decay exponentially through the life of the system. These factors may seem incredible, but experience shows otherwise. If you pick any $500,000 software job at random, it is likely to be a $1,000,000 software job done well or a $200,000 software job done poorly. The fact is that the cost of the software often reflects more directly the capability of the team than it does the size of the real job to be done.

As was already mentioned, exceptional performance is possible only through working smarter, not working harder. It requires more powerful techniques, both conceptual and organizational. The key to exceptional performance is intellectual control, not only by individuals, but by an entire organization. For that reason, organizational techniques of work structuring are as important as conceptual techniques of program structuring.

In software the only way to do more work is by working smart. When people work hard and long hours, they start making excuses for themselves, make mistakes, and end up doing lots of rework. And when they are doing rework because of mistakes that they excuse because they were working hard, it becomes a vicious cycle. Program debugging is rework, no matter what programmers want to think. I expect new programs to work the first time tested and from then on. Debugging not only shows a lack of concentration and design integrity, but is also a big drag on productivity. If somebody writes a hundred lines of code in one day and then takes two weeks to get it debugged, they have really only written ten lines a day.

The ultimate limitations to exceptional productivity are not ability or know-how; the limitations are found in the social and business institutions around us. These limitations begin in school, where it is not smart to be too smart because that makes it hard on other students. They continue into industry through all kinds of formal and informal arrangements, with peer pressure not to show up one's associates. In software engineering, where jobs are usually unique and no one knows their real size anyway, there is a definite motivation to inflate the size of jobs to make them look more important. Managers are usually paid by how many people they manage, rather than by how much they do with the people they have. But that is another long story itself.

Index

A
Abnormal operation termination, 136
Abnormal storage termination, 136
ACM curriculum '78 [2], 261
AIT, 74–77, 79
Aledort, Marvin M., 32
Alexander, C., 233
Algebra of functions, 217
ALGOL, 25, 27
Alternation equation, 226
Argument, 123, 175
Artificial intelligence, 174
Ashcroft, E., 220
Assert, insert, and test, 74
Atanasoff, 216

B
Backup programmer, 65–69, 110
Baker, F. T., 211, 244
Barzilay, Robert A., 32
Basili, V. R., 244
Bigelow, 216
Block structure, 27
Block-structured programming languages, 120
BNF, 31
Böhm, Corrado, 211, 218, 220
Bottom up, 111
Bottom up programming, 105
Brinch Hansen, P., 257
Brooks, F. P., 258
Brown, P. J., 211
Burks, 216

C
Central Media Bureau, Inc., 32
Character-based program content, 59–60
Chief programmer, 65–70, 104, 110, 113
Chief programmer team, 65–70, 104, 258
COBOL, 27
Collecting node, 128, 131
Composition equation, 226
Computation problem, 226
Computer program, 126
Computer programming, 254
Computer science, 254
Control flow, 127
Control graph, 127–128, 130, 136, 139, 143
Control language, 85
Control lines, 131
Control logic, 92–95, 99, 104–105, 108, 110, 146
Control logic statements, 97
Control logic structures, 108
Control node, 127
Control structures, 92–93, 99
Cooper, D. C., 218, 220
Core, 30
Correct program, 194–195, 198
Correctness, 72
Correctness proofs, 122
Correctness theorem, 120, 121, 161, 167

D
Dahl, O. J., 257
Data space, 126
Data states, 130
Decomposition, 125
Denning, P. J., 211
Design, 257
Design review team, 23
Design-to-cost, 231, 248–249
Development, 257–258
Development accounting, 187
Dijkstra, E. W., 210, 212, 219, 223, 240–241, 257
DO-WHILE, 28
Documentation, 183–184
Domain, 123

E
Eckert, 216
Engineering, 254
Equivalent, 134
Error day, 189, 246, 248

Exception code, 112
Execution, 127, 132
Execution content, 61–62
Execution trace analyzers, 62
Expansion, 135
Expansion theorem, 121, 168, 170
Expansion theorem (set theoretic version), 170
Expansion theorem (verbal version), 169

F
Ferrentino, A. B., 257
Final data, 132
Final value, 127
Flowchart, 128, 130–132, 141, 143, 217–218, 220–221
Floyd, R. W., 211
Formal grammar, 31
Formula, 138
FORTRAN, 15, 27
Function, 175
Function completion, 126
Function composition, 125
Functional programming, 120
Functional specification, 94, 98, 100
Functional subspecification, 92–93

G
Gannon, J. D., 246
GO TO, 27–30
Goldstine, H. H., 216

H
Hardware, 58
Henrici, P., 216
Hoare, C. A. R., 211, 241, 246, 257
Horning, J. J., 246
Householder, A. S., 216
Houston RTCC, OS/360, 23
Huggins, W., 212

I
IBM, 13, 16
IBMer, 14
Identity mapping, 131
IF-THEN, 12
IF-THEN-ELSE, 11–12, 28–29
Indeterminate algorithms, 174
Indeterminate instructions, 175
Indeterminate program, 175
Indeterminate program execution, 175
Indeterminate program relation, 175
Individual programmer, 14, 16–25
Information statistics analyzers, 62
Information theory, 58
Initial data, 132
Initial value, 127
Input lines, 127
Instructions, 126
Intermediate data, 132
Irons, Edgar, 25
Iteration equation, 227
Iterative IF (IIF), 11

J
Jackson, M. A., 240–242
Jacopini, G., 210, 218, 220
JCL (job control language), 83–86, 88

K
Kelley, J. R., 211
Kernel system, 23
Kernihan, B. W., 211
Knuth, D. E., 211
Kosaraju, S. R., 220

L
Language processor, 85
Large system, 91
LEL (linkage editing language), 83, 85
Librarian, 68
Linger, R. C., 257
Linkage editing, 85
Liskov, B., 212, 240
Load modules, 85
Loop qualification, 165, 167

M
Main-line programming, 112
Management, 257–258
Manna, Z., 220
Marshall, William F., 32
Mathematics proof, 196
Mauchly, 216
McCarthy, J., 211, 216
McGowan, C. L., 211
Mills, H. D., 211–212, 257
Minsky, Marvin, 216
Multilanguage processor, 83–84

N
Natural language, 8, 44–45, 51
Naur, P., 211
Newell, Allen, 216
Next instruction, 127
Node, 127
Noonan, R. E., 243
Normal termination, 136

O
Object modules, 85
Olsen, Robert S., 32
ON ENDFILE, 28
OS/360, 13–15, 83–85
Output lines, 127

P
Parnas, D. L., 243, 257
Partial rule, 125
PERCENT (%) INCLUDE, 30
Pinzow, Daniel, 32
Pinzow, Susan L., 32
PL/I, 14–15, 27–30
PL/360, 25
Plouger, P. J., 211
Pomerene, 216
PPL, 67–69
Predicate function, 130
Predicate node, 128, 130
Primitive forms, 11
Process node, 127, 130, 133, 135, 138
Productivity, 265–270
Program content, 59, 62
Program correctness, 71, 160, 193, 200, 212
Program formula, 141
Program function, 127, 141
Program schemas, 128
Program segments, 97, 120
Program stubs, 92
Program tree, 159–161
Programming librarian, 65–66, 68–69
Programming measurements, 58
Programming practices, 193
Programming problem, 226
Programming production library (PPL), 66
Proper program, 132–133, 136

R
Randell, B., 212
Range, 123
Relation, 174
Reliability, 72
RETURN, 30
Roget's, 33
Rothman, John, 32
Royston, R., 32

S
S-structured, 158
SAGE, 14
Segment, 93, 120
Simon, Herbert, 216
Software, 58, 254–255
Software engineering, 251–252, 254–256, 258–262
Software gap, 253
Software productivity, 265
Source program analyzers, 62
State space, 126
State vector, 131
Stepwise refinement, 223, 225
Structure theorem, 119–120, 146–147, 158, 168
Structured program, 223
Structured programming, 91, 99, 110, 115–119, 121, 181, 193–194, 200, 210–212, 215–217, 240–241
Structured programs, 122, 161, 211
Subprogram, 127
Subprogram execution, 127
Subprogram function, 127
Symbol-based program content, 59
Symbol-character-based program content, 61
Syntactic-based program content, 60

T
Table lookup, 125
The New York Times, 31
Top down, 92–93, 111, 231, 244–245, 249
Top down corollary, 120
Top down programming, 3–4, 105–106, 110, 112, 121
Top down structured programming, 187, 189
Trent, George D., 32
Turner, A. J., 244

V
Value, 123, 175
Virtual machine, 180
Von Neumann, J., 216

W
Weinberg, Gerald M., 258
Wilder, R. L., 212
Wilkinson, J. H., 216
Williams, 216
Wirth, N., 211, 223, 242, 246, 257
Witt, B. I., 257

Y
Yohe, J. M., 211

Z
Zilles, S., 240
Zurcher, F., 212